Rx Hollywood

THE SUNY SERIES

HORIZONS OF CINEMA

MURRAY POMERANCE | EDITOR

Also in the series

William Rothman, editor, *Cavell on Film*
J. David Slocum, editor, *Rebel Without a Cause*
Joe McElhaney, *The Death of Classical Cinema*
Kirsten Moana Thompson, *Apocalyptic Dread*
Frances Gateward, editor, *Seoul Searching*
Michael Atkinson, editor, *Exile Cinema*
Paul S. Moore, *Now Playing*
Robin L. Murray and Joseph K. Heumann, *Ecology and Popular Film*
William Rothman, editor, *Three Documentary Filmmakers*
Sean Griffin, editor, *Hetero*
Jean-Michel Frodon, editor, *Cinema and the Shoah*
Carolyn Jess-Cooke and Constantine Verevis, editors, *Second Takes*
Matthew Solomon, editor, *Fantastic Voyages of the Cinematic Imagination*
R. Barton Palmer and David Boyd, editors, *Hitchcock at the Source*
William Rothman, *Hitchcock: The Murderous Gaze, Second Edition*
Joanna Hearne, *Native Recognition*
Marc Raymond, *Hollywood's New Yorker*
Steven Rybin and Will Scheibel, editors, *Lonely Places, Dangerous Ground*
Claire Perkins and Constantine Verevis, editors, *B Is for Bad Cinema*
Dominic Lennard, *Bad Seeds and Holy Terrors*
Rosie Thomas, *Bombay before Bollywood*
Scott M. MacDonald, *Binghamton Babylon*
Sudhir Mahadevan, *A Very Old Machine*
David Greven, *Ghost Faces*
James S. Williams, *Encounters with Godard*
William H. Epstein and R. Barton Palmer, editors, *Invented Lives, Imagined Communities*
Lee Carruthers, *Doing Time*
Rebecca Meyers, William Rothman, and Charles Warren, editors, *Looking with Robert Gardner*
Belinda Smaill, *Regarding Life*
Douglas McFarland and Wesley King, editors, *John Huston as Adaptor*
R. Barton Palmer, Homer B. Pettey, and Steven M. Sanders, editors, *Hitchcock's Moral Gaze*
Nenad Jovanovic, *Brechtian Cinemas*
Will Scheibel, *American Stranger*
Amy Rust, *Passionate Detachments*
Steven Rybin, *Gestures of Love*
Seth Friedman, *Are You Watching Closely?*
Roger Rawlings, *Ripping England!*

Rx Hollywood
Cinema and Therapy in the 1960s

Michael DeAngelis

Cover image: *Bob & Carol & Ted & Alice*. (Paul Mazursky, Columbia Pictures, 1969).

Published by State University of New York Press, Albany

© 2018 State University of New York

All rights reserved

No part of this book may be used or reproduced in any manner whatsoever without written permission. No part of this book may be stored in a retrieval system or transmitted in any form or by any means including electronic, electrostatic, magnetic tape, mechanical, photocopying, recording, or otherwise without the prior permission in writing of the publisher.

For information, contact State University of New York Press, Albany, NY
www.sunypress.edu

Production, Eileen Nizer
Marketing, Michael Campochiaro

Library of Congress Cataloging-in-Publication Data

Names: DeAngelis, Michael, 1957– author.
Title: Rx Hollywood : cinema and therapy in the 1960s / Michael DeAngelis.
Description: Albany : State University of New York Press, 2018. | Series: SUNY series, horizons of cinema | Includes bibliographical references and index.
Identifiers: LCCN 2017015615 (print) | LCCN 2017033038 (ebook) | ISBN 9781438468532 (ebook) | ISBN 9781438468518 (hardcover   ) | ISBN 9781438468525 (pbk.   )
Subjects: LCSH: Psychoanalysis in motion pictures. | Psychoanalysis and motion pictures. | Psychiatry in motion pictures. | Motion pictures—United States—History—20th century.
Classification: LCC PN1995.9.P783 (ebook) | LCC PN1995.9.P783 D33 2018 (print) | DDC 791.43019—dc23
LC record available at https://lccn.loc.gov/2017015615

10 9 8 7 6 5 4 3 2 1

For Andrew, my prince

Contents

List of Illustrations	ix
Acknowledgments	xi
Introduction	1
1 Analyst/Patient Relationships: Psychotherapeutic Dynamics	15
2 Therapy and the Sexual Block	55
3 Marriage Therapies and Women's Liberation	83
4 Psychedelic Therapies	121
5 Therapy and Confession	153
Conclusion	187
Notes	195
Works Cited	207
Index	217

List of Illustrations

Figure 0.1	*On a Clear Day You Can See Forever* (Vincente Minnelli, Paramount Pictures, 1970)	6
Figure 0.2	*Wild in the Streets* (Barry Shear, American International Pictures, 1968)	10
Figure 1.1	*A Very Special Favor* (Michael Gordon, Universal Studios, 1965)	42
Figure 1.2	*Coming Apart* (Milton Moses Ginsberg, Kaleidoscope Films, 1969)	48
Figure 2.1	*Reflections in a Golden Eye* (John Huston, Warner Bros/Seven Arts, 1967)	65
Figure 2.2	*Carnal Knowledge* (Mike Nichols, Embassy Pictures, 1971)	73
Figure 3.1	*A Guide for the Married Man* (Gene Kelly, 20th Century Fox, 1967)	95
Figure 3.2	*Bob & Carol & Ted & Alice* (Paul Mazursky, Columbia Pictures, 1969)	104
Figure 4.1	*The Love-Ins* (Arthur Dreifuss, Columbia Pictures/Four-Leaf Productions, 1967)	136
Figure 4.2	*Skidoo* (Otto Preminger, Otto Preminger Films/Sigma Productions, 1968)	150
Figure 5.1	*The President's Analyst* (Theodore J. Flicker, Paramount Pictures., 1967)	168
Figure 5.2	*The Boys in the Band* (William Friedkin, Cinema Center Films/Leo Films, 1970)	185

Acknowledgments

I first developed an interest in this project through discussions with the students in my "Hollywood in the 1960s" course at DePaul University, and I continue to be grateful to have an academic position that puts me in contact with such bright, engaged, and reflective students. I am equally grateful to my dean, Salma Ghanem, who authorized and supported a two-quarter academic leave that the University Research Council awarded me, and without which this book could not have been completed. And I am lucky to have such amazing and generous colleagues as Bruno Teboul, Carolyn Bronstein, Lexa Murphy, Kelly Kessler, Blair Davis, Paul Booth, and Luisela Alvaray, who have made me feel welcome in the community of the College of Communication ever since I started there in 2010. I offer special thanks to my friend and distinguished colleague Dusty Goltz, who helped me to stay on track with the project even when I felt less than motivated. Wonderful conversations with my colleague Jim Motzer after Group Ride class at Galter LifeCenter consistently reaffirmed my enthusiasm and appreciation for the wildly diverse cinema of the 1960s.

It has been entirely a pleasure to work with SUNY Press, and I am indebted to the two anonymous manuscript readers for providing generous, detailed, and insightful feedback that helped to make the manuscript revision process feel smooth and organized. I am very grateful to James Peltz and Rafael Chaiken for their kindness and support throughout this project. And I owe so much to Murray Pomerance, the editor of this series and a remarkable colleague ever since I met him twenty years ago, who has always had a boundless reserve of confidence in my abilities.

Carol Coopersmith, Susan McGury, Peter Forster, and Miriam and Yoav Ben-Yoseph are lifelong friends and amazing human beings whose joy, love, generosity, and support always remind me about how lucky I am to be a part of a world whose presence they grace. And Teresa Mastin continues to be a supreme force who inspires me with her warmth and wisdom.

As if it weren't wonderful enough that a research facility like the Margaret Herrick Library of the Academy of Motion Picture Arts and Sciences even exists, the kindness, generosity, organization, professionalism, and exceptional expertise of everyone who works there have made the experience of conducting research an absolute pleasure. I only wish it were a bit closer to Chicago!

Ken Feil, Steven Cohan, Pamela Robertson-Wojcik, and Mary Desjardins are friends and scholars of unassuming brilliance that inspire me whenever I read anything that they write, or when I have the privilege of connecting with them. They have all been role models to me in this writing process, as has Harry Benshoff, who first turned me on to *Skidoo* over twenty years ago. I have never been the same, and I can't thank him enough.

My personal trainer and close friend, Jesse Berg, has motivated me through the various stages of this project much more than he could ever know. Through our welcome conversations each Monday morning, he has helped me to think through and organize many of the governing ideas of this book, lending me his curiosity, interest, and insight as a careful listener and discerning critical thinker. I also greatly appreciate his father Gaius, who generously took the time to meet with me for a long, productive, and enlightening conversation about confession and spirituality.

Finally, and most emphatically, I thank Andrew Ramos, my partner of thirty-two years (and much more recently, my spouse), for the confidence, love, and support he has always shown, not only by agreeing to watch and discuss *Rosemary's Baby*, *The Hospital*, and *Carnal Knowledge* with me during his very limited free time on weekends, but by doing much, much more than his fair share of our daily chores so that I could have more time to write. Every night when he comes home from teaching Pilates, I count my blessings for being with a man with such integrity, intelligence, judgment, and exceptional beauty.

As noted, a portion of chapter 2 comprises an expansion of material originally published in "1972: Movies and Confession," *American Cinema of the 1970s: Themes and Variations*, Rutgers University Press, 2007.

Introduction

"WE HAVE A LOT OF SICK PEOPLE in this country," President Johnson suggested in a June 11, 1968, address, "but the country is not sick" (Young, A9). By the time of this declaration, however, just six days after Robert Kennedy's assassination, and two months after the assassination of Martin Luther King, the nation had been bombarded with arguments to the contrary. Eight months earlier, Arkansas Democratic Senator J. W. Fulbright proclaimed that "the Great Society has become a sick society," one committed to an unjust war overseas while lacking any similar commitment to resolving the racial unrest and social inequities prevailing in the United States (SM, 30). Fulbright's proclamation was ironic given his history as an advocate of racial segregation in schools,[1] yet Americans on both sides of the racial divide were affirming this diagnosis of the nation's pathology. Despite its title, "Most in Poll Say U.S. Is Not 'Sick,'" a July 1968 report on a recent Gallup Poll indicated that more than one-third of Americans considered the United States to be a "sick society," with blacks (48%) and supporters of segregationist Alabama Governor George Wallace (42%)—who received 46 electoral votes in his run as an independent candidate in the 1968 presidential election—among the two largest sectors of the population to concur with this label of social illness. Much of the "sick society" discourse focused upon racism, and religious leaders along with President Johnson himself would continue to emphasize the urgency to eradicate social injustice to honor the legacy of the recently assassinated public figures. The scope of the "sick society" label, however, extended beyond the parameters of racial unrest, the Vietnam War, and the assassination of high-profile political figures, with the social metaphor of illness also being applied to recreational drug use, rising divorce rates, and moral indecency, as well as the heavily publicized mass murders that had exacerbated national anxiety in recent years. The notorious culprits included Richard Speck, who strangled eight student nurses in a dormitory on the south side of Chicago in 1966, and Albert DeSalvo, who killed thirteen women in Boston between 1962 and 1964. "We have to make an effort to understand, to go beyond these rather difficult times," Robert Kennedy pleaded in a public address on the night of Martin Luther King's assassination. "What we need in the United States is not division; what we need in the United States is not hatred; what we need in the United States is not violence or lawlessness, but love and wisdom and compassion toward one another. . . ." Yet the silencing of Kennedy's political voice just two months later would only heighten the despair of an American public that across the decade had also worried about the prospect of nuclear destruction, and that continued to bear witness to a technocracy that overvalued notions of technological expertise and "progress" that were contributing to the individual's sense of personal and social alienation—to what humanistic psychologist Carl Rogers would call "the increasing dehumanization of our culture, where the person doesn't count" (10).

Kennedy's plea for Americans to promote the values of empathy, unity, and connectedness was also a call for a remedy or treatment to counteract the pervasive spirit of fear, hatred, loneliness, and division that often characterized the human condition during this decade—a plea for citizens to reach out beyond themselves, to connect, to listen, and to value the perspectives of others with similar or disparate fears, in the hopes of counteracting the prevailing social pathology. This goal was consonant with a politically progressive belief in the value of promoting alliances over divisions and differences. This study demonstrates that "therapy"—as a field of applied psychology undergoing a process of historical transformation, and as a cultural "restorative" that formed provisional alliances with other fields of inquiry—served as a most appropriate response to Kennedy's call by offering Americans the prospect of connection through human, interpersonal communication. With its emphasis upon reflection, contemplation, and insight, psychotherapy had traditionally been characterized as an inward-directed process; in the context of historically concurrent developments in fields of inquiry including pharmacology, sociology, organized religion, and the scientific study of human sexuality, however, "therapy" in the 1960s promised a clearer understanding or "healing" of the self that also anticipated a movement outward, extending to embrace what lies beyond the realm of the individual, a process of "reaching out" in order to form connections and alliances with communities, support networks, organizations committed to political resistance, family members, friends, priests, and other likeminded individuals who might provide a needed sense of belonging.

Broadly speaking, therapy's adaptability to this phenomenon of "reaching out" emerged through the field's gradual transition from the preferred method of psychoanalysis to a different set of psychotherapeutic approaches that outwardly highlighted interpersonal communication and social interaction as integral to the therapeutic process. This transition did not erase the practice of psychoanalysis from the therapeutic or cultural scene, and as John Burnham notes, Freudian psychology continued to stress the importance of the individual's adjustment to both "internal and external reality" (62). At the same time, the era maintained a perception that as a method of inquiry, psychoanalysis focused upon the workings of the subject's past through the excavation of repressed memories, in contradistinction to other emerging therapies' emphasis upon "unlearning" forms of dysfunctional behavior, upon problems that could be solved with less time or financial resources, and upon the pursuit of change and progress in the present. Indeed, speaking about encounter groups, Carl Rogers noted that a crucial indicator of therapeutic progress was the group's ability to move away from a focus upon the "there and then" of past feelings and experiences, to the immediacy of the "here and now" of the present (16). While most models of treatment ultimately required the subject to apply psychotherapeutic principles outside the therapeutic setting, the therapeutic process prescribed in emerging humanistic, client-centered, community, group, encounter, and many behavioral models also emphasized interpersonal interaction within the context of the therapist/patient relationship, preparing the patient for a transition to the world outside.

At the same time that the field of psychotherapy was changing and refocusing, the American film industry was undergoing its own process of transformation. Precipitated by the advent of television and other demographic and cultural shifts, the postwar box office decline reached a critical point during the 1960s. Phenomenal as it was, the success of such roadshow productions as *West Side Story* (1961), *Lawrence of Arabia* (1962), *Doctor Zhivago* (1965), and especially *The Sound of Music* (1965) proved difficult to replicate, and attempts to repeat their formulas resulted in a number of high-budget releases yielding low box-office returns. By the end of the decade, many of the major studios would be driven to bankruptcy and takeover by corporations with little previous exposure to the film industry.[2] Hollywood was also confronting the harsh reality that since the 1950s, some sectors of the audience were attending the cinema much less frequently than others, and it was no longer possible or financially feasible to continue to produce films designed to appeal to an undifferentiated, "general" audience. Having regulated its own content to avoid censorship since the 1930s according to the standards of permissible representation determined by the Production Code Administration (PCA) in conjunction with powerful organizations like the Catholic Legion of Decency, the film industry's ability to respond to the growing demand for films with "adult" subject matter—products that could also be differentiated from television programming—was severely compromised. The industry continued to confront these problems of self-regulation in the early years of the decade, as such directors as Elia Kazan (*Baby Doll*, 1956) and Otto Preminger (*The Moon Is Blue*, 1953; *The Man with a Golden Arm*, 1956; *Advise and Consent*, 1962) repeatedly tested the boundaries of industry self-censorship. By the mid-1960s, the demise of the Production Code was imminent, and in 1968 the industry converted to a rating system that would assess films according to their suitability to specific age groups and levels of maturity.

The transition from psychoanalysis to other psychotherapeutic models never comprised a clean break between therapeutic strategies, and throughout the 1960s innovative therapeutic methods were often based upon combinations of two or more approaches. Marked as it was by such definitive milestones as the establishment of the concept of "variable obscenity" with the release of Mike Nichols's 1966 adaptation of *Who's Afraid of Virginia Woolf?*, the American film industry's transition from the longstanding Production Code to the rating system was no more instantaneous or seamless. Despite new thematic and representational liberties regarding subject matter that was suitable only for mature audiences, the industry's transition from generalized to age-differentiated audiences remained a financially unpredictable one, and especially given the matter of already declining studio profits, cinema of the 1960s includes numerous examples—both before and after the inception of the rating system—where the attempt to address one group of viewers without alienating another group resulted in a "schizophrenic" approach to target marketing and narrative construction. Other cases evidenced the industry's tendency to hold on to time-worn strategies of securing broad-based audience appeal while simultaneously attempting to embrace the new realities of demographics and audience composition, despite the inherent contradictions of such an approach. The movement toward a differentiated, adult-focused cinema involved a constant struggle among studios, audiences, and agencies of content regulation.

Psychotherapy's increasing emphasis upon the notion of "reaching out" beyond the parameters of the self, and the prospect of behavioral change focusing upon the present moment, correlate with the film industry's attempt to devise effective strategies for addressing adult audiences who were eager for films that reflected change and confronted contemporary issues—and also for pleasing critics who were demanding that such issues be treated frankly and realistically. Therapy itself comprises a cogent example of a subject of great public interest during this era, and one whose cinematic expression was affected by factors both external and internal to the film industry. This book seeks to illuminate how the concept, dynamic, and practice of therapy was incorporated into the themes, representations, and narrative strategies of a changing film industry by focusing upon five socially pertinent fields of psychotherapeutic inquiry that American cinema addressed in the 1960s and early 1970s: the dynamic between therapists and patients; the diagnosis and treatment of male and female sexual dysfunction; the treatment of marital discord and dysfunction in the context of shifting gender relations; the therapeutic use of hallucinogenic drugs; and the dynamics of "confession" in the interwoven contexts of psychotherapy and organized religion. The study is organized around two interrelated questions: (1) In what ways is therapeutic discourse informed by other (legal, political, sociological, and religious) discourses during this period of profound social change? (2) How do these historically intersecting discourses bear upon the narrative strategies of an American cinema facing the necessity of new adjustments during the 1960s and early 1970s? Through the examination of concerns and strategies of therapeutic discourse in the context of these five fields of inquiry, I propose that a common tendency emerges—a tendency for the subject/patient's therapeutic treatment to extend beyond the point of self-insight such that it continues in a process of opening up to the world—working toward the formation of stronger interpersonal, community/social, and political engagement, thereby counteracting social division and alienation with the spirit of connection, unity, and community. This tendency emerges as the contemporary culture reframes and reconfigures therapeutic issues as problems of human communication, thereby enabling the development of tangible treatment strategies that promise to address and alleviate individual psychological problems *as* social problems. The study offers an analysis of the alliances and disparities that develop among sets of correlated historical discourses, illuminating changes in perspective that develop over time, while also revealing alliances that emerge from perspectives that had developed along skewed paths only later to converge at a specific historical moment to address a specific problem. As a constant, discourses remain unstable, susceptible to shifts and deviations, and the study of these convergences and divergences helps to illuminate the ways in which cultures attain and challenge ideological consensus.

Each chapter centers upon therapeutic discourse relating to one of the five primary fields of inquiry chosen for the study. After complicating a widely accepted notion of psychotherapy as primarily conformist and ideologically normative, chapter 1 focuses upon changes in the dynamic between therapist and patient that were occurring between the late 1950s and early 1970s. The move away from psychoanalysis that began in psychotherapy of the late 1950s and early 1960s is not diachronically replicated in cinematic representations of the analyst/patient relationship; instead, the early years of the decade witness cases in which contemporary social and political topics such as racism and the threat of nuclear annihilation are grafted onto the analyst/patient relationship. Early films depict a variety of psychotherapeutic approaches, and the patient's search for connections to the outside world prevails in these films, most of which were critically reviled for electing sensationalism over the realism that was expected to support the theme of social justice. In the face of an escalating Vietnam War around which political consensus could not be reached, or a remedy be established, by the middle of the decade the film industry had largely disempowered and trivialized the role of the psychotherapist, as the representation of patient/therapist relations shifted genres from sociopsychological drama to romantic comedy, where these relations would become more insular and contained. As the restrictions of the Production Code further receded, the new comedic context also sexualized these therapeutic relations, converting sex into a "problem" to be resolved, usually in conjunction with a backlash against the burgeoning second-wave feminist movement and its challenges to traditional gender roles. In films as generically disparate as *Coming Apart* (Milton Moses Ginsberg, 1969) and *On a Clear Day You Can See Forever* (Vincente Minnelli, 1970) cinema at the close of the decade witnessed a new willingness to politically critique the therapist/patient relationship in narratives that continued to sexualize this relationship while stressing

Figure 0.1. Daisy Gamble (Barbra Streisand), liberated from the constraints of psychotherapy at the end of *On a Clear Day You Can See Forever* (Vincente Minnelli, Paramount Pictures, 1970). Digital frame enlargement.

the value of interpersonal and social communication as a key component of the therapeutic process.

The subsequent chapters focus upon psychotherapeutic relations whose examples in cinema are not confined to representations of patients and analysts in formal or professional therapeutic settings. Extending from the noted tendency to sexualize psychotherapeutic relations, chapter 2 focuses upon an area in which sex literally *comprises* the problem: the new sex therapies designed to treat men and women experiencing sexual dysfunction. Here, the gradual historical movement away from the psychoanalytic model diachronically aligns with the course of cinematic representation of the era. Through the first half of the decade, psychoanalytic models dominate in films such as *The Chapman Report* (George Cukor, 1962) and *Marnie* (Alfred Hitchcock, 1964) that problematize female sexual dysfunction (or "frigidity," as it was referenced at the time), and whose methods invariably comprise investigations into childhood traumas that the therapeutic subject has repressed. In these cases, an invested male figure (one without any therapeutic credentials) initiates the subject's "cure," upon which she is delivered to his hands, her return to psycho-physiological health now rendering her suitable for sexual relations and marriage. Aligned with the successful treatment strategies of Masters and Johnson, the move to behavioral models later in the 1960s accommodates a greater cinematic emphasis upon therapy as a vehicle for psychological change stemming from a confrontation with present conditions. This move correlates with themes and narratives that are attuned to contemporary social conditions and historical developments, especially the women's liberation movement that was also influencing representations of the patient/therapist dynamic. Consonant with Masters and Johnson's own methods, enhanced interpersonal communication (both verbal and tactile) serves as the remedy for eliminating the anxiety that causes sexual dysfunction. Despite the new liberties in sexual representation that the move to the film rating system accommodated, however, films of the late 1960s and early 1970s such *Midnight Cowboy* (John Schlesinger, 1969), *The Hospital* (Arthur Hiller, 1971), and *Carnal Knowledge* (Mike Nichols, 1971) continue to focus upon sexual pathology rather than sexual freedom, with the pathological subject now a male figure plagued by what the popular press would label as the incurable "New Impotence" initiated by feminism. It is only in the politically contentious realm of early 1970s hardcore pornography where economies of narrative construction readily accommodated resolutions to problems of sexual dysfunction.

While chapter 2 confronts a largely incontrovertible problem, chapter 3 focuses upon marriage therapies, where the problem/solution dynamic becomes more complex because of the institution's uncertain status in light of second-wave feminism and the women's liberation movement. Models of marriage therapy adhered to the previously noted gradual transition away from psychoanalysis, while emerging methods in this area combined aspects of the psychoanalytic method with other schools of thought, integrating a focus upon present-day change with the investigation of repressed memories. While sociological studies that tied marriage to capitalism and materialism remained skeptical about the continued value of the institution in the contemporary sociopolitical context—and also more resistant to the notion that failing marriages could be treated effectively by hard "work"—most therapeutic studies consistently maintained that marriage was worth saving and entirely salvageable when dysfunction was addressed as a problem to be resolved. Across the decade, therapeutic models conducted both within and outside the therapist/patient context increasingly focused on collaboration and enhanced interpersonal communication strategies as essential components of treatment, culminating in the late 1960s and early 1970s with the emergence of humanistic therapies, including the popular encounter group model developed by forerunners in behavioral psychotherapy.

As an extension of postwar ideologies that promoted the preservation of male sexual freedom, cinematic treatments of male marital anxiety occur much earlier than the treatments of male sexual dysfunction. At the start of the decade, the representation of marital anxiety tends to be more consistently comedic than dramatic, influenced by Italian marital satires such as *Divorce Italian Style* (Pietro Germi, 1961) and *Marriage Italian Style* (Vittorio De Sica, 1964) that had gained popularity in the United States. If the women's liberation movement was positioned as the primary cause of male impotence, the treatment of women in the mid-decade American, male-centered marriage comedies often bordered on misogynistic accounts of her ceaseless demands for a monogamous relationship, even while the films would ultimately reaffirm the integrity of the marriage institution by making couples responsible for acting as their own therapeutic agents to repair dysfunction through open communication. Acknowledging the advances of second-wave feminism, therapeutic marriage films of the late 1960s and early 1970s such as *Diary of a Mad Housewife* (Frank Perry, 1970) adopted female perspectives on the burdens of marital confinement, yet the film industry was soon to take recourse in marital dynamics that travestied the advancements of the feminist movement in films such as *Lovers and Other Strangers* (Cy Howard, 1970) and *The Marriage of a Young Stockbroker* (Lawrence Turman, 1971), which reworked the progressive politics of consciousness raising according to increasingly popular humanistic therapeutic models that promoted self-actualization.

While chapters 2 and 3 confront issues of interpersonal alienation that occur in intimate relationships, chapter 4 addresses forms of social disconnection for which psychedelic drug use was presented as a potential remedy, promoting empathy, compassion, understanding, and the celebration of human difference as counteractives to the profuse alienation of technocratic culture. Situated at the heart of the generation gap, the controversial topic of hallucinogenic drug use was rendered even more socially divisive by the realities of its recent history as an agent of mind control that the CIA (and later, the military) had used as a tactic of interrogation and torture at the height of the Cold War. Here, the rhetoric of "control" and psychological destruction came into direct conflict with the rhetoric of liberation through psychological insight in various psychotherapeutic settings in the late 1950s and early 1960, as therapies used psychedelic drugs as viable accelerants in the understanding of schizophrenia and the treatment of alcoholism and other addictions. Initially conducted in an academic context, the behaviorist experiments of Dr. Timothy Leary expanded the scope of psychedelic therapy to address problems of recidivism and to promote spiritual transcendence. The popular press configured Leary's controversial departure from Harvard University as the basis for a humiliating public scandal that pathologized the researcher's therapeutic efforts. With the increasing popularity of LSD and other hallucinogens in youth culture, Leary would soon be cast as the key figure in a backlash against American "family values," even as the scientific community would defame his reputation by counterposing his subjective and indulgent "pseudo-science" with real, objective and authoritative science, in the spirit of the technocracy. The national illegalization of LSD in 1966 further delegitimized therapeutic discourse as the government curtailed scientists' access to the drug, and these same efforts would soon transform the "hippie" into contemporary America's prototypical "loser."

The film industry's treatment of hallucinogenic drug use occurred during the second half of the decade, after the drug was made illegal. Attempting not to alienate either side of the generation gap, and aware of the consequences of voicing any single, definitive perspective on a cogent, controversial issue with great potential for exploitation, the industry produced films that, like *Wild in the Streets* (Barry Shear, 1968), took *both* sides on a controversial issue in the context of the same narrative, using a variety of strategies to address the inherent contradictions of this approach (see fig. 0.2). These paradoxical treatments were often the result of contending voices within the film industry as it struggled to negotiate the still unestablished boundaries of post-Code cinematic representation. As a social corrective, however, the psychedelic cinema

Figure 0.2. Millionaire LSD producer Max Frost (Christopher Jones, center) and boy-genius accountant Billy Cage (Kevin Coughlin, left) dose Senator Johnny Fergus (Hal Holbrook) and the entire U.S. Senate with LSD in *Wild in the Streets* (Barry Shear, American International Pictures, 1968). Digital frame enlargement.

of the late 1960s ultimately emphasized the value of interpersonal communication as both a product of and an alternative to LSD use in such films as *Skidoo* (Otto Preminger, 1968), before hallucinogens would be re-pathologized in conjunction with the Manson murders of 1969.

Whereas chapter 4 concerns the ultimately compromised efforts of psychotherapeutic discourse to intervene in the negotiation of a controversial issue—that is, to be recognized *as therapy* rather than as a problematic symptom of a larger sociopsychological disorder—chapter 5 addresses an area in which therapeutic discourse, with less resistance, largely succeeds in expanding and opening up possibilities of connection through a singular process of confluence, by merging with another discourse to which it had long been opposed. Previously limited to the realms of the legal system and the Catholic Church, the discourse of confession would align religion with psychotherapy by the late 1950s due to parallel developments in the two fields. The Church drew upon the discourse of therapy as it began to develop a new sense of commitment to connect with the social problems of the world outside its domain, especially with the advancements of the Second Ecumenical Council (Vatican II) in the early 1960s. As concurrent, emerging psychotherapeutic approaches were emphasizing the importance of the patient's reflection upon present-day realities as a prelude to larger interpersonal and social change, the Church was gradually moving away from a dynamic that positioned confessor and penitent in a unidirectional, "monologic" relationship, in preference for a system in which the verbalization of transgression became a matter of therapeutic "disclosure" closely aligned with interpersonal communication. At the same time, with Pope Pius XII taking an interest in cinema's role as a medium of education and dialogue, the Church was also drastically changing its stance regarding the products of the film industry, moving away from the moral condemnation and judgment that had long characterized the Legion of Decency and its role in upholding the standards of the industry's Production Code. These efforts paralleled the film industry's commitment to adapt to the present-day changes in viewer demographics that ultimately led to the Code's dissolution. The chapter analyzes a group of films from the mid-1960s to the early 1970s which, in accordance with these recent changes in the Church and the film industry, focus upon the phenomenon of confession as a theme, a style, a narrative device, and an interpersonal dynamic conducted far beyond the confines of the confessional booth. In films ranging from *The President's Analyst* (Theodore J. Flicker, 1967), to *Five Easy Pieces* (Bob Rafelson, 1970), to *The Boys in the Band* (William Friedkin, 1970), confession becomes not only a crucial vehicle for the painful disclosure of truth, but also among the only means of forging interpersonal and social connections, by fostering intimacy, sincerity, and transparency in an alienated culture.

The book is structured as a historical discourse analysis that foregrounds specific contexts of meaning, seeking to illuminate places of correlation and tension among a set of interconnected discourses at play during the 1960s and early 1970s. Wodak and Meyer explain that "critical discourse analysis is characterized by the common interests in de-mystifying ideologies through the systematic . . . investigation of semiotic data (written, spoken, and visual)," and the "semiotic data" that I focus upon here comprises two sets of texts (3). The first includes the scientific research pertaining specifically to the subject of therapy and the fields of inquiry with which this subject connects, including religion, hallucinogenic drug use, marriage, feminism, and sex research. These texts include publications primarily addressed to the psychotherapeutic professional community, books and articles that professionals write in an effort to disseminate their findings to interested "lay" readers, and popular press articles that synthesize this research for the broader American public, according to its perceived relevance and interest to contemporary society. The second set of texts includes both the films themselves and written materials pertaining to the film industry, including critical reviews that illuminate reception strategies of the historical moment, and internal industry correspondence and studio publicity materials that highlight marketing strategies. While some of this scientific and cinema-related material includes more recent publications, I have chosen to focus mainly upon texts written in the 1960s and early 1970s, since they best reflect the discursive strategies at play during this historical period.

Although this book does not fully align with the methods or perspectives of earlier critical work on this subject, I offer it as a complement to Janet Walker and Dana Cloud's important research on the intersection of therapy, politics, and popular culture. In *Control and Consolation in American Culture and Politics*, Dana Cloud defines the therapeutic enterprise as wholly invested in a form of "healing" that strives to reconcile the subject to the terms and circumstances of her own oppression, rather than providing any foundation for social change. Therapy directs the subject's focus inward to the individual and the family as it "translates political questions into psychological issues to be resolved through personal, psychological change" (xx–xxi). Focusing upon the post-Vietnam era, Cloud analyzes a diverse set of instances of therapeutic discourse such as the "family values" rhetoric of political campaigns, the media's dissemination of news about support groups in its coverage of the Persian Gulf War, and the discourse of consciousness-raising in key feminist texts as well as the 1991 film *Thelma and Louise*. Countering the notion of therapy as solely a mechanism of ideological control and containment, Janet Walker's *Couching Resistance: Women, Film, and Psychoanalytic Psychiatry* examines operations of power that develop as the institutions of psychoanalysis and Hollywood cinema converge in defining woman as object in therapeutic relations from the late 1940s through the early 1960s. Walker argues that both institutions accommodate negotiations of this definition, bringing to light the strains of both ideological resistance and adjustment in the field of therapy and its cinematic representation.

My intention in this study is to bring into focus the alliances and divergences among discourses that interweave and accumulate around therapy as a clinical, social, scientific, and cultural phenomenon that resonates strongly enough in the United States during the 1960s and early 1970s to extend its reach beyond the realms of psychiatry and psychology, to a broad set of cultural models and practices, ultimately including a cinematic medium that has developed its own institutional, political, and narrative criteria for determining this discourse's relevance and palatability to American audiences. Rather than simply absorbing or replicating this interwoven and accumulated material to make it available for audience consumption on a rectangular screen, this cinema both synthesizes and negotiates these discourses. As the following chapters show, the analysis of neither the specific discourses themselves nor their interplay as they coalesce around the field of therapy is structured to highlight principles of causality; instead, I seek to map out the developments, intersections, and divergences in terms of their power (or lack thereof) to resonate as meaningful and important during an era of profound cultural change.

All of the films of this study were released between 1961 and 1972, a period that is broad enough for me to shape the analysis to accommodate the major shifts in content self-regulation that occurred in the mid to late 1960s, along with the concurrent developments in psychotherapy and related fields that inform this analysis of the therapeutic dynamic in cinema. In chapters 4 and 5, the historical time span of the films is by necessity much shorter: all of the relevant psychedelic films covered in chapter 4 were released between 1966 and 1968, after the criminalization of LSD possession; and "post-booth" forms of Catholic confession did not materialize until shortly after the conclusion of Vatican II in 1965. Both of these chapters, along with the others, ultimately frame their specific cinematic time spans in broader, lengthier historical terms. While the period under consideration includes the release of many more films that pertain to the subject of therapy, practical considerations have guided the decision to limit my selection to a manageable number of primary films that best illustrate the patterns I discuss.

1

Analyst/Patient Relationships

Psychotherapeutic Dynamics

Discussing the burgeoning field of community psychiatry in his 1970 study, *The Politics of Therapy*, University of Wisconsin student-health psychiatrist Seymour Halleck explains that "Although I want to believe that I have no visions of how I want my patients to change, I am regularly amazed (and perhaps pleased) to note that my patients gradually move toward value systems that are closer to mine. While there are some exceptions, most of my radical patients become a little less radical and my conservative patients become a little less conservative" (96). Such an admission might appear to reinforce the convictions of cultural theorists such as Dana Cloud, who asserts at the outset of *Control and Consolation in American Culture and Politics: Rhetorics of Therapy* that "psychotherapy is a rhetoric that exhorts conformity with the prevailing social order" (2)—one that has been operating by means of a "language of healing, consolation, and adaptation or adjustment" (3), especially in the post-1968 era (51). Far from celebrating this phenomenon as a victory for the psychiatric profession (despite his admission about being pleased), however, Halleck positions this inherently ideological dimension of psychotherapeutic practice as a central tenet of a therapeutic model that, if used responsibly, supports the altering of inequitable sociopolitical conditions for the greater good, and that is essential for all therapists to foreground to their patients, lest they find themselves being swayed unknowingly to a political position antithetical to their own values. As Janet Walker argues, Halleck's work is aligned with "a changing view of the relationship between society and the individual" (21). From this perspective, to recognize and admit outright that therapeutic discourse is political is an attempt at transparency, and one that enables an open therapeutic process in the evolving relationship between analyst and patient.

Halleck's work emerges from one of the politically engaged, contextual therapeutic models that by the 1960s had gradually gained prominence over the psychodynamic model that had dominated American psychotherapeutic practice since the late 1940s (Cautin 33). While Freudian psychoanalysis had traditionally centered upon a probing of the patient's past, seeking to expose the source or origin of aberrant psychological conditions in early childhood trauma, emerging behavioral and client-centered models that ultimately assumed prominence focused more intently on the analysis of the patient's present condition, with behavioral therapists positing that "most abnormal behavior can be modified through social learning principles" (DeLeon 110). While psychoanalysis confronted forms of psychic victimization sufficiently devastating to patients such that they developed elaborate repressive mechanisms to disavow their traumas, many emerging therapeutic models of the 1960s valued the basic principle that because undesired, dysfunctional behavior is acquired and learned, patients can overcome psychic obstacles by learning and adopting more functional and adaptive behavioral strategies to replace those that have not served them well.

In *The Politics of Therapy*, the crucial value of the therapist's role as guiding educator, along with the openness and transparency with which he must foreground his own political constitution and belief system, are principles that also encompass the broader set of progressive psychotherapeutic practice of the late 1960s and early 1970s—practices rooted in social, cultural, and political developments in America in this era. Halleck's prescription for psychiatry becomes emblematic of a larger call for forms of interpersonal connection and communication that might bring individuals with diverse beliefs and expectations based upon differing social, economic, and political conditions into more productive and meaningful contact with one another. Halleck highlights the importance of encouraging such contact in the context of prominent social movements of the era that were still striving to elevate a cultural awareness of the severe socioeconomic disparities that persisted across the United States. His sensitivity to the prevalence of the consolation and adjustment motives highlighted by Cloud resonates in this historical context. In his selection of examples and case studies Halleck is careful to emphasize that therapeutic "solutions" must inevitably vary across races and cultures. His commitment to foregrounding the political dimension of psychotherapy also correlates with other historically specific—and specifically politicized—cultural phenomena of this period. His work emphasizes the importance, within the therapeutic context, of a hyper-awareness of environmental stress factors, of *listening* to others, of devoting oneself to discerning and appreciating multiple perspectives, and of accomplishing these goals when possible in therapeutic settings that permit "patients" to learn from each other, whether the contexts include a set of strangers in a group therapy session, or the collective members of one's immediate nuclear family. "The family therapy model . . . enables family members to learn how they actually communicate with one another and gain a clearer understanding of each other's problems," Halleck explains. "Each person in the family also learns something about how the others view him, and it is often possible to untangle the twisted web of relationships that has led one or more persons in the family to experience emotional suffering" (57).

This chapter argues that such matters of transparency, openness, connection, and understanding serve as a most suitable thematic context for interpreting American cinematic representations of the therapeutic process in the 1960s and early 1970s. This suitability arises not because these representations mirrored or traced the gradual cultural deferral of Freudian psychoanalytic therapy to other therapeutic models during this period. In fact, as the chapter will demonstrate, rather than highlighting the emergence of alternative therapeutic approaches as the psychoanalytic model lost prevalence (Nordcross/Cautin 33), most of the psychotherapists cinematically represented during the 1960s and early 1970s were clearly identified as Freudian psychoanalysts, and even when they were not, they adhered to a therapeutic method fully consonant with the psychoanalytic method in its focus upon the interpretation of dreams and the investigation of deeply rooted trauma, the resolution of which comprised what Glen Gabbard has aptly named the "cathartic cure," the psychic revelation that dovetails so effectively with classical Hollywood cinematic structure (2001, 366). It is tempting to interpret these developments as merely an indication that Hollywood was behind the times regarding contemporary developments in the field of psychotherapy, and that the American film industry was continuing to cling to individualistic therapeutic models that hegemonically upheld the aims of consolation and adjustment while American culture was busy becoming more overtly and radically politicized. Exploring further, however, what does emerge in the study of cinematic analyst/patient relationships, especially in a comparison of representative films of the early 1960s and the early 1970s, is a search for meaningful and fulfilling forms of interpersonal connection—sometimes between analyst and patient, but just as often in broader contexts, between patients themselves, or between patients and others outside of the therapeutic setting. These connections often emerge as positive outcomes of the therapeutic process; at other times, the value of openness that might facilitate connection and communication emerges as a result of what either patients or analysts *fail* to achieve within the one-on-one therapeutic dynamic and are consequently forced to seek elsewhere. In either case, what transpires is the grafting of sociopolitically emergent themes of connection so firmly established throughout this period *onto* the one-on-one analyst/analysand model of psychoanalysis.

Simultaneously during this period, however, the emphasis upon the value of human connection and mutual understanding derived through psychotherapy is mined by a Hollywood film industry that, at least in the eyes of contemporary film critics, was guilty of exploiting and sensationalizing mental illness, especially given that as the 1960s progress and the strictures of the Production Code lessen, the therapeutic setting guarantees an intensifying, frank, and often sexual intimacy. Indeed, as Gabbard suggests, "the presence of the psychotherapist allows the protagonist to share an inner world on the screen that would otherwise not be available to the audience" (2001, 365). During the early 1960s, the parameters of exploitation are confined to what is critically perceived as the too graphic and overly exaggerated depictions of antisocial and pathological behavior resonating in a culture that still remains as anxious about totalitarianism as about the racial inequities that American culture was addressing in the civil rights era. As the decade advances, however, the terms of onscreen exploitation of psychotherapy become more firmly rooted in themes and frank depictions of sexuality that dovetail with historical developments of the sexual revolution. Consistently, cinematic depictions of patient/analyst relationships throughout this period evidence the workings of a film industry caught in a struggle to determine how to formulate workable (and profitable) alliances—between audiences and critics accustomed to the still tenuously upheld moral restrictions of the Production Code, and a new audience base whose preferences for frank, adult subject matter often exceed the limits of the industry's longstanding system of self-regulation. Ultimately, the industry's representation of analyst/patient relations evidences problems of dovetailing, reconciling, and often mismatching historical trends involving changes in audience expectation and content regulation, as well as in the methods and models of psychotherapy itself.

While the inception of the era of sexual revolution is usually designated as the mid- to late-1960s, a treatment of pertinent analyst/patient films from the first years of the decade helps to illuminate the historical and cultural contexts in which thematic and representational trends developed. Gabbard and Gabbard describe the early 1960s as the "Golden Age" of psychiatry in American cinema, when the psychiatric profession and professional enjoyed their highest level of unquestioned authority (1999, 75). Contemporary critical assessment of films in this era accentuates a broad cultural acceptance of psychiatry by an American public well-versed in the profession's terminology. A 1963 *Commonweal* review of John Huston's controversial biographical drama *Freud* (aka *This Secret Passion*, 1962) explains that "although they are not named at the time, the film illustrates various concepts of hysterical illness, psychological traumas, repressions, free association, transference, infantile sexuality, and other now familiar terms of psychiatry" ("Sang-Freud," 389). Gabbard suggests that after the representational boundaries of the Production Code had been successfully tested and expanded during the 1950s—a period that corresponded with the dramatic increase in television viewership and ownership, and a further decrease in Hollywood's box-office receipts—the presence of the psychiatrist "could legitimize sexuality in films" (1999, 24–25). In *Couching Resistance*, Janet Walker supports this claim of legitimization with her recounting of *Freud*'s struggle to gain acceptance by the Production Code Administration: after an initial denial of the seal of approval on the sole basis of the script, technical adviser Dr. Harold Loomis enlisted the authority of the American Psychological Association (APA) to address issues at the crux of the PCA's resistance. Additionally, the support of theologians and religious leaders—many of whom were themselves psychiatrists—was obtained to secure an alliance with the Legion of Decency, the Catholic organization that continued to hold sway over the film industry (Walker 1993, 144–50).

The cultural resonance of psychiatry at the height of this "Golden Era" is evident by sheer volume alone, with approximately twenty films centering upon analyst/patient psychotherapeutic relations being released between 1962 and 1963. In addition to Huston's landmark biopic on the "father" of psychoanalysis, the films of this period are historically significant for their linkages between internal, psychic states and external, societal conditions, thereby challenging even early in the decade the notion that psychotherapeutic representation was focusing exclusively upon the personal at the expense of the political. Many of these narratives also support Walker's claim that Freudian psychoanalysis is not necessarily oriented to the terms of social adjustment, its insight-directedness harboring the capacity for social resistance rather than ideologically imposing any single world view (40–42). Furthermore, in Huston's biopic, Freud's (Montgomery Clift) own comment to Joseph Breuer (Larry Parks) that "Society would collapse in a day if sexuality were allowed free expression" is prescient regarding the moral and social concerns that would surface later in the decade, even if the film's concentration upon the early period of Freud's life and professional development during which the theories of infantile sexuality and the Oedipus complex were formulated, appears to place Huston's work at a historical remove from the climate of the early 1960s.

Continuing with a trend that is traceable to the 1950s melodramas of Nicholas Ray (*Rebel Without a Cause*, 1955; *Bigger than Life*, 1956), Vincent Minnelli (*The Cobweb*, 1955; *Tea and Sympathy*, 1956), and Douglas Sirk (*Imitation of Life*, 1959), many of the early 1960s films root their political orientation in traumas emerging from the dysfunctional nuclear family, years before family therapy had been introduced as a psychotherapeutic practice. Aligning social, political, and domestic matters in this way, the films superimpose the sometimes ambiguous distinctions between sanity and insanity with the socially rendered differences between the normal and abnormal. Released in the United States just two weeks after *Freud*, Frank Perry's critically acclaimed *David and Lisa* (1962) begins as the mother (Neva Patterson) of the film's eponymous central male protagonist David Clemens (Keir Dullea) returns her son to a boarding school for the mentally ill. When head psychiatrist Alan Swinford (Howard Da Silva) interviews her about David's illness and symptoms, David's mother responds defensively, deflecting any suggestion that she is responsible for her son's aberrant behavior. Although the doctor does not definitively diagnose David's condition, David's curt verbal responses to others, stiff mannerisms and stilted movements and gestures convey an anti-social predisposition, with his irrational fear of even the most casual forms of physical contact. When David discusses his dreams in the therapeutic sessions, Dr. Swinford unsuccessfully attempts to encourage him to explore the connection between the fear of touch and his fear of being loved, but his subsequent interactions with his mother on her infrequent visits to the school illustrate the connection all too clearly: rather than being curious about her son's progress, she chastises him for his impertinent and disrespectful behavior, and refuses to perceive any similarities between David and the "crazy" students at the institution. Indeed, she finds the school and its students so distasteful that she soon arranges for David to move back to the family's home, the suffocating nature of which is conveyed in a claustrophobic, symmetrical medium-shot of a conservatively suited David at the dining room table, with furrowed brow and blank stare, neatly aligned with the floral centerpiece immediately before him, tall, lighted candles narrowly framing his rigid body while china cabinets rise up at the extreme left and right portions of the cinematic frame, his parents' idle welcome-home dinner conversation audible from the immediate offscreen space. "It's terrible when you're not here," his mother later confides, yet the imposing domestic setting clearly compromises any sense of his "presence" there: as it turns out, his mother has decided that David must enroll in a more elite and respectable place of learning, one where she will not have to suffer the embarrassment of others in their social circle who might recognize her son's "'condition." David's father Stewart (Richard McMurray), clearly incapacitated in the presence of his domineering, opinionated spouse, makes an effort to reach his dispassionate son. Speaking to him privately about his alienation from his own (disinterested) father, and expressing genuine concern regarding the reasons for David's anxieties, he discusses the sense of renewed possibilities he felt when David was born: "I wanted to make the world over so that those eyes could never see anything that—so that nothing ever could scare you, or disappoint you." Yet David's reticence to respond to his father's suggestion that the two of them reconcile by taking a road trip suggests that his problems are too deeply rooted to be resolved by diversions and casual encounters.

At the start of the film David demonstrates his disrespect for the psychiatric profession, and he boldly makes his feelings known to Dr. Swinford, referencing the "idiot psychiatrists my mother drags me to" in one of their first therapy sessions. At the same time, David is exceptionally well-versed in psychotherapeutic terminology (while Dr. Swinford refrains almost entirely from using it) and is soon offering his diagnoses of several fellow students as well as Dr. Swinford. Once he is forced back into a routine with his parents, and continuing to be haunted by a dream in which he struggles to control the movements of a gigantic clock's minute hand fitted with a guillotine blade and about to decapitate his acquaintances, however, it isn't long before David decides to leave home and return to Swinford's care. Especially after David's return, the psychiatrist, who opposed the mother's decision to remove him from the school, demonstrates an even stronger influence upon David's emotional and social behavior. As Gabbard and Gabbard suggest, in the film "the psychiatrist functions as the best hope in a fallen world without the consoling promise of eternally nurturing families" (1999, 88). Unlike David's parents, whose interest in their son's well-being remains too tied up with a perception of their own failings, Dr. Swinford proves to be a much better role model, not by imposing any standard of "normalcy" by which David will be expected to abide and conform, but rather by listening and affirmation. "The most important thing is what I think of myself," he proclaims to Dr. Swinford, with whom he has grown comfortable with smiling and making eye contact. That David appears to be progressing in his treatment is nowhere more evident than in a later scene in which he asks Dr. Swinford if he might ever be well enough to go to medical school, adding that he is considering a career in psychiatry.

Although Mrs. Clemens's behavior clearly aligns with the pattern of "Momism" established and sustained through the 1950s whereby the stilted emotional development of male children conveniently traces back to the influence of domineering, over-protective, and overly class-conscious mothers, *David and Lisa* is less interested in assigning blame for David's condition than in exploring the barriers to social interaction that sustain mental illness and isolation. Foremost among these are obstacles that prevent empathy and communication: in contrast to the uneasy interactions between David and his parents at home—interactions that take place in cramped quarters and windowless rooms, and that comprise parental directives and confessions to which David remains impervious—his meetings with Dr. Swinford in the second half of the film resonate with openness, light, and less structured and imposing configurations of *mise en scène*. More importantly, they comprise actual conversations in which David willingly participates and does most of the talking.

Most remarkably, however, David's successful psychological transference—his construction of Dr. Swinford as an ideal father figure—is positioned not as a sign of an ultimate "cure," but rather as a necessary first step in a safe, controlled environment that he needs to master before attempting less certain or predictable relationships in the "outside" world—mainly, with Lisa. Given that she is, even by David's own diagnostic account, a "chronic schizophrenic" with two distinct personalities, only one of which is verbally communicative (and *only* in rhyme), the situation presents a formidable challenge. Given these circumstances, David's layman influence proves to be effective: Lisa's interactions with him break down the barriers that had left her a victim of her own isolation. "Love" does not cure either of them, but by the ending she has begun to experiment with verbalizing to him without rhyme, and in the final moments of the film, he reaches out to her, both physically and verbally, with what was earlier perhaps the most difficult expression for someone so mortally terrified by the prospect of human contact: "Take my hand."

With its opening title, "Dedicated to the caretakers whose research and sacrifice discover truth," *The Caretakers* (Hall Bartlett, 1963) articulates the connections among psychic trauma, domestic circumstances, and political issues in a more overtly pro-social context.[1] After a credit sequence featuring expressionist sketches of exaggeratedly shadowed, isolated, faceless figures covering themselves up to hide from view, the narrative begins with a harrowing scene in which an eye-darting, profusely perspiring, clearly panicked Lorna Melford (Polly Bergen), wincing and contracting at the loud traffic noise, darts about the city streets until happening upon a movie theater where she decides takes refuge.

Once ushered to her seat, however, a series of shot/reverse shots in extreme close-up accentuate her terrified reactions to deafeningly loud newsreel sequences depicting the launching of a rocket and a violent protest involving the police and an unidentified mob. Suddenly bolting from her seat, she dashes down the aisle toward the screen, quavering and gesticulating wildly as she faces the audience, her body juxtaposed with the screen action behind her depicting racing cars in whose direct trajectory she has become situated, her resounding screams drown out by the revving of the car motors onscreen.

After the unresponsive Lorna is admitted to the Canterbury State Hospital, she is placed under the care of head psychiatrist Donovan MacLeod (Robert Stack), who has struggled with administrative authorities to run and maintain an experimental "borderline" ward for patients whom he determines to be at least potentially capable of successful re-socialization. In the scenes depicting Lorna's private sessions with MacLeod, the therapeutic investigation of trauma bears some similarity to David's treatment in *David and Lisa*: family trauma is at the root of her problems, as Lorna reveals that as a child she was put in the untenable position of arbiter in arguments between a "cold" mother and a father who was always on the verge of abandoning home. The narrative suggests that Lorna's childhood feelings of helplessness have left her even less equipped to cope with the recent death of her daughter in an automobile accident. Compared to Dr. Swinford, however, the psychiatrist in *The Caretakers* is more fully personalized, and the less restrictive narration permits the audience access to the doctor's own, more severe family trauma resulting from his father's suicide after suffering from a debilitating mental illness. "I buried my feelings—the guilt, the shame," MacLeod admits to a sympathetic nurse, and when he adds that "a place like this could have saved him—and so many more," the film connects his investment in patients like Lorna to the greater personal and professional mission of a man who has managed successfully to surmount debilitating trauma to the benefit of others.

The core of the film's distinctive representation of therapy, however, lies less in the traditional one-on-one psychodynamic process than in progressive group therapy sessions that were still experimental in the early 1960s. *The Caretakers* modifies *David and Lisa*'s strategies of patient socialization so that it depends entirely upon the development of successful interpersonal relations among patient inmates. With a life together in the ward apart from more severely afflicted and isolated patients who cannot be helped as readily, the women take on the characteristics of a community whose cohesion and flexibility are tested and ultimately reinforced by the often uncomfortable dynamics of group therapy. Patients plagued by their own sense of isolation become aware of each other's habits, patterns, and obsessions: Edna (Barbara Barrie) hasn't spoken a word in over seven years; Connie (Sharon Hugueny) has invented a series of warm, sympathetic letters from her mother that were never actually written; Marion (Janis Paige) is especially contemptuous of MacLeod's probing questions; but Irene (Ellen Corby), an elderly patient who is clearly the most lucid of the group, lends compassion and balance to the group with her declaration that "No one's crazy here. We're alone. All alone." MacLeod himself is depicted as a maverick heavily invested in a therapeutic philosophy that requires the facilitation of trust among all group members (himself included), and the group sessions become an extension of his belief in the power of empathy and understanding as invaluable therapeutic tools. "The group fights to destroy the abnormality" in the brain of the mentally ill, he argues, adding that "'Maybe it's because the group is a whole, and the people in it begin to realize that they need and care for each other. Our job is to understand these people. To learn to see with their eyes. To hear with their ears. To feel with their needs."

The fact that patient "progress" in this experimental setting is much more gradual and developmental than immediate or "cathartic" might make the depicted methods seem more realistic to those viewers encountering the film over half a century after its release. As the stunned reaction of the group of nurses observing the sessions remotely via television monitor evidences, however, in its contemporary context MacLeod's methods are depicted as wholly radical—a turning point in the profession, marking the shift from longstanding methods of incarceration, separation, and seclusion of the mentally ill from the rest of society, toward a philosophy of re-integration and inclusion that emphasizes connectedness and communication. This shift paralleled contemporaneous developments in the history of psychotherapy in the United States: in *From Asylum to Community: Mental Health Policy in Modern America* (1991), Grob traces this movement away from sequestration in state hospitals toward re-integration through newly funded community mental health centers. MacLeod's dream of constructing a day hospital that would permit patients such as those in the borderline ward to stay at home with families at night echoes the intentions of the Community Mental Health Centers Act (passed in 1963, the same year as *The Caretakers*'s release) (DeLeon 41). And although it includes no direct references to the Civil Rights Movement, in its emphasis on the virtues of empathy and compassion and its harsh warnings about the social dangers of stereotyping and injustice, the film serves as a plea for understanding wholly consonant with the era's spirit of political reform. This spirit is most evident in the integrity with which *The Caretakers* depicts these proponents of change as they struggle to surmount the debilitating, regressive views of powerful head nurse Lucretia Terry (Joan Crawford), who insists that the safety of her nursing staff is more important than any investment in new therapeutic methods and guidelines. "Never trust a patient," she warns her nurses as she trains them in mandatory judo classes for their own protection. "The patient must know that you are in control." Lucretia's predisposition to "the intelligent use of force," along with her vindictive determination to subvert MacLeod's progressive plans ("Don't you understand what you're doing? Clinging to the past?" he asserts), marks her as a totalitarian presence in the film—a figure without empathy or compassion plagued by outmoded and ineffectual ideals of separation and control.

The film reinforces the larger social dangers of such beliefs that are now being rendered archaic by extending their reach beyond the confines of the state mental institution. Echoing a scene in *David and Lisa* where patients on a supervised outing encounter an aggressive and belligerent father whose efforts to "protect" his family from them results in a needless confrontation in a train station, the anxieties of both patients and the society from which they have been sequestered become aggravated with the occasional easing of "border" restrictions in *The Caretakers*. As Lorna sits peacefully alone beneath a tree on a hillside during a picnic beyond the institution's grounds, a young boy runs up to her to retrieve a ball. A wholly pleasant exchange between them is interrupted when the boy's father runs over to him in alarm, screaming, "I told you to stay away from them. Do you want to get hurt?" as he drags the boy away. In both films, the parent's abrupt and needless interventions to ensure family "safety" are presented as signs of a debilitating, widespread problem of communication and understanding that American society remains reticent to address, at least in mainstream cinema of this period. *The Caretakers* subverts distinctions between sanity and psychopathology most effectively by contrasting the sense of ignorance-based fear and stereotyping that parents sometimes pass on to their children, with a much healthier sense of family closeness that develops in the borderline ward. The most powerful instance occurs in the closing moments of the film, when Lorna intervenes to comfort Edna after a potentially disastrous incident in the ward. "You're gonna get well. We want you," Lorna promises, approaching Edna with direct eye contact and a widening smile. "We're your family now," she continues, inducing Edna to utter her first words in seven years: "Good. So Good." Indeed, these final developments are sufficiently groundbreaking to win over not only the skeptical Marion (Janis Paige), who concedes that "You were right, Doc. You were right all the time," but also one of the nurses whom Lucretia had deployed to act as a spy overseeing the developments in the borderline ward.

Samuel Fuller's *Shock Corridor* (1963) continues the era's probing of social injustices, adding to the mix the contemporary anxieties regarding global nuclear destruction, in the less welcoming environment of a ward reserved for the most extreme sufferers from mental illness in a state mental institution where investigative journalist Johnny Barrett (Peter Breck) poses as an inmate to solve the murder of one of the patients, in an effort to win the Pulitzer Prize. Once he finds an opportunity to interview the only three inmates who witnessed the crime, his efforts to gather information from them are complicated by Johnny's awareness of the guards' surveillance, the severity of the traumas that the witnesses have suffered, and his own descent into madness that is complete by the end of the film. Strumming his acoustic guitar and singing songs of the old South as he idles through the asylum's corridors, the delusional Stuart (James Best) reveals to Johnny that during his military service in the Korean War, he was captured by communists and subsequently brainwashed into an allegiance with their cause. Drifting in and out of an awareness of where he is now and where he came from, and struggling to account for the traitorous actions that ultimately resulted in his dishonorable military discharge, Stuart identifies his own parents as the perpetrators of a form of social injustice that ultimately poisoned him: "I liked my home. No, that's a downright lie. Ever since I was a kid, my folks fed me bigotry for breakfast and ignorance for supper, and never, not once did they ever make me feel proud of where I was born. No knowledge of my country, no pride—just a hymn of hate." The circumstances of trauma surrounding the third witness, the nuclear physicist Dr. Boden (Gene Evans), are also rooted in the irrationality of contemporary military conflict, or in this case, the threat of conflict that world superpowers deploy as weapons: Boden's institutionalization appears to have resulted from an epiphany regarding the potentially drastic consequences of his work on nuclear projects, through which he has realized the senselessness of the Cold War and the arms race, themes that permeated American culture during this period and that were also being dramatized in contemporaneous films including *The Manchurian Candidate* (John Frankenheimer, 1962), *Fail Safe* (Sidney Lumet, 1964), and *Dr. Strangleove, or How Learned to Stop Worrying and Love the Bomb* (Stanley Kubrick, 1964). Dr. Boden's exhortation to Johnny resonates less as indecipherable pathological rambling than an example of too lucid and insightful reasoning: "We've become too sophisticated in the art of death. There's a sense of doom and crisis. We have too many intellectuals who are too afraid to use the pistol of common sense."

The fact that *Shock Corridor* was released in the United States on September 11, 1963, approximately one year after a Supreme Court ruling impelled the University of Mississippi to admit its first Black student, and precisely three months after Alabama Governor and presidential hopeful George Wallace blocked the entrance to the Foster Auditorium on the University of Alabama campus in an audacious and notorious move to protest new policies of school desegregation, makes Johnny Barrett's encounter with the second witness to the murder more prescient and more challenging. Before the camera reveals the face of Black inmate Trent (Harry Rhodes) himself, we see him marching through the corridor holding a large sign reading "Integration and Democracy Don't Mix. Go Home, Nigger." Trent steals the ward's pillowcases and converts them to Ku Klux Klan hoods, convinced that he is the organization's founder. The low-angle shots of hood-clad Trent bellowing "White supremacy" and "America for Americans!" incite the fervor of other patients whom he rouses into a mob, ordering them to attack the Black patient who has just materialized at the far end of the corridor. Waking in the middle of the night straight-jacketed to his bed, Trent reveals to Johnny the nightmare that jolts him back to an awareness of reality: as the only Black student in a southern university shortly after the Supreme Court's order of desegregation, he found himself unable to withstand the scorn and derision that he was forced to endure. His psychotic symptoms thus comprise an extreme reaction to a racial trauma that has transformed victim into oppressor. The much calmer and rational Trent of this scene describes racial hatred as "the disease carried to those yet unborn"—a direct warning about the legacy to which today's citizens will be held accountable.

Released in December of 1962 with the tagline "Some men and some motion pictures just won't conform," *Pressure Point* offers an even sterner alert to the historical dangers of intolerance, as it addresses the issue of psychotherapeutic professionals' political responsibility through the conflict between an unnamed African-American prison psychiatrist (Sidney Poitier) who is commissioned to treat a similarly unnamed, White supremacist and Nazi sympathizer inmate (Bobby Darrin) sentenced to three years in prison for sedition in 1942, and referred to the psychiatrist's care because of insomnia. Like *David and Lisa* and *The Caretakers*, the film investigates childhood trauma—in this case brought about by a tyrannical, sadistic, alcoholic father who brings women home while his terrified wife and son are forced to bear witness, and a mother who relies too exclusively upon the affection and comfort she derives from her son's presence. The film also shares with *Shock Corridor* a sense of the ease with which racial hatred can proliferate when it is fueled by stubborn ignorance. In addition to the highly combatant relationships between doctor and patient, however, *Pressure Point* is also distinctive for its more nuanced and ultimately more ambivalent investigation into the efficacy of psychotherapy in the treatment of social disorders.

Despite the scorn that the patient demonstrates from the start at the idea of a Black psychiatrist, Poitier as therapist achieves success in alleviating the patient's immediate symptom: once he gets the patient to acknowledge that his uneasy, complexly orchestrated dreams indicate a hatred of his father, he is "cured" midway through the narrative in that he no longer experiences sleep issues. Yet the now-treated symptom masks the much larger problem of the patient's profound, all-encompassing racial hatred—a "problem" that the patient himself can much more easily conceal, since from his perspective his belief system is entirely justified rather than sociopathological. The situation is exacerbated when his willingness to accept that he hates his father (a revelation effected through the psychiatrist's discerning diagnostic skills as a "cathartic cure") fails to bring about any insights regarding his broader, social hatred of Blacks and Jews. Yet *Pressure Point* never suggests the professional failure of the psychiatrist, even while it harbors unconditional support for psychiatry's pronounced capacity, investment, and responsibility in addressing the social, ethical, and political problems that often accompany psychopathology.

Pressure Point perceptively explores social and professional factors that facilitate the spread of racial prejudice. As the film opens in the present day (1962), Poitier, who has assumed a position of head psychiatrist outside the penal system, is confronted by the pleas of the younger (unnamed) psychiatrist (Peter Falk), who tells his superior that after more than seven months, he has made no progress in treating his Black patient, pleading with Poitier to take him off the case and reassign it to a "negro" psychiatrist. Demonstrating the film's commitment to disrupting the segregationist logic of Falk's request, Poitier bluntly refuses, yet he empathizes with the young doctor's plight: Falk's dilemma makes him recall the psychotherapeutic treatment of Darrin twenty years earlier, and his own reticence to continue treating a patient who exhibited such personal scorn for his therapist. Poitier denies Falk's request not because he considers him to be a racist, but because he refuses to admit defeat in the face of another psychiatric case involving human ignorance and misunderstanding. Indeed, this feature-length flashback to America at its point of entry into the World War II conflict is framed as a history lesson: 1962 audiences were well aware of the atrocities committed abroad and at home in the name of segregation and the maintenance of racial purity during the war years, and connecting these to the more contemporary manifestations of these issues in the early 1960s becomes a means of disrupting cycles of oppression across history. Then and now, the film argues, addressing and overcoming hatred requires the diligent and tireless effort of the psychiatric professional, an effort that cannot be abandoned even when failure seems unavoidable. And in one sense, Poitier *has* failed: against his wishes and protestations, the shrewd Darrin is ultimately granted parole by the board of myopic, White psychiatrists whom he manages to convince that he is no longer a threat to society. While Gabbard and Gabbard's contention that "The insuperable difficulties faced by Poitier in treating Darin contradict his optimistic belief that Falk can overcome the intractable resistance of a black patient" (1999, 90) seems logical to some extent, the narrative also positions Poitier as a figure who, on the basis of such encounters, remains unyielding in his conviction that they can only strengthen the committed psychotherapeutic professional's resolve.

Poitier's dilemma is at once, personal, professional, and political: how does one treat a patient who abhors his own psychiatrist not because of his credentials, but because of his racial difference? His proposed solution is to acknowledge the patient's resistance without validating or exacerbating it, assuming as much of an "objective" position as possible. This is precisely how Poitier proceeds in the first half of the film, while refusing to succumb to his patient's strategies of undermining his authority and belittling his professional standing. Poitier articulates this exclusively to the viewer, through voiceover narration that diegetically connects back to the story that he is relating in the present day to Falk. When Poitier becomes momentarily unable to maintain this semblance of objectivity during the therapeutic sessions, however, he assumes the fallback position of a figure who is not only a psychiatrist, but an official of a penal institution—one whose authority *must* be respected or at least acknowledged lest Poitier decide to have him incarcerated indefinitely once his sentence has been served. "All I can do is help you to remake yourself," Poitier exclaims, but rather than exemplifying a menacing tactic of "mind control" to ensure his compliance, however, *Pressure Point* positions the methods of the psychiatrist as the only means of facilitating Darin's awareness of, and subsequent recovery from, the all-too-convenient forms of mind control to which he has already willingly, yet perhaps unknowingly, submitted. As such, Poitier's moral and ethical strengths sharply contrast with Darin's weakness—his susceptibility to an illogic of hate that renders the entire Jewish race suspect of malice because of the narrow-mindedness of one Jewish father who deemed him unsuitable to court his daughter. Ultimately, Darin's weakness is revealed to reflect a concern about a larger cultural predisposition to totalitarianism, to a herd mentality that liberates mankind altogether from obligations of clear and sound reasoning by providing alliances to countless others who are similarly embittered, and who require only a convenient scapegoat and a charismatic leader to guide them. "If one-hundred disgruntled and frustrated individuals fall in line behind one psychopath, then in essence we are concerned with the actions of 101 psychopaths," Poitier explains to his superiors, as the camera pans up to a portrait of Hitler at a Nazi rally before dissolving to a close-up of Darin's face.

Despite these considerable obstacles, *Pressure Point* remains just as committed to advocating for the power of empathy, connection, and communication as *David and Lisa* or *The Caretakers*. Even if the film denies the Poitier/Darin conflict a positive resolution, its portrayal of a psychiatrist's resolve to reach out to his patients unconditionally remains intact. "More than I wanted to kill you, I wanted to help you!" he explains to Darin in their final confrontation, and although he remains unsuccessful in fulfilling this intention, by the end of the film his revelation of a career-transforming experience with psychotherapy has at least had the desired effect on Falk, who vows to try again (and harder) with the patient who has frustrated him. And if his experience with Darin comprises a failed attempt at connection, the film ultimately suggests that, at least from Poitier's perspective, the failure stems more from the patient's weakness, since so many others who have suffered far worse than Darin have "managed to become a normal part of society."

With Poitier's final declaration of faith in his country's commitment to pursuing moral and ethical justice, *Pressure Point* certifies that such disastrous lapses into weakness can never defeat the spirit of the America in which he believes, despite his (ex-) patient's insistence that he has been paroled because the all-white board ultimately took the side of the "white, Christian American": "No matter how many of you there are," he warns Darin, "you'll lose because the country's good and strong, and goodness will prevail!" Anna Everett suggests that during the Kennedy administration, when the president vowed to put an end to racial discrimination in housing and to take additional progressive steps on this front after the conservative Eisenhower era, the early 1960s films of the Civil Rights Movement reflected the American society's growing receptivity "to confront America's complex racial politics on both the cultural and political fronts" (47). *David and Lisa*, *The Caretakers*, *Shock Corridor*, and *Pressure Point* evidence the emergence of a new, more controversial, adult-oriented cinema which, as Everett argues, was willing to take on contemporary social issues in a more realistic way than was then feasible in fictional series television, in relation to which Hollywood was continuing to see its box-office receipts steadily decline (46–47). Everett also brings attention to a coterminous development in the advancing medium of the small screen, a development to which Hollywood struggled to respond positively and profitably: while early 1960s series television may have been forced to steer clear of provocative subject matter, technological advances had made it all too well prepared to bring its vivid, disturbing news images of racial and social conflict into the living rooms of the American public on a nightly basis, representing "realism" in its most heightened, raw, and non-fictitious form.

This infiltration of the political into the realm of the domestic provides a useful context for interpreting critical reactions to the patient/analyst films of this period—reactions that highlight problems in psychotherapeutic representation. *David and Lisa*, a small-budgeted, independently financed film, and the only one of these four films to earn a significant profit, is also the only film of the four that received virtually universal critical praise, largely rooted in its advancement of perceptions of interpersonal connection that are capable of promoting the value of understanding.[2] "The film's message is clear," reports William Trombley of the *Saturday Evening Post*. "People can change" ("Small-budget triumph"). Comparing the film positively to the "coldness" of *Freud*, Arthur Knight praises *David and Lisa*'s "warm and profound sense of human beings reaching out toward each other, and in that contact gaining strength and serenity" ("SR Goes to the Movies: View from the Couch," 30). And *Time* magazine celebrates especially the film's closing moments, in which "David turns to Lisa, one lost child turns to another lost child and stammers the three little words that make him a member of mankind: 'Take my hand'" ("Children of Darkness" 64).

The ready association of subtlety and understatement with warmth and innocence, and the ability to root all of these concepts under the broader heading of "realism," make the largely negative critical reactions to the other three films more understandable. One of the only positive contemporary reviews of *Pressure Point* emerges from Hollis Alpert, who praises Sidney Poitier's performance as a "believable figure of strength and humanness" ("SR Goes to the Movies: A Wandering Samurai," 26); in a similar vein, *New York Times* film critic A. Weiler finds the performances in *Shock Corridor* to be realistic (32). The antithesis of believability, however, is firmly rooted in artifice, and more damagingly, shock and sensationalism. Referencing the former, the *New York Times*'s Bosley Crowther expresses disdain for *Pressure Point* because its narrative form is misaligned with its content: the use of the flashback structure is insufficiently "simple" and "direct" for this subject matter, and ultimately "the ugly truths of [the film] are blurred with too many theatrical contrivances" ("The Screen: Story of the Thief," 47). Conceding that Fuller was attempting to formulate "some comment on our times,"

Arthur Knight aligns with Crowther in faulting *Shock Corridor* for its "contrived framework" ("SR Goes to the Movies: Who's Morbid?," 34). Despite his acknowledgment that the U.S. Senate selected the film for preview, and that the film was influential in the passing of the Mental Health and Mental Retardation Act (SR 46), Knight also sharply criticizes *The Caretakers* for its "moments of voyeuristic indulgence," including the graphic depiction of electroconvulsive therapy, and for the opening movie theater sequence depicting Lorna's hysteria, which prompts the audience to "safely prepare for melodrama, not documentary" (46). And *Commonweal* critic Philip Hartung voices a similar contention about the film's reliance upon shock and sensationalism, arguing that "the subject should really be treated sanely and intelligently, not hoked up for melodrama ("The Screen," Jan. 4, 1963, 48). Interestingly, however, using similar criteria and standards of evaluation the *Film Daily* review finds that the film successfully conveys a sense of realism: "Scenes of the hospital and its methods have the force of honest reporting. Indeed running through the picture is a sense of conviction. . . . At times it is of the nature of a documentary, but never to the point where the story loses its vital human quality or its super-charged conflict of viewpoints and procedures" (Herbstman).

In the early 1960s, then, realism serves as the common denominator for successfully aligning the Hollywood film industry's venture into an adult-themed, politically conscious and progressive cinema. Whether or not they were directly connected to the contemporaneous Civil Rights Movement, Hollywood films focusing upon the psychotherapeutic analyst/patient dramatized issues of normality and abnormality in ways that were at least potentially consonant with the demand for realism, and it dovetailed elegantly with the theme of social injustice as a problem that needed to be interrogated, explained, and ultimately overcome. Enhanced interpersonal communication and connection were deemed capable of bringing about a world that would no longer have need nor excuse for intolerance. The umbrella of realism thus provided the possibility of aligning cultural expectations with the products of the film industry, but only if handled appropriately, within the parameters of good taste: as critical responses demonstrate, no matter how noble the filmmaker's intentions, the excessive, the sensational, and the shocking were considered unwelcome and inappropriate to a realistic exploration of mental illness or its treatment within the psychotherapeutic dynamic.

Critics have advanced several viable explanations of the shift in the representation of therapist/patient relations that occurs in the mid-1960s. Gabbard and Gabbard argue that the Golden Age of psychiatry in American cinema was at least partially a product of an unsustainable back-to-values move on the part of the Hollywood film industry as film audiences continued to fragment and dwindle (1999, 77): "The Golden Age also seems to be related to Hollywood's desperate attempt at preserving its familiar paradigm of reconciliation, an undertaking that made great demands on the healing powers of cinematic psychotherapists" (1999, 105–06). Speaking specifically of the psychiatric treatment of women, Janet Walker argues that during the mid-1960s, with the inception of second-wave feminism, "the status of psychiatry fell, in proportion to its growing perceived inability to define femininity or the female role in the context of the social parity for which many had begun to call" (1993, 20). Cloud suggests that, with its roots in consolation and adjustment, the rhetoric of therapy was entirely incongruous with an era of great social and political change. A close look at the social-political developments of the era, however, reveals a different set of factors relating to this representational shift, with transitions occurring in conjunction with two major "agenda" items of the decade: the protection against the impending threat of nuclear confrontation and disaster, and the struggle for civil rights. Anxieties regarding the former waned to some extent after the successful resolution of the Cuban Missile Crisis and the related concessions that the United States made to the Soviet Union. The Civil Rights Movement, however, would continue to progress and thrive after 1963: the efforts of the Freedom Rides of 1961, the March on Washington of 1963, and the Freedom Summer of 1964 culminated in the passing of the Civil Rights Act, followed in 1965 by the Voting Rights Act, and indeed, it would be naïve to suggest that even with the passing of this landmark legislation, problems of racial and social inequity were resolved, when instead they intensified. Yet after 1963, Hollywood largely suspends its interest in producing narratives that support the efficacy of psychotherapeutic practice—either in one-one-one or group sessions—in addressing or rectifying social injustice.

As part of President Kennedy's "New Frontier," the two most prominent issues on the national agenda—widespread nuclear destruction and racial injustice—were incontrovertible: no one was arguing in favor of world annihilation, and while the issue of eradicating racial injustice met with strong resistance, the concept of injustice itself remained a problem that needed to be addressed, and that was still deemed incompatible with the fabric of American values, traditional or progressive. As long as analyst/patient psychotherapy continued to align with the national political agenda, the theme found a comfortable place in a Hollywood cinema that was committed to avoiding the politically contentious and that was still invested in playing to the mainstream, even if now more exclusively to the "adult" end of this spectrum.

Nuclear destruction and racial injustice remained prominent as agenda items after Johnson took office; indeed, Johnson's Great Society platform centralized a commitment to eradicating poverty, and his Republican opponent Barry Goldwater's perspective on the nuclear annihilation of the enemy largely contributed to his loss of the 1964 election. But the era offered no definitive, clearly envisioned stance that psychotherapy—and more specifically, psychiatry—might without controversy strive to rectify on the Hollywood screen. As J. Hoberman suggests, the issue of civil rights became more divisive with increasing instances of violent protest at home, exacerbated by 1965 with the country's ever-growing investment in an overseas war whose goal of avoiding the spread of Communist ideology would soon fail to register as justification of the nation's growing financial investment, military deployment, and body count (129–30). The split of perspectives on these issues was accompanied by the growth of protest movements that highlighted the tensions between powerful and powerless, rich and poor, young and old, and Black and White. Where, then, to position any potentially relevant and effective psychotherapeutic discourse that wouldn't risk alienating some audience sectors?

The film industry was already in trouble, with box-office receipts declining each successive year of the decade. Most of the major award-winning films were either throwbacks to an era growing more obsolete or efforts to replicate successful formulas, and the industry was losing audiences both to television and international cinematic movements that provided greater freedom of artistic experimentation and fewer restrictions regarding theme and subject matter. Amidst these developments, the industry elected to neutralize the political efficacy of one-on-one psychotherapy by rendering psychiatrists as catalysts of the more provocative sexual subject matter that was finding its place in American cinema in the middle of the decade. In some ways, this constituted a bold move that attempted to shift psychotherapy from the realm of the ethical to the moral, through representational license that became more liberal as the decade progressed, especially after 1966 with the impending demise of the Production Code and the opening up of new avenues for adult-oriented cinema brought by the new MPAA rating system. And indeed, by the end of the decade, under radically different historical and cultural conditions, this decision allowed the patient/analyst film to recoup the sense of intimacy of communication that it had retained in the early 1960s, with the one-on-one psychotherapeutic dynamic ultimately aligned with investigations of contemporary issues of psychiatric ethics, along with new ties to the women's movement.

Fueled by an awareness of its potential for inviting moral controversy and also by the promise of product differentiation from television, however, the sexualization of one-on-one therapist/patient representations of the mid-1960s turned out to provide only limited appeal to audiences and popular critics. One confounding issue was that, unlike nuclear holocaust or social injustice, sex did not readily qualify as a "problem" amenable to "realistic" treatment in onscreen representation—at least not until the early 1970s, with more frank depictions of sexual subject matter in such films as *Carnal Knowledge* (Mike Nichols, 1971, discussed in chapter 2). In the meantime, however, the one-on-one analyst/patient film of the mid-1960s attempted to problematize sex through gender-focused configurations of power in which men strove to have more sex with women who, via the developments of the sexual revolution and the guideposts of second-wave feminism, struggled to contain male sexual energies. The period witnessed a film industry still struggling to determine how to address adult audience sectors without alienating the mainstream, and to embrace emerging perspectives on sexual openness without going "too far" and potentially offending more conservative audiences.

This sexualization of analyst/patient therapy materializes at least as early as 1964 with the release of Robert Rossen's controversial *Lilith*, which concerns the complex relationship between Vincent (Warren Beatty), an occupational therapist-in-training at the private and exclusive Popular Lodge sanitarium, and Lilith (Jean Seberg), one of the patients to whom he is assigned. While the attraction between therapist and patient is noticeable at first glance, Vincent's sexual obsession with her soon intensifies to the point where he can no longer tolerate her relatively harmless infatuation with fellow patient Stephen (Peter Fonda), who commits suicide after Vincent cunningly orchestrates a scenario to convince him that Lilith does not reciprocate Stephen's affection. Much more than "just" an infatuation to Vincent, Lilith comes to encompass what Janet Walker aptly describes as "a bisexual, nonmonogamous world where desire is free-floating" (118), as she liberally dispenses her affections to a fellow female patient Yvonne Meaghan (Anne Meacham) and even insinuates the seduction of little boys of the small neighboring town while Vincent compulsively struggles to master and possess her through an effort that culminates in her destruction. Hysterical as he aimlessly roams the sanitarium grounds after finding Lilith in a catatonic state, Vincent runs toward his psychiatric superiors as he utters the desperate words "Help me" before the film's final freeze frame. As Walker clarifies, *Lilith* is only one of a series of films of the early 1960s to suggest the pathological nature of the therapist, here exacerbated by the uncanny resemblance that Lilith bears to Vincent's mentally unstable mother, and Walker suggests that the film may be read "as [a] narrative reconfiguration of the growing social ambivalence about psychiatric power and women's subjugation to it" (121). Emblematic of Vincent's increasingly desperate powerlessness is his conspicuous inability to communicate, to get outside of his own head long enough to forge the meaningful connections necessary to making himself understood to *anyone*: his relationship with Lilith devolves into a desperate power struggle marked by expressions of sex and death, and he is no less helpless to express or clarify his feelings regarding a prior, intimate relationship with Laura (Jessica Walter), who appears to have been devastated by his unexplained departure years earlier, and on whose doorstep he appears unannounced one night, before once again fleeing from her sexual advances as he had inexplicably done years earlier.

The film received mixed reviews, with the sharpest criticism referencing a false sense of poignancy, and of "deliberate artiness [and] the pretentious lifelessness of Rossen's direction" ("Willfully Delicate," 116A). *Time* magazine faults the film's too extensive reliance upon the "techniques of modern moviemaking," including expressive cinematography and several especially slow dissolves to rivers and streams, commenting that "it does seem silly to deliver the same old Hollywood sexology in a fancy wrapper marked resh kavawn," referencing words of the secret, untranslatable language that Lilith has scrolled on the wall of her room ("Schizoid Sensations,"144).[3] As an investigation positioned at the intersection of psychotherapy and sexuality, however, *Lilith* strives for a nuanced portrayal of the therapeutic process and its capacity for dangerous forms of transference and counter-transference: especially noteworthy here are the frank and open debriefing sessions with the head psychiatrists that punctuate Vincent's training period, in which he is prompted to acknowledge his susceptibility to the same desires that ultimately ruin him and Lilith.

Relocating the therapeutic setting outside the boundaries of state hospitals and sanitariums, and striving to politically isolate the therapeutic process itself—or at least to resituate it under the headings of gender, sex, and power—other American films of the mid-1960s offer less nuanced and more exploitative representations of analyst/patient relationships. Released three months before *Lilith*'s premiere at the New York Film Festival, J. Lee Thompson's *What a Way to Go!* (1964) marked a popular trend of reducing a now largely stereotypical psychiatrist to the function of plot catalyst—in this case, for a series of three extended therapy-session "flashbacks" that comprise the story of the thrice-widowed Louisa May Foster (Shirley MacLaine), an advocate of the "simple life" whose mental illness resides in the illogical determination to donate to the Internal Revenue Service her multi-billion-dollar fortune accumulated by ex-husbands whom she found wholly compatible until she inadvertently inspired them to become compulsive fortune seekers, their unquenchable greed leading to tragic ends. While Richard Schickel's mostly negative review of the film remarks that it offers a "little comment on the inescapability of affluence in America these days" ("Running a Good Thing into the Ground," 14), the narrative is aligned with a "problem-as-non-problem" framework prevalent in the representation of therapist/patient relations in this period, compounded by a correlative tendency to render the therapist ineffectual (Gabbard & Gabbard): except for the moment when he acts on a perceived opportunity to date Louisa, entertaining the prospect of sharing her about-to-be forfeited inheritance, the psychiatrist, Dr. Victor Stephanson (Robert Cummings), functions primarily as a diegetic surrogate for the viewer, a baffled and bemused listener helpless either to affect or effect the story's outcome. Indeed, the positive resolution in *What a Way to Go!* remains entirely disconnected from the therapeutic dynamic and framework, as Louisa ultimately happens upon Lennie Crawley (Dean Martin), the ex-magnate in the retail industry who had unsuccessfully courted her when he was rich, but who was subsequently driven out of business by her increasingly competitive first husband Edgar's (Dick Van Dyke) machinations. Steeped in humility, and now rendered financially destitute and reduced to the position of janitor in Dr. Stephanson's office building, Edgar becomes Louisa's perfect mate.

Even as it integrates the psychiatrist as a more active participant in the workings of its plot, the therapeutic framework of the highly successful yet critically reviled bedroom farce *What's New Pussycat?* (Clive Donner and Richard Talmadge, 1965) offers a yet more insidious extension of the problem-as-non-problem formula that renders the therapeutic process ineffectual.[4] Woody Allen's first feature-film screenplay brings fashion editor Michael James (Peter O'Toole) to enlist the services of cartoon-cut Freudian psychoanalyst Dr. Fritz Fassbender (Peter Sellers) for treatment of a malady that reads more like a playboy's fantasy scenario: Michael is irresistible to women and himself unable to resist their sexual advances—an especially inconvenient problem given that he is steadily dating ESL instructor Carole (Romy Schneider) and afraid of committing to her or any woman exclusively. Agreeing to "treat" Michael, Dr. Fassbender is actually more interested in figuring out how to emulate his successes, and the narrative soon devolves into a complex series of mistaken identities, replete with marital and sexual deceit. As in *What a Way to Go!*, the story forcibly eradicates therapy from its contemporary political context, functioning as a feature-length titillation that mocks both the therapeutic profession and those who are drawn to seek treatment from it. Consonant with a strain throughout much of

Allen's work that derives humor from the combination of a base-level fascination with philosophical schools of thought and a blatant, scathing anti-intellectualism, the film heavily invests in stereotype in the name of cleverness: the aims of group therapy are displaced when one of the female group members becomes enamored of Michael; Dr. Fassbender reveals that his father is a Viennese gynecologist recently arrested on morals charges; and one running joke tames the forces of the sexually aggressive poetess Liz (Paula Prentiss)—who presents Michael with a poem that she wrote "at Hillside hospital after my fourth nervous breakdown"—by having her commit a series of suicide attempts in his honor as the narrative progresses. Consonant with the demands of bedroom farce, and in a conspicuous alliance with Allen's mentor Ingmar Bergman's 1955 romantic comedy *Smiles of a Summer Night* (many of whose plot twists it shares), the film ultimately—and predictably—rescinds its passionate support for the unbridled sex that it initially posited as pathological, concluding as Michael marries Carole and vows to abandon his womanizing ways, thankfully exclaiming to Dr. Fassbender that he has been "cured."

Extending the analyst/patient film's experimentation with more open yet still morally conflicted sex, *A Fine Madness* (Irvin Kershner, 1966) grounds its black comedic narrative in contemporary Manhattan, in a story involving budding poet Samson Shillitoe's (Sean Connery) struggle to overcome writer's block and complete his masterwork, aided by the unflinching support of his waitress wife Rhoda (Joanne Woodward), but thwarted by the pesky government agents who devote their energies throughout the film to serving Samson with a subpoena that will force him to pay alimony to an ex-wife. Like Michael in *What's New Pussycat?*, and certainly consonant with the 007 persona that Connery had by this point already honed through a series of four films, but which here stems more directly from the open expression (or repression?) of "creative energies" than from the perks of international espionage, Samson revels without remorse in his talents as a womanizer, unapologetic for the extramarital sexual services he frequently and liberally offers, even when Rhoda ultimately discovers his infidelity.

Also like *What's New Pussycat?*, *A Fine Madness* encapsulates Hollywood's contemporary inclination both to exoticize and to eroticize the attribute of European-ness that, especially in the context of the burgeoning sexual revolution, can be readily contrasted with a perception of sexual expression in America as fraught with outmoded "hang-ups"—a trend stemming as much from America's puritanical heritage as from European cinema's still notorious insusceptibility to the thematic and representational strictures of the Production Code Administration.[5] In *A Fine Madness*, however, the aims of the psychiatric profession intersect with these expressions of liberated and constrained aspects of sex in more puzzling and paradoxical ways. Samson's yielding to therapeutic treatment comes only at Rhoda's insistence, after she watches a television interview promoting the talents of Dr. Oliver West (Patrick O'Neal), a psychiatrist who specializes in the treatment of creatively blocked patients, and whose professional notoriety instills in Rhoda a fear that her husband may resort to suicide unless those blocks are successfully cleared. Declaring to Dr. West that "you protect what is, while I envision what can be," Samson maintains a stalwart resistance to treatment: selected by West as an ideal case because of the distinction of his symptoms from those of other patients, the poet agrees to be confined at West's ominous Para Park Hospital only because the seclusion will provide him with the time and space to finish his creative work, with the added benefit of slowing his pursuit by the authorities. Even after involuntarily undergoing the experimental lobotomy that Dr. West authorizes after discovering wife Lydia (Jean Seberg) having sex with Samson in the hospital's hydrotherapy pool, Samson remains resolute and wholly unscathed by therapeutic efforts to tame his creativity; in fact, that he emerges entirely unaffected by the archaic surgical procedure serves as much as a testament to the victory of the creative impulse as a triumph of contemporary masculinity.[6]

The selection of Connery for the role of Samson is especially notable for its cementing of a perception of resilience, and the string of sexual conquests accumulated by the swarthy, rugged, deep-voiced, muscular, hairy-chested Scotsman might mark him as an entirely valiant, exotic hero but for the fact that he more fully embodies the qualities of a rogue, fleeing from responsibilities and obligations, devoid of empathy, and indifferent to his wife and friends except when he needs their help (or their money) to get out of a jam. The film's power relations of gender become less clearly decipherable, however, by the accumulation of so many other elements in the film that register as "foreign" but that do not also qualify as "exotic"—namely every psychiatrist working at the Para Park Hospital except for the ineffectual and American Dr. West, whom Samson appropriately vanquishes by inadvertently "winning" Lydia from him such that she leaves her husband and pays off Samson's entire alimony debt. The lecherous Dr. Freddie Vorbeck (Werner Peters) liberally gropes and fondles Lydia, even attempting to blackmail her by threatening to reveal her sexual tryst with Samson to Dr. West. Accordingly, *A Fine Madness* struggles to maintain two distinct masculinized forms of mastery that it ultimately correlates—one through a psychotherapeutic process that is rendered barbaric, archaic, and ultimately ineffectual; the other through aggressive sexual advances that enforce its energies through conquest. And if *What's New Pussycat?*

closes with a deeply ironic yet barely plausible suggestion of a "cure" to the malady of pathological (male) sexual indiscretion, the therapeutic resolution of *A Fine Madness* resonates as even more arbitrary, as the now debt-free poet, his masterwork finished, takes his wife home, reassuring her that he is not "mad" at her after her meek, anxious revelation that she is pregnant with his child.

Both *What's New Pussycat?* and *A Fine Madness* take strides to fully contain the communicative potential of the therapeutic dynamic by relegating it to the aim of servicing sexual relationships. "World disarmament should start out in the bedroom" is the telling political pronouncement of *A Very Special Favor* (Michael Gordon, 1965), a romantic comedy that extends this strategy of sexualizing therapy, both by designating the "battle of the sexes" as the only battlefield that American society was having to cope with in the late summer of 1965—by which time President Johnson's rapid acceleration of the Vietnam War effort was taking full force—and by offering a reactionary disavowal of the burgeoning revelations of a second-wave feminist movement, whose proponents Helen Gurley Brown and Betty Friedan had begun directing the nation's attention to the double standard that had effectively demeaned women for engaging in the same polyamorous behavior that designated men as triumphant sexual warriors. The film's opening segment outside a Parisian courthouse acclimates the audience to the modernized sexual mores and attitudes that the film ultimately aims to subvert: as Northern Oil Company troubleshooter Paul Chadwick (Rock Hudson) shares a passionate, midday kiss with a woman (Jay Novello) in a convertible after the two have finalized arrangements for a tryst later that evening in her apartment, an American woman in her fifties, clearly aghast at this public display of affection (or at least by the woman's part in it), proclaims, "You won't find women like that in Cedar Rapids," to which her just-as-surprised husband woefully replies, "No matter how hard you try." The battle lines are drawn, and sex is once again the problem. But if by 1965 gender polarity was already a staple of Hollywood romantic comedy, *A Very Special Favor* explicates polarity on a much broader scale—one that ultimately encompasses contemporary issues of nationalism and the American film industry's conflicted position on sexual content.

As it turns out, the woman in the convertible is the barrister presiding over a corporate court case involving Chadwick's suit against a French company. Colleagues have warned Paul that, as an American in a French judicial system, he has little chance of winning, but these skeptics have clearly failed to realize the persuasive powers of heartthrob Rock Hudson, who knows exactly what he wants and how to get it—in this case, by having promised to show up that night at the Barrister's apartment if she "throws" the court case in his favor. On the plane back to New York, Paul encounters Michel Boullard (Charles Boyer), whose witnessing of Paul's sexual courtroom manipulation has left him duly impressed. Michel has returned to New York to visit the daughter whom he has not seen in over thirty years after losing a custody battle with an ex-wife, an American who caught him in the act of marital infidelity and then sued him. Upon their return to America, after witnessing the inexplicable transformation of his psychiatrist/daughter Lauren (Leslie Caron) into "a thirty-year-old spinster" whose domineering attitude toward docile and overly accommodating fiancé Arnold Plum (Dick Shawn) brings back unpleasant memories of his own ex-wife, his laudatory approval of the American's methods leads him to request a favor: "save my daughter" by being the man "who will gently knead her into a romantic adventure, an emotional interlude from whose fires a woman can evolve."

The polarities of this complex dynamic come to encompass the realms of gender, professional, and national identity—one in which "French-ness" harbors the requisite "exotic" realm where id-centered sexual drives may roam and cathect freely. Michel's national identity bears witness to this phenomenon, and the fact that his daughter has not inherited the same propensity for pleasure is configured as the undue influence of his American ex-wife. Paul's in-court, gender-conquering sexual performance, however, leads Michel to the paradoxical conclusion that only this man, an American, can restore in his daughter, by demonstrating his romantic skills and sexual energies, qualities that are authentically French. Michel's proclamation to Paul that "You must have some French blood in you" is, in the context of the developments of American culture and its dominant film industry in the middle of the decade, a most telling one, offering to American audiences in the era of a burgeoning sexual revolution the opportunity to sample some permissive European sexual hijinks played out by a Hollywood actor who was still being cast as the industry's foremost representative and firmest embodiment of a romanticized masculinity. Sexually speaking, *A Very Special Favor* plays upon America's already firmly rooted associations of European sexual energies as liberated and unbridled by such trifling annoyances as consent, fidelity, or trust—annoyances that in their American context have resulted in elaborate lawsuits, costly alimony payments, and worst of all, women who sexually dominate men.

Like Michael in *What's New Pussycat?* and Samson in *A Fine Madness*, Paul Chadwick is irresistible, and this quality serves as his entry point for a psychotherapeutic relationship with Lauren that is from the beginning entirely a ruse, but that nonetheless demands "treatment" in an elaborate game involving strategies that constantly subvert the integrity of the seeming opposites of European/American, male/female, and analyst/patient. In a throwback to not-so-distant, pre-feminist perceptions of the working woman, Lauren's embodiment of a domineering, almost elitist stuffiness becomes linked to the attributes of objectivity, dominance, and power that the film imagines as endemic to the psychiatric role (see fig.1.1). Her professional methods are actually quite contemporary: she initially directs Paul to attend her group therapy sessions not only because she has no room in her schedule left for private appointments, but also because she finds group sessions to be a more successful form of treatment. When she does agree to meet privately with Paul (who feigns embarrassment about admitting his irresistibility in the context of a group setting), she elects a behavioral therapeutic approach to his problem. Complaining that he dare not resist the women who cannot resist him because the one woman whom he did resist ended up committing suicide, Lauren compels him to break the cycle by ordering the next would-be seductress to leave his premises immediately.

Paul's strategy is based upon what he considers to be a keen understanding of the psychotherapeutic dynamic: to play the role of a patient by rendering himself vulnerable to the authoritative pronouncements of his therapist. The strategy aims to reverse the power dynamic by making the patient assume a position of control, feigning a passivity and helplessness that Paul also shrewdly frames as feminine traits: "Do you know what it feels like to be loved just because of your body?" he

Figure 1.1. Dr. Lauren Boullard (Leslie Caron) counsels and diagnoses Paul Chadwick (Rock Hudson) in *A Very Special Favor* (Michael Gordon, Universal Studios, 1965). Digital frame enlargement.

asks Lauren. "I've become a love toy." In fact, Paul puts himself in the position of therapist by framing this role as the agent with an objective shared by an entire class of mid-1960s romantic comedies about dysfunctional marriages which will be discussed more extensively in chapter 3: to ideologically rectify an out-of-kilter society that permits women to behave like men, and men to lapse into femininity. Indeed, Lauren's fiancé Arnold has already fallen victim to this lapse, taking orders from both Lauren and his mother, donning an apron at home as he cleans and cooks meals, and resigning himself to an impending marriage without children who might interfere with her professional life—behavior so revolting that Michel proclaims to his friend Etienne (Walter Slezak) that Arnold will have become "the ideal" American husband after [Lauren] is through with him."

While the therapist/patient power struggles play out rather predictably, *A Very Special Favor* remains remarkable as a case study illuminating a paradox that the industry was continuing to face in the middle of the decade—one involving a commitment to embrace a culture of emerging sexual permissiveness while refraining from offending viewers who might find such openness offensive. An abrupt turn in the plot trajectory that occurs midway through the film embodies this dilemma. Michel has been keeping his identity hidden from Lauren while Paul carries out his favor for the father, but he unexpectedly witnesses the drastic effect of the scheme he has put in place: seeing his daughter crying, humiliated and defeated in the lobby of Chadwick's apartment building, Michel suddenly decides to reveal himself as her father, and also to reveal the deception that Chadwick is playing out at her expense—without, of course, admitting to his own role as the orchestrator of the intrigue that has directly resulted in Lauren's manipulation by her irresistible patient. That he so abruptly turns the tables on his own plan becomes attributed to his role as a "father" who cannot stand to see his daughter suffer, and he vows to help Lauren seek revenge on her oppressor. If, realistically, the turn is something of a stretch, it yet elegantly emblematizes the "self-checking" tendency of a cinema intent upon experimenting with the "lure" and open embrace of sex while simultaneously (or, in this case, sequentially) condemning it for having become so uncontained. Once Lauren knows about Paul's plan, the "revenge" that her father so eagerly anticipates takes the form of another power reversal in which, in an effort to re-affirm the monstrousness of second-wave feminism, she demoralizes her oppressor by intimating his complete failure as a sexual performer. Indeed, Paul's devastation is sufficiently extreme to send him on a bar-crawl bender where a posse of henpecked males gathers round, charging him to serve as their advocate in a final showdown between the sexes, offering a new spin on the sexual revolution that is not so new at all, gleefully anticipating the celebration of a return to male dominance that they are convinced has been lost: "the army of liberation is on its way," announces one patron, while another proclaims that "someday you're gonna be able to tell your grandchildren that the revolution started in your bar!"

Ultimately, however, *A Very Special Favor*'s sexual revolutionary fervor collapses under the weight of its own disparate aims, gender and generational collisions, and ideological contradictions. The film's concluding sequences find Michel now urging the demoralized Paul to do him the additional favor of submitting himself to the same social institution that brought about Michel's own undoing, by marrying the woman whom he has grown to dislike so profoundly. "Keep her pregnant all the time," Michel suggests, and when Paul protests that "I don't even like her," his prospective father-in-law exclaims that "that's part of the revenge." In the final scene, the father has gotten his wish—or almost: with Lauren giving birth to her sixth daughter, Michel asks for the final favor of another try, so that he might have a grandson. *A Very Special Favor* ultimately deploys the analyst/patient psychotherapeutic dynamic to valorize the sexual appetite of that ogling, envious husband from Cedar Rapids while simultaneously playing to his wife's complaint that the new permissiveness is wholly contemptible; to indict marriage as a constraining, outworn institution while simultaneously protesting for the urgency of its perpetuation; and, in the process, to celebrate these contradictory tendencies under the heading of a domesticated yet "liberated" American spirit that ultimately now owes nothing to the advocates of unbridled sexual license across the Atlantic.[7]

If the goals of social and interpersonal connection dominating the landscape of one-on-one psychotherapy in the early 1960s fall victim to such mid-decade efforts to reduce the therapeutic process to addressing the interests of an ultimately domesticated sexual realm—one that actively undermines productive communication between analyst and patient, and that no longer prompts the patient to reconceptualize social connections with the world beyond the analyst's office—the close of the decade evidences yet another shift in America's cinematic engagement with the politics of psychotherapy. While sex and sexual relationships continue to dominate films that foreground the therapeutic process, the industry yields a number of films that formulate a more critical and analytical approach to the contradictions and paradoxes that the mid-1960s films evidenced yet never succeeded in dissipating or resolving. Rather than constituting a "re-politicization" of therapy, however, it would be more accurate to describe the turn as a renewed willingness to struggle with the interpersonal dynamics of the patient/therapist relationship, while eliminating any recourse to appropriating this dynamic to reinforce prevailing ideological claims of power in gender and sexual relations. These films range from a police procedural on a historically recent serial killer, to an independent production centering upon a troubled psychiatrist, and to the cinematic version a Broadway musical about a woman who enlists a therapist to help her quit smoking.

Capitalizing on the national attention that was being devoted to high-profile murderers, Richard Fleischer's fact-based police procedural entitled *The Boston Strangler* was released in October of 1968, just one month before the introduction of the MPAA's new rating system, and bearing next to its MPAA seal the advisory "Suggested for Mature Audiences." The largely negative reviews focused, predictably, upon the film's sensationalism and stereotypical representations of what *Newsweek* described as "a few gray-haired psychiatrists [who] mumble Viennese voodoo, all to legitimize the film as something more than a thrill" ("Doing the Garrote," 114). Despite such criticisms, however, the film remains notable for its attempts to approach the subject of criminal pathology from both a psychological and a social perspective—to make connections that extend beyond the realm of the psychopathological mind itself in a way that addressed contemporary concerns over the labeling of the United States as a "sick society." Bordering upon pro-social forms of address, some of these attempts seem heavy handed, most notably a closing title announcing that "the film has ended, but the responsibility for the early recognition and treatment of the violent among us has yet to begin." Yet *The Boston Strangler* succeeds in more broadly contextualizing violence and murder than the final sequence of Hitchcock's *Psycho* (1960), where Dr. Fred Richman (Simon Oakland) authoritatively explains the criminal psychopathology of Norman Bates (Anthony Perkins) through a hermetic, Freudian discourse that limits the scope of the diagnosis to the realm of the "diseased" mind. While *The Boston Strangler* certainly rewrites the actual history of the pursuit of Albert DeSalvo (Tony Curtis), the film is also quite attentive to historical context: when a press reporter asks newly appointed special investigator John Bottomley (Henry Fonda) for his opinion on the current "talk" about the importance of treating mental illness before it develops into criminal behavior, he responds, "A lot of talk is exactly what it is. What more can you expect from a society that itself spends 44% of its tax dollars on killing?" If, as Leslie Abrahamson asserts, "the film foregrounds the horrific as an empirical condition of modern culture" (203), the fact that the scene takes place even before the United States escalated the Vietnam War effort accentuates its resonance and relevance in the late 1968 context, echoing as it does the country's mounting investment in an increasingly unpopular war.

At the same time, however, *The Boston Strangler* also makes a desperate plea for empathy and understanding. Whatever might be considered as exploitative elements are contained to the film's first half, which focuses entirely upon the ruthless tactics and misguided efforts of the Boston police force to wrest confessions from religious zealots, obscene phone callers, known sex offenders, and torture-fascinated "faggots" whose underworld the plot flagrantly exposes as the body count continues to rise. Given this context, the subsequent switch to DeSalvo's own narrational perspective is notable for its *lack* of sensationalism, as it begins with the killer embracing his young daughter while both bear witness to the televised JFK funeral, immediately after which DeSalvo leaves home to commit a crime. DeSalvo is depicted as a mild-mannered, soft-spoken man suffering from a debilitating schizophrenic condition that has left him unaware of the brutal crimes that he has proven capable of committing. Once he is apprehended, the film frames the matter of exacting a confession as a conflict in which criminal, legal, moral, and psychological perspectives on pathology interact: the police urge for the "connection" of the "two Alberts" to make sure that the suspect remains incarcerated, while the psychiatrists emphasize that his case is "a medical problem, not a legal one." Ultimately, the decision to compel DeSalvo to reenact his own crimes while in custody—presented to him rather duplicitously as an opportunity for the needed cathartic release that confession will provide—ultimately proves unsuccessful: once he reaches the point of recognizing what he has done, he never succeeds in "integrating" his personality in a way that would permit him to successfully communicate his actions or his emotions to the authorities. Throughout the process, however, DeSalvo remains fully cooperative, and the sensitive depiction of his character, coupled with socially and politically cogent scripting, results in a film that strives to reconnect psychotherapy with issues of public mental health, imbuing them with social urgency and importance in ways that reflect portrayals of the field earlier in the decade.

As chapter 5 will further elaborate, in the context of the therapeutic dynamic the act of confession constitutes an attempt not only at catharsis but also self-revelation, constructed as a connection that involves both personal discovery and a reaching out, a communicative act that promises to extend beyond the boundaries of the analyst/patient relationship. If *The Boston Strangler* ultimately suggests the failure of therapeutic confession in this context—as the patient remains trapped in a non-communicative state, cut off from the authorities, the psychiatrists, and even from himself—the controversial independent film *Coming Apart* (Milton Moses Ginsberg, 1969) brings analyst/patient confessional expression to an even more devastating moment of crisis by explicating the more constrictive and disconnective process that ensues when the psychiatrist Joe (Rip Torn) rents a studio apartment in his ex-lover Monica's (Viveca Lindfors) Manhattan high-rise and conducts a never fully articulated experiment of self-analysis, setting up a hidden camera that records a series of his encounters with patients, lovers, and other sexual partners, punctuated by Joe's own occasional editorial interventions. "Everyone seemed to be seeing a psychiatrist," Ginsberg suggests in a supplemental essay included in the DVD release, and his intention was to "project a character who suffered this fissure—between the ideal doctor his patients saw and the faulted one he saw in the mirror—to such a degree that he breaks in two; even as he tries to hold his psyche together by making a film about the rent of his soul" (*Film Comment*, 5).[8] The design and configuration of the psychotherapeutic space was inspired by the television series *Candid Camera*, on which Ginsberg had worked as an assistant. All of the action is contained to the rectangular studio space, with the static camera placed upon a long table underneath a set of broad windows overlooking the New York skyline, and aimed directly at an opposite wall housing a mirror so large that it encompasses the boundaries of the cinematic frame. A couch is placed against the wall and directly below the mirrors, and a slightly oblique camera angle becomes sufficient to produce the effect that two characters seated on opposite sides of the room (one at the couch, the other at the window) appear to be facing each other (with one character's face always visible only as a reflection), rather than having the character on the couch face the camera straight on, which would result in a semblance of direct address reserved only for instances in which Joe is alone in the studio, commenting directly through the camera's recording device.

This spatial/cinematic configuration effects a complex set of power relations organized by the operations of seeing and being seen. Aligned with Joe's experimental purpose, the central protagonist/therapist is always aware of another set of "eyes" looking back at him as he looks out at his patients or the world beyond, and this sense of induced reflection becomes a more prominent aspect of the set-up than any purely voyeuristic or fetishistic use of the recording format—that is, as a potentially compromising "sex tape" or a primer for masturbation, neither function of which appears to interest Joe even remotely. Still, there remains a distinct power imbalance between Joe and anyone else who enters into the space—for the most part, his wife, current and former psychiatric clients (all female), and current and former lovers, some of whom are or have been Joe's psychiatric patients (see fig. 1.2). Occasionally, Joe exploits this balance in ways that remind viewers of their own privileged position within the film's hierarchy of knowledge—a position actually superior to Joe's own. When a young model who has come to the studio to show him her photography portfolio inquires about the object which we know to be the camera, Joe describes it as a "kinetic art object"; feigning the professional identity of a photographer, he explains to the model that he's "interested in reality" and in photographing situations "as they happen."

Control itself does not register as a sexual turn-on for Joe; instead, it extends the dynamic with which he has grown most comfortable by professional orientation, and here he remains unyielding. When one client complains that it seems unfair that Joe always asks about her life, while she cannot ask about his, he responds merely by posing more questions to her. As the progressive disengagement and disorientation of the central protagonist begins to elicit the concern of others, however, the power dynamic is disrupted in ways that also unsettle the boundary between analyst and patient. "You're really in torment, Joe," one client suggests. "You must have had some mother, baby. You keep searching for your mother." To such pronouncements, including Monica's more desperate interrogations later in the film as her ex-lover becomes more incommunicative, Joe remains verbally unresponsive. His demeanor changes, however, when he perceives disruptions of the power dynamic to be too

Figure 1.2. Karen (Phoebe Dorn) confronts her husband, "Glassman" Joe Glazer (Rip Torn), about his infidelities in *Coming Apart* (Milton Moses Ginsberg, Kaleidoscope Films, 1969). Digital frame enlargement.

threatening. In a sex scene that finds Joe and ex-patient Joann (Sally Kirkland) facing the mirror ("It's like an orgy," Joann remarks), when she impulsively grabs her camera in an effort to capture and luxuriate in the reflexive dynamics between seeing and being seen, Joe startlingly commands her to put down the camera; retreating to a chair facing the window, he remains indifferent to Joann's protestations that "You're not as strong as I thought," "You're frightened," and "You're weak-willed." Following a tense, extended interlude of maintained physical distance, however, Joann resumes the seduction by performing a striptease that fails to produce any erotic response until Joe regains control of the encounter by tapping her buttocks with his lit cigarette. Joann then bends down on the floor to submit to his advances, while her photographic camera remains visible on the sofa in the foreground of the frame, a conspicuous reminder of Joe's only tenuous "command" of the scene's proceedings.

If the patient/analyst films of the early 1960s yielded strong connection and interpersonal communication both within and beyond the therapeutic setting, *Coming Apart* even more forcefully testifies to a disconnection that isolates and ultimately destroys its central protagonist. Extending cinematic formulas that posit sex at the heart of the therapeutic encounter, it is not until several scenes have passed that the viewer becomes able to distinguish psychiatric clients from sexual hookups, especially since Joe is so adept at transforming one type of visitor into the other. While the mid-1960s films focus upon sex exploitatively as a non-problem, in the world of *Coming Apart* sex has become both a distraction and a meager substitute for interpersonal connection. As graphically depicted as it is, the sex in the film is itself disconnected and disengaged: in several of the sex scenes (including a notorious instance of fellatio in cinema of this decade) Joe remains dispassionate and disaffected, and in other instances he appears to be asleep. In an early sequence, the intense arousal of a woman who attempts to seduce Joe by proposing that they engage in sadomasochistic and fetishistic rituals ends up becoming a source of parody when Joe's response fails to move beyond awkwardness and confusion. The sexual act seems inevitable yet always mistimed: in most cases, one participant is always either less (or more) engaged than the other; in other instances, the "peak" of sexual desire has already passed by the time of the encounter, as is the case with Monica, who repeatedly rejects his advances with blunt pronouncements that "I don't love you anymore" and "it's too late."

Ultimately, even the video camera, the technological mechanism at the center of the narrative and Joe's experiment, echoes the sense of dislocation that its author and orchestrator experiences, articulated perhaps nowhere more directly than in the film's opening line, "I am frightened and wonder to find myself here," spoken as Joe tests the microphone. If his high-rise apartment setting finds him progressively trapped in a network of gazes—including the looks of the camera, the audience, his visitors, and even himself—his interactions with the recording device take on a tone of intimacy rendered tenuous and subject to failure by distortions and technical glitches. Indeed, the results of Joe's "self-analysis" and therapeutic work are condensed into one brief scene midway through the film, in which he begins to address the mirror, the camera, and the viewer with what appears to be a confession: "the odd thing is that I can pretend that I'm there now watching this, watching all of the film so far—" after which sound distortion renders the remainder of his words inaudible, resuming only at the speech's conclusion with the pronouncement that "I'll never change." The actual scope of the experiment remains unrevealed to the viewer, and the clarity of expression that Joe attempts always fails because he is using a device that denies him the feedback that he consistently refuses from his friends, thereby exacerbating his isolation and despair. Yet *Coming Apart* also emphasizes that these failures and disconnections do not simply comprise experiences that have "happened" to Joe; instead, as Bruce Kawin clarifies, at every turn the narrative elects "to emphasize the antihero's responsibility for his own situation" (*Mindscreen* 67). All of the "actual" professional interactions—those involving current psychiatric patients who see him at his office—are rendered through brief audio-only interludes where the image is reduced to total darkness, not through any technical glitch, but rather from some deliberate strategy of exclusion on Joe's part, a decision not to make visible the professional life that threatens to invade the space of this "retreat." In two of these scenes, female patients plead to make an appointment with him, insisting that they have been improving under his care, yet Joe dispassionately dismisses them by announcing without explanation that he has simply decided to reduce his afternoon appointment schedule. By the end of the film, the psychiatrist, who has been operating under the pseudonym of "Glassman," and who now appears to be unemployed, is forced to abandon the experimental confines of his rented studio; his sexual exploits having been discovered by his wife, who ultimately asks for a divorce. All that is left to destroy is the therapeutic setting itself, carried out in the final scene by Joann, who trashes the studio and completes the task by hurling a paperweight at the mirror that has provided us access to the therapist's reflections.

As a sexually explicit film with a self-imposed X rating, this dark and tragic depiction of a psychiatrist's dissolution seems far removed from the therapeutic dynamics of the more upbeat *On a Clear Day*

You Can See Forever, a relatively lighthearted, G-rated musical romantic comedy released in 1970, and based upon a relatively successful Broadway musical of the same name that premiered in 1965. And indeed, the films' conclusions about the efficacy of the patient/analyst relationship are quite different: while *Coming Apart* ultimately registers a communicative failure that extends from the internal, to the interpersonal, to the cultural, *On a Clear Day* counters with the therapeutic success of patient and analyst, both of whom, through intricate machinations of transference and counter-transference, effect "cures" to their own (and each other's) psychological maladies. And unlike the always ill-defined and perpetually deferred self-analysis of *Coming Apart*, *On a Clear Day* represents the personal, reflective process of its protagonist at its most functional. Peculiarly, however, the cures offered by the end of the film seem largely disconnected from the "symptoms" that initially bring patient and analyst together.

Janet Walker's observes that "by the mid 1960s, the face of American psychiatry became less authoritarian, more self-critical, and less liable to dictate prescriptive roles for women, with . . . changes occurring in an atmosphere of political activism, including feminist activism" (14). If *Coming Apart*'s progressive annihilation of the psychotherapeutic professional brings such self-criticism to a moment of crisis by forcing him to be aware of the consequences of his actions upon the world of women around him, *On a Clear Day* comprises the apotheosis of concerns across the previous decade about the efficacy of the one-on-one, analyst/patient psychotherapeutic dynamic. While the film never overtly frames these concerns in the context of the women's movement, *On a Clear Day* implicates a perspective that encourages "diagnosed" women to recognize the conditions under which the consultation of a psychiatric professional becomes unduly constraining and counterproductive. *On a Clear Day* uniquely interrogates Freudian psychoanalytic methods, as new therapeutic strategies and paradigms emerge to provide alternatives better suited to respond to the psychopathology of contemporary culture. If *The Caretakers* anticipates a transition from Freudian to behavioral and community psychotherapy, *On a Clear Day* hybridizes Freud with emerging therapeutic enterprises extending to the realms of hypnotherapy, self-help, and the human potential movement, all of which had emerged as popular phenomena by the end of the decade, as evidenced especially by the 1969 release of Thomas Harris's longstanding bestseller *I'm OK, You're OK*, a guide for self-enlightenment that uses as its foundation the resilience of debilitating yet formative childhood memories throughout life, and the struggle for the development of a "healthy" adult self, capable of successfully negotiating learned and inherited roles of parent and child. While Dana Cloud marks the popularity of Harris's book as "emblematic of a shift away from activism [which peaked in 1968] toward personal healing and self-fulfillment" (50), *On a Clear Day You Can See Forever* imagines an instance in which the promise of personal healing also constitutes a political act of reaching out that is not antithetical to social change.

The film's convoluted plot centers upon early '20s New Yorker Daisy Gamble (Barbra Streisand), who enlists the services of Columbia psychology professor Marc Chabot (Yves Montand) to help her to quit smoking. An initial interview with Daisy leads him to suspect that she is clairvoyant, and once he engages her in hypnotherapy (only marginally successful regarding its intended outcome), Chabot uncovers Daisy's previous identity as Melinda Winifred Tentrees, an early nineteenth-century Englishwoman whose own clairvoyance was exploited by her second husband Robert (John Richardson), ultimately leading to her public execution upon suspicion of witchcraft. Chabot's bewilderment at the intrusion of such parapsychological phenomenon of reincarnation into his objective, scientific, academic practice leads to additional treatment sessions in an effort to either affirm or definitively discount the legitimacy of Daisy's past-life identity. If the clairvoyance seems to have survived the transition of Melinda's reincarnation as Daisy, so has a pattern of usury at the hands of insensitive men. Daisy's motivation for quitting smoking is unrelated to health concerns; instead, her fiancé Warren (Larry Blyden) has directed her to curtail her habit because an executive who shares business interests with Warren, and with whom they are scheduled to dine, finds smoking repulsive. Blathering on about financial security, retirement, and pensions, the manipulative and self-serving Warren instructs Daisy to express no opinions and to drink no martinis during the dinner.

The psychotherapeutic power dynamics of *On a Clear Day* closely resemble those of *Coming Apart* in many ways. Like Joe's female "visitors," Daisy is initially characterized as weak and impressionable: unlike her therapist, Daisy has no college degree, and as Chabot is placing a student under hypnosis when she meets him during one of his class sessions, Daisy becomes hypnotized telepathically. Apparently lacking the willpower to control her five-packs-a-day smoking habit, she surrenders to a male authority figure for a quick fix so that she can meet the deadline set by her demanding male partner. Chabot himself is depicted as not only dominant and self-assured, but also ethically suspect: under the guise of maintaining scientific objectivity, he refrains from revealing anything about Melinda to Daisy, and he never explains that his actual reasons for continuing their therapeutic sessions are more for his benefit than hers.

Once she discovers Melinda's "identity" (after happening upon one of the audiotaped therapeutic sessions in Chabot's office), however, Daisy comes to see that her relationships with Chabot and Warren evidence the same "problem"—a longstanding tendency to devalue her own needs for self-interested men. This realization, along with Chabot's preference for the stronger-willed Melinda over her, serves as Daisy's epiphany and call to action: having willingly renounced everything that makes her unique—including her powers of extrasensory perception, her past lives, and an uncanny ability to make flowers grow *very* rapidly, she breaks off her relationship with Warren and calls Chabot on his own duplicity. The closing sequences find Chabot confessing that Daisy has inspired him to reconcile with his wife ("I used to be in love with answers, but since I have known you, I am just as fond of the questions. I think the answers make you wise, but the questions make you human."), and Daisy revealing in a final hypnotherapy session that she and Chabot will be together and married in the next life (2038, precisely, as Laura and John Caswell), even though the fact that the revelation occurs in the hypnotic state appears to leave Daisy unaware of what will be happening sixty-years ahead. The ending of the film, however, marks one of the first occasions when a female psychiatric patient emerges as triumphant and transformed *after* ceasing treatment with her male therapist, rather than *because* of his efforts. Connected to the lucid, vibrant colors of lush floral abundances that thrive on rooftop gardens and college campus lawns—indeed, wherever she walks—Daisy is ultimately offered no "cure" from Chabot; but unlike the wrecked protagonist of *Coming Apart*, the therapeutic process has provided Daisy with the impetus for her own emergence. By joyously transcending the limits of interior spaces that have sequestered and defined her as the object of scientific inquiry for men who have grossly underestimated her potential, Daisy rejoices upon the "clear day" of her final musical number—a day of perceptual insight to be sure, and also a day entirely clear of the influence of male suitors, husbands, and therapists.[9]

Over the course of the decade, the function of one-on-one analyst/patient psychotherapy shifted from a model in which psychological, social, and political problems were directly addressed within the therapeutic dynamic, to a function that would be better described as catalytic—one whose changes and insights might be *motivated* by the analyst/patient relationship, but whose benefits to its patients more often ultimately result from insights that the therapist himself has not directly brought about—insights that make the continued relationship with the therapist either unhealthy or inconsequential, and that attest to the therapeutic subject's agency to determine the conditions of her own "cure." If the film industry had found opportunity to sexualize the psychotherapeutic dynamic since the mid-1960s, the next chapter focuses upon a context in which the sexual act itself becomes the problem that draws patients to the therapist's office.

2

Therapy and the Sexual Block

> The cotherapists are fully aware that their most important role in reversal of sexual dysfunction is that of catalyst to communication.
>
> —William Masters and Virginia Johnson,
> *Human Sexual Inadequacy* (1970)

THIS CHAPTER EXAMINES AMERICAN sexual culture's transformation during the late 1960s and early 1970s through the lens of emerging psychotherapeutic developments in the diagnosis and treatment of "sexual block," a term that encompassed male impotence and female disorders classified early in the 1960s as "frigidity," but later described with the more scientifically neutral and less denigrating terminology as "orgasmic dysfunction." The study of human sexual function in the early 1960s continued to be dominated by Freudian psychoanalysis, yet new behavioral and cognitive treatment strategies would assume a position of prominence within psychotherapy later in the decade. This gradual movement away from the therapeutic model of psychoanalysis paralleled a conterminous shift in the film industry's new representational liberties after the dissolution of the Production Code in the mid-1960s and the inception of the Motion Picture Association of America's new movie rating system in 1968 which, in accordance with the *Ginsberg v. New York* decision by the Supreme Court in the same year, supported Hollywood's treatment of adult-oriented subject matter by validating a notion of "variable obscenity" whereby material deemed unsuitable for children and teenagers might be considered acceptable for adult audiences. Among the most profound ironies of Hollywood's engagement with the sexual revolution, however, was that as such new opportunities for thematizing and representing sexual pleasure became available as the 1960s progressed—bolstered by landmark legal decisions in the publishing industry—the film industry became more intent in focusing upon psychosexual pathology than in celebrating sexual freedom. The exploration of human sexual dysfunction served as a viable means of containing the expression and performance of sexual desire within familiar and established ideological boundaries. In the case of sexual block, the containment of sexual response correlates with what professional and popular psychotherapeutic discourse would describe as new manifestations of male sexual anxiety brought about by the women's liberation movement and also by an explosion in the discourse of sexual deviance and pathology, that ultimately precipitated reactionary forces against sexual license and plurality in mainstream cinema of the era, and that exacerbated anxiety about the increasingly accepted notion of sexual intercourse as the utmost expression of human communication. As this chapter will demonstrate, even as American cinema was experimenting with more frank and explicit in the treatment of sex by the late 1960s, the film industry continued to constitute sex as a "problem" of interpersonal communication that needed to be discussed, investigated, and resolved, rather than something that could be celebrated in the context of the sexual revolution. And the therapeutic discourse of sexual block provided a most suitable context for the cinematic narrative problematization of sex.

Therapeutic Treatment Strategies

According to Alfred Kinsey's findings published a decade earlier, "frigidity" was a pervasive problem affecting as much as one-third of American women, and a 1964 literature review in the *Psychoanalytic Review* categorizes the disorder as "female psychosexual development," incorporating Freudian notions of sado-masochism, narcissism, and penis envy. Acknowledging the limitations of the psychoanalytic method's efficacy and its failure to account for "the role of society in limiting the opportunities of women for direct sexual gratification . . . as well as the interesting question of the effect of relatively greater equality of women in our modern world" (Moore 346), the review highlights the method's disconnection from contemporary social developments that were challenging traditional designations of gender. Popular therapeutic discourse of the era was also highlighting two other significant limitations of psychoanalysis: first, its preoccupation with the patient's past experiences and traumas, to the relative exclusion of the present moment; second, its requirement of a long-term investment of time, energy, and financial resources to carry out its purposes. Behavioral and cognitive therapeutic alternatives to psychoanalysis gained popularity by the middle of the decade, even though the origins of behavioral therapy stretched back at least to 1958 with South African psychiatrist Joseph Wolpe, who would develop the popular and influential stimulus-response approach known as "systematic desensitization," involving the subject's structured exposure to a hierarchically arranged set of anxiety-inducing stimuli, the ultimate goal of which exposure is to entirely neutralize and eliminate the anxiety.

Intimating the limitations of psychoanalytic approaches to the treatment of sexual dysfunction, this same 1964 review acknowledges that "frigidity appears to be somewhat uncertainly defined. It could not be otherwise so long as the phenomenon of female orgasm is itself not clearly understood" (Moore 345). The requisite clarification of misunderstanding came with the 1966 publication of William Masters and Virginia Johnson's monumental volume *Human Sexual Response*, which articulated a four-stage model of the human sexual response cycle, eliminated once and for all the erroneous concept of the vaginal orgasm, and explained that unlike men, women were capable of experiencing multiple orgasms because of the longer post-climactic refractory period in males. While Masters and Johnson would not prescribe a treatment regimen for sexual dysfunction until the release of their even more popular 1970 book *Human Sexual Inadequacy*, the efficacy of cognitive-behavioral treatment regimens was being proposed before the end of the decade. For example, a June 1967 *New York Times* article details behavioral therapy's break from psychoanalysis in the treatment of neurosis, and suggests that "even such classically difficult disorders as extreme aversion to sexual relations are usually easily curable, in Wolpe's view" (Hunt, "Freudians Are Wrong," SM20). Still, it would not be until the early 1970s that such methods gained public attention for the treatment of male and female sexual dysfunction, with *Human Sexual Inadequacy* used as a model that inspired a proliferation of therapies. Sharing Wolpe's harsh criticism of psychoanalytic methods, Masters and Johnson prescribed an intensive therapeutic strategy carried out during a two-week stay at the Reproductive Biology Research Foundation in St. Louis. The therapeutic method certainly took account of the patient's past, as the treatment began with a series of interviews along with two extensive history-taking sessions designed to reveal to the therapists the patient's "sexual value system." Unlike psychoanalysis, however, the method primarily emphasized behavior modification strategies designed to gradually relieve sexual anxiety and ultimately to eliminate instances and patterns of sexual dysfunction that were not rooted in physiological conditions.

Masters and Johnson's therapeutic objective was not only the elimination of dysfunctional sexual anxiety but also the promotion of enhanced interpersonal communication. Interaction between husband and wife was a crucial component of a therapy that required both verbal and sexual communication. "There is no such thing as an uninvolved partner in any marriage in which where is some form of sexual inadequacy," the therapists clarified. "Isolating a husband or wife in therapy from his or her partner not only denies the concept that both partners are involved . . . but also ignores the fundamental fact that sexual response represents . . . interaction between people" (Masters and Johnson, 1970, 8). The commitment to productive interaction is similarly evident in the requirement of a cotherapist "team" comprising a man and a woman (Masters and Johnson themselves, and later, teams that they would train) that promoted gender-based identification and freer exchange in the therapeutic setting. *Human Sexual Inadequacy* foregrounds that "the cotherapists are fully aware that their most important role in reversal of sexual dysfunction is that of catalyst to communication," and that "the ultimate level of marital-unit communication is sexual intercourse" (14). The communication strategies incorporated a "give-to-get" dynamic that emphasized the participant's immersion in the pleasure of giving pleasure to a partner rather than the expectation of reciprocation (198). Yet the discourse of connection and communication extended to each step of the therapeutic process outlined in the second book, from periodic roundtable discussions that served the largely educative function of challenging myths and correcting prejudices of the patients' value systems through "nonjudgmental evaluation," to the "sensate focus" sessions that prompted couples to enhance each other's pleasurable responses through tactile communication, focusing on eliciting excitement in a controlled, pressure-free environment without activating the performance anxiety associated with sexual intercourse. Even after a five-year follow-up period, Masters and Johnson boasted a success rate of over 70 percent in their two-week treatment regimen—several times greater than that of psychoanalysis.

The team's methods and strategies were not universally accepted, and despite their protestations that the technical nature of the sexual discourse was necessary in order for them to avoid accusations of indecency,[1] some found the detached, analytic tone in which they described sex to be alienating and even morally suspect.[2] Still, it would be difficult to overestimate the impact of their methods and findings upon contemporary American perspectives on functional sexual health and access to sexual pleasure. Proposing that "sexual problems of one kind or another affect at least half the married couples in the U.S. today," a 1972 *Newsweek* article entitled "All About the New Sex Therapy" credited Masters and Johnson with making the "sex clinic" into "a vital part of the modern hospital and the intensive care unit" (65). The article further affirmed the success of the team's strategy of directly addressing and engaging the sexual problems of American couples, explaining that "The two-to-four-month waiting lists at most sex clinics are ample proof that thousands of people are rapidly losing their reticence and are fully prepared to shed their inhibitions" (66). By the early 1970s, the team was also being at least partially credited with the advent of "comprehensive mental health clinics" that were bringing more widespread attention to "marital problems which involve as a focal factor either impotence or frigidity" (Levit 56).[3]

Both before and after the two initial studies of Masters and Johnson, psychoanalytic and behavior therapies were often co-administered,[4] yet in popular contemporary discourse the two methods were more often dichotomized. Psychoanalysis could be a long and expensive process; the benefits of behavior therapy were more immediate, and ultimately cheaper. Behavior therapy was portrayed as centering upon communication and human interaction—both within the unit of the heterosexual couple, and between analysts and patients—as compared to the more authoritative and hierarchically structured method of Freudian analysis. As Janet Walker has noted, from the immediate postwar period through the first years of the 1960s the configuration of psychotherapy had been moving from a focus upon the self to a broader embrace of the social context in which the subject interacts. This progression, along with psychoanalysis's focus on excavating the past in comparison to behavior therapy's more direct address of the patient's present and future, informed the film industry's use of the discourse of sexual block later in the decade, with psychoanalysis characterized as a form of inquiry that remained largely removed from the contemporary cultural developments of an increasingly turbulent decade, and cognitive-behavioral therapeutic approaches accommodating the broader sociopolitical context of the sexual revolution.

The Psychoanalysis of Sexual Dysfunction

Several films released from the early to mid-1960s integrate prevailing psychoanalytic characterizations of sexual dysfunction. Plagued with demands for censorship by both the Production Code Administration and the Catholic organization the Legion of Decency, George Cukor's 1962 film *The Chapman Report* comprises one of the decade's first attempts to come to terms directly with the implications of treating sex as science.[5] Released between the publication of two key feminist works of the decade—Helen Gurley Brown's *Sex and the Single Girl* and Betty Friedan's *The Feminine Mystique*—the film acknowledges neither the celebration of female sexual liberty promoted in the former work nor the interrogation of women's traditional place in marriage articulated in the latter. More clearly rooted in "old Hollywood" demands of condemning the sexual freedoms that it simultaneously appears to embrace, *The Chapman Report* remains ambivalent about the frank treatment of sexual dysfunction with which the industry would continue to struggle even after the inception of the new rating system later in the decade and the broader representational liberties regarding adult-oriented subject matter that it promised. Asked by a reporter at the start of the film to comment upon what happens when a woman finds herself disappointed in the relationship with her husband, Dr. George Chapman (Andrew Duggan), the head of a sex research team whose methods and findings clearly resemble those of Alfred Kinsey, confidently rattles off the only four possible responses: "divorce, a lover, an analyst, or a bottle." And indeed, the film follows through by dramatizing at least three of these possibilities in its case-study focus upon four upper-middle-class southern California women who come to express dissatisfaction with their sexual experiences. While the film never dramatizes the sole remaining option of consulting an analyst, the ensuing relationship between the widowed Kathleen Barclay (Jane Fonda) and sex researcher Paul Radford (Efrem Zimbalist, Jr.) comes to resemble a patient/analyst relationship closely enough, replete with complications of transference and countertransference that culminate in Paul's declaration of love and a proposal of marriage.

The Chapman Report evidences a conflicted perspective on the notion of "progress" in sexual research. As her now-deceased husband "Boy" (John Baer) describes it, Kathleen's dysfunction has branded her with the label of "femme de glace," and the infiltration of her community by the eager sex research team exacerbates her own self-perception as a hopeless, pathological case—or, as she describes herself, "half a woman."[6] During her interview, in which Paul remains behind a screen and entirely invisible to her, thereby permitting the camera's unyielding, static focus to exacerbate her sense of anxiety and entrapment, Kathleen responds erratically to the series of "objective" questions posed by the fact-finding sex researcher. With Kathleen wearing a formal white dress and a fancy white hat that obstructs the audience's view of part of her face, the *mise-en-scène* over-determines the same sense of impermeability that her husband found so intolerable. Yet *The Chapman Report* is less interested in designating Kathleen's condition as untreatable than in correlating the two debilitating processes of sexual "coding" that have victimized her—the first articulated by her aggressive and insensitive husband (and also by her controlling father, with whom she has been living since her husband's death), and the second organized by the system of research and analysis that Chapman's team practices in the name of sexual science. As a product of Hollywood in 1962, the film wholly embraces and even exploits the contemporary nature of its subject matter, yet any immersion in the progressive contemporaneity of its therapeutic advances in sexual research remains held in check by a pronounced suspicion that sexual science is more concerned with producing categories of statistical significance than with understanding the relationship problems of actual human beings. From a credit sequence visually articulated as a series of computer punch cards, to Chapman's initial directive to his team that in their interactions with interviewees they are to imagine themselves as "fact-finders" speaking as an "uncritical machine," *The Chapman Report* posits "statistics" as a generalized category that ultimately suggests something alienating and potentially sinister because of its failure to account for the crucial, complex variable of "love," configured as a universal component of functional romantic relationships that can neither be reduced nor translated into data points. As the skeptical Dr. Jonas (Henry Daniell) informs Paul during a consultation after acknowledging that his feelings for Kathleen have exceeded the boundaries of professional interaction, "Someone has got to make her understand that statistics do not make morality. You have the one and only cure: love. Real love."

Charged with the task of containing anxieties around a new age of sexual science that threatens to reduce human beings to categories of normality or abnormality, the film's remedy for this problem is to emphasize that love transcends statistics, and that the contemporary woman's best bet is to make sure that she marries the man who will ensure that her relationship remains within the 89 percent majority of women who love their husbands—a majority that Paul and Kathleen are about to join by the ending of the film, along with two other of the case study couples, the strength of whose marital love has also been tested and affirmed by the wives' revelatory experimentation with extramarital affairs. Ironically yet strategically, it is Chapman himself who ultimately proclaims that the cases of "bad" relationships remain so vivid to the public that we lose sight of the fact that the vast majority fall into the column labeled "Happily Married Women—and Men." Progressive as the film aims to be in its stance on sexual science, *The Chapman Report* conspicuously evades the specific parameters of concern over women's livelihood and independence that form the foundation of Brown and

Friedan's protestations: none of the four wives needs to work in order to survive, and children are referenced yet never presented as factors that complicate marriages or compromise women's identities. In fact, the film expresses a similar anxiety over diagnostic frenzy that would plague American culture more profoundly a few years later in the wake of Masters and Johnson's research findings. The distinctions afforded by the realities of 1962 psychotherapeutic culture were such that virtually *any* category of sexual dysfunction—including those, like Kinsey's, which were intended to obscure rather than reify discrete classificatory distinctions between normal and abnormal sexual behavior—would be relegated to a popular therapeutic discourse that situated crucial traumatic events in the patient's past as the cause of present behavioral patterns. Accordingly, from her own perspective, Kathleen's dysfunctional sexual condition is one that she believes to be rooted in a trauma whose origins she cannot articulate—that is, until the intervention of a professional (Paul Radford) triggers the requisite catharsis that liberates her from the constraints of her father and her deceased husband.

Psychoanalysis's focus on excavating the past in comparison to behavior therapy's more direct address of the patient's present and future, cumulatively informed the film industry's perspective on sexual block in this era, with the psychoanalytic method characterized as a familiar yet insular form of inquiry that remained largely removed from the contemporary cultural developments of an increasingly turbulent decade. Aligned with psychoanalytic investigations of the female sexual psyche of this period, *The Chapman Report* structures the prospect of the cathartic breakthrough as largely outside the scope of the suffering woman's agency or control: had Paul Radford not materialized as an intervening force in Kathleen's life, she might never have been liberated from the pathological sense of abnormality that her husband had so effectively imposed upon her. Kathleen witnesses the process of bringing about her own cure without ever actually participating in it or directing its course; indeed, the film's preference of extended flashbacks to frame its explications of trauma emphasizes her role of victimized, passive witness.

If a trauma that is sufficiently severe or intense to have interminably prevented the woman from accessing sexual pleasure becomes a staple of Hollywood's films about sexual block early in the decade, the sense of women's helplessness and lack of agency certainly correlates with a significant gap in the understanding of female psycho-physiology. The aforementioned 1964 professional literature review on frigidity illuminates the nature and scope of this gap, with the author acknowledging that "frigidity appears to be somewhat uncertainly defined. It could not be otherwise as long as the phenomenon of female orgasm is itself not clearly understood" (Moore 345). Such lack of understanding allows the perpetuation of trauma's status as a psychic "unknown" that can and must be excavated and revealed by painstaking therapeutic probing. Unlike his earlier *Psycho*, whose criminal psychologist neatly wraps up an assessment of Norman Bates's psychopathology in Freudian terms during its closing sequence, Hitchcock's 1964 *Marnie* features no representations of psychotherapeutic professionals, and unlike *The Chapman Report*, it even lacks a male figure with marginal qualifications or credentials to assess the symptoms or causes of female sexual dysfunction. Nonetheless, the relationship between its eponymous, central, sexually dysfunctional female protagonist (Tippi Hedren) and Mark Rutland (Sean Connery), the rich and powerful man whose fascination with this kleptomaniacally criminal subject compels him to take such complete charge of her care, is steeped in psychoanalytic discourse consonant with the film's emphasis upon sexual trauma. During one of their many heated arguments, Marnie's response to her protector's method of investigative analysis is epitomized by her comment "You Freud, me Jane?," and Marnie is always quite perceptive in her assessment of the power that Mark has convinced himself that he holds over her: "Oh men," she exclaims. "You say no to one of them, and bingo, you're a candidate for the funny farm."[7] In the context of Marnie's keen suspicions about Mark's motivations, his seemingly impulsive decision to jumpstart Marnie's progress on the path toward mental health by raping her during their honeymoon voyage (despite the fact that earlier in the voyage he promised his ice-blue-nightgown-clad bride that he would honor her request for separate sleeping quarters and agreed not touch her) serves paradoxically as a violent act of penetrative control under the guise of a "breakthrough" physiological shock treatment designed to free her from frigidity even as it promises to curtail his own growing sexual frustration. In this context, Marnie's subsequent suicide attempt in the ship's immense, built-in swimming pool registers as both an ultimate act of capitulation to her husband-captor and a larger act of defiance and refusal to be contained[8]—indeed, a refusal that also resonates with prevailing psychoanalytic explanations of frigidity as the execution of a wish to disappoint the man that arises out of penis envy (Moore 341), or that, according to Deutsch, involves sado-masochistic fantasy (Moore 343).

Despite Marnie's well-informed claims and protestations, her sustained victimization by not only Mark but also by the repressive operations of her own psyche—which reveals pieces of its puzzle only through troubling dreams, flashbacks triggered by the sound of thunder, and a terrifying, arresting symptomatology centering upon the color red—marks her as entirely cut off from a past whose revelation comprises the only hope for the catharsis that might elicit her cure. The therapeutic process that the film offers is one stemming entirely from isolation and disconnection, the denial of access to the past traumatic moment framed by Marnie's mother as an act of grace (Marnie has "blocked out" her murder of the sailor), and protection (she is convinced that Marnie is better off not remembering what happened), and it is left undisclosed until Mark forces the truth from the mother in her daughter's presence. If the ending of the film presents the audience with a cathartically "cured" Marnie, the cure emerges less as a result of her own agency than through a process of exhaustive degeneration that has impelled others to act on her behalf.

While male sexual dysfunction in the mid-1960s received less extensive treatment than female "frigidity" in Hollywood cinema, a similar sense of dysfunction's association with disconnection and disempowerment permeates the characterizations of John Huston's 1967 adaptation of the Carson McCullers novel *Reflections in a Golden Eye*. Released shortly after the official demise of the Production Code but before the inception of the new MPAA rating system in 1968, the film bore the seal of approval the MPAA with an accompanying advisement "Suggested for Mature Audiences" which would later serve as the official descriptions of the organization's brief-lived "M" rating. Its designation of mature subject matter seems warranted primarily by the suggestions of homosexuality and impotence of its central protagonist, Major Weldon Penderton (Marlon Brando), and indeed these two conditions—the first denoting a "perversion" and psychological disorder by the American Psychological Association until 1973, and one for which shock and desensitization treatments were still regularly administered by psychiatrists[9]—are conspicuously correlated in the narrative through a reciprocal causal connection. Penderton comes to embody insularity and disconnection, evident in the overdetermined, almost pathetic narcissism with which he surveys his own broad physique in the bedroom mirror after visibly struggling to work out with barbells that are too heavy for him (see fig. 2.1). The more elemental and less "deviant" sexual energies of the handsome, mostly silent Private Williams (Robert Forster) become associated with the strong, majestic, elegant, and gracefully moving horses that he has been charged to groom and tend at the Pendertons' stables, and that he also rides bareback or entirely naked. As his wife Leonora (Elizabeth Taylor) scornfully delights in reminding him, Penderton is clumsy and relatively inept on his horse, and he cannot keep up with his wife and his best friend, Lt. Colonel Morris Langdon (Brian Keith), when the three ride together. Penderton's "dysfunctional" riding skills are brought to a breaking point when he ventures out with his wife's favorite horse on his own: failing to control his speeding stallion's gallop, he is thrown

Figure 2.1. Major Weldon Penderton (Marlon Brando) admires his post-workout physique in *Reflections in a Golden Eye* (John Huston, Warner Bros/Seven Arts, 1967). Digital frame enlargement.

from the animal and proceeds to beat him violently with a whip until a naked Williams makes an almost ethereal appearance and silently escorts the seriously injured animal back to the stables.

Penderton's sexual dysfunction manifests itself as both an inability to effect the requisite connections that result in sexual pleasure, and as a form of "deviance" from normative sexual expression: he is compelled to witness his wife's blatant flirtations with Langdon without ever registering the affective response to disrupt or condemn what he perceives, and he is victimized in the face of the scorn and sadistic mockery with which Leonora carries out a striptease before her wholly unaroused but ultimately enraged and humiliated husband's gaze. Like *Marnie*, as well as Kathleen in *The Chapman Report*, Penderton's anhedonia leaves him closed-off and largely unresponsive to the network of potential interpersonal connections that surround him, yet the addition of homosexuality to the protagonist's profile of psychopathology unleashes a "perverted" sexual energy whose expression seems limited (at least by 1967 standards of cinematic representation) to an almost predatory voyeuristic surveillance of the private with whom he almost never directly interacts, and an equally sinister penchant for fetishism that finds the major collecting not only postcards depicting erotic Asian art, but the silver spoon that he has stolen from the artistic, effeminately coded Captain Murray Weincheck (Irvin Duggan), along with the Baby Ruth candy bar wrapper that Williams discards while Penderton tracks his movements through the streets of the military base. Consonant with the construction of a psychoanalytically informed "neurosis" that encompasses his two interrelated maladies, as a psychopathological case study Penderton seems less a character than a set of accumulating symptoms presented to the audience without ever being explicated: lacking backstory to frame his estrangement from his wife, and denied anyone in whom he might confide, he is left to navigate the fields of jealousy and desire entirely on his own, his impotence and homosexuality fused to represent a deadly psychological affliction that finds release only in murder.

Behavioral/Contextual Approaches to Sexual Dysfunction

A shift in Hollywood cinema's strategies of dramatizing issues of sexual dysfunction occurs late in the decade, correlated with the increasing popularity of behavioral and cognitive therapies and the relative decrease in reliance upon "pure" Freudian psychoanalytic models. Accordingly, a new system of discourse emerges to incorporate and contain this sexual function. Indeed, Masters and Johnson's revolutionary transformation of sex through science invites a metaphorical description of uninhibited flow, with processes of systematic desensitization, relaxation, and verbal and tactile communication all anticipating a resulting healthy orgasm—a specific moment when a profound sensation (or series of sensations) should occur if the sexual system is operating smoothly and optimally, liberated from the misfires, gaps, and disruptions of flow that disrupt intimacy and precipitate a state of self-consciousness that the therapist team describes as the "spectator effect," the sense that one is observing oneself go through the motions of sexual intimacy rather than immersing oneself in it. Effective therapeutic methods are intended to generate momentum within this complex system. Extending far beyond the dynamics of the patient/therapist relationship, however, the problematization of sexual response (serving as the condition of cure) becomes a mechanism that generates as much anxiety as hope. The increasing demand for therapists resulted in a need for a proliferation of therapies, and advances in treatment prefigure more descriptive and precise language to talk about sex. Published in 1974, the first sustained piece on sexual dysfunction in *Psychology Today* (which itself commenced publication in 1968) evidences this trend, with author Helen Kaplan Singer promoting a soon-to-be-released book entitled *The New Sex Therapy*, even though her new methods almost entirely reiterate those of Masters and Johnson, except for the designation of seemingly more specific categories to denote types of disorder, including a distinction between "primary prematurity" and "secondary ejaculator" as discrete categories of male sexual dysfunction (78). This discursive explosion also precipitated more anxiety about sexual performance, which ultimately demanded more recourse to therapy: a

1973 *Ladies Home Journal* article entitled "My Impotent Husband," for example, lists and describes more than fifteen factors that might contribute to male sexual dysfunction, including those conducive to treatment via the newly emerging therapies (e.g., misinformation about aging, newlyweds with performance anxiety) and those that curiously recall psychoanalytic conditions requiring more extended therapeutic treatment (e.g., the combination of a clinging mother and an ineffectual and neglecting father, which, the author explains, could result in homosexuality). If the goal of therapy is to remove the block to sexual climax that is also a barrier to effective communication, then this discourse seems constantly in the process of refining its own strategy for dramatizing successful and unsuccessful means of both treating and describing the problem of sex.

In addition to witnessing the emergence of a more refined discourse to describe and circumscribe the field of sexual dysfunction—a discourse that breaks new ground in the understanding of the physiological, psychological, and social dimensions of sexual behavior even as it risks generating more anxiety from the perspective of patients because of its ever more specific and refined terminology—the growing preference for psychotherapies emphasizing that maladaptive behaviors can be "unlearned" gradually steers the treatment of sexual dysfunction away from its longstanding reliance upon an investigation of the past via psychoanalysis, and toward an analysis of the present-day, context-oriented behavior modification, focusing more intently upon what is happening with the patient right now—or, that is, "then," in an era of shifting gender relations, of greater social and political awareness, and ultimately, of greater demands for effective communication strategies. The more emphatic focus on the present in therapeutic discourse translates to a greater receptivity and awareness of contemporary social conditions as contexts of behavior.

Among the social conditions that become foregrounded in American popular cultural discourse on sexual dysfunction is the overturning of the gender-based "double standard" that was being challenged by the women's liberation movement. Indeed, Masters and Johnson remain attentive to the interaction of their own research findings with the social and cultural factors that both unite and differentiate sexual response by gender throughout *Human Sexual Inadequacy*, especially in a chapter entitled "Orgasmic Dysfunction." Acknowledging outright that "the concept that the male and female also can share almost identical psychosocial requirements for effective sexual functioning brings expected protest" (215), they proceed to explain that the "negation of female sexuality, which discourages the development of an effectively useful sexual value system, has been an exercise of the so-called double standard and its sociocultural precursors" (216). Asserting that female sexual dysfunction has prevailed largely because the woman has been forced to "adapt, sublimate, inhibit, and even distort her natural capacity to function sexually in order to fulfill her genetically assigned role" (218), Masters and Johnson seem wholly aware of the sexual and social problems involved in rectifying these gender inequities, yet it is in the arena of popular cultural discourse on sexual block, where negotiations of sex and gender play out, that the implications of this disruption of the double standard are most pronounced. And despite the research team's conviction that greater sexual equality promises greater orgasms for all, popular literature addressing both male and female audiences tends to emphasize the debilitating effects of such notions of equality, specifically upon men. A 1972 piece in *Mademoiselle* strategically exploits the issue in "Impotence: The Result of Female Aggressiveness—or What?," and a 1973 *McCall's* article entitled "When Men Lose Interest in Sex" emphasizes that the notion of "sex as communication" induces anxiety because the man must actively consider whether or not he is actually pleasing a female partner who may now be more comfortable with openly expressing to him the extent and status of her own (dis)pleasure. "Sexual openness and the idea that the problem is soluble have brought impotence out of the closet" (30), the author argues, before proceeding to acknowledge the importance of refraining from suggesting that women's demands might ever get "so out of hand that men turn impotent en masse" (36), and ultimately backpedaling further through her assessment of Masters and Johnson's influence: "The double standard meant that sex was something the male did *to* the female, so inevitably the male was concerned about his sexual performance. Then we became 'enlightened.' Sex became something that the male did *for* the female. That still gave him fears of performance. If the liberation of women gives us anything, it will be that sex is something that male does *with* the female, in which case an awful lot of concern for performance will be eliminated" (36).

If the matter of rectifying longstanding gender imbalances in the production of sexual pleasure takes on an idealistic and even utopian tone here, the potentially debilitating effects of this crucial component of the sexual revolution upon the American male are exacerbated in Philip Nobile's provocative 1972 *Esquire* piece entitled "What Is the New Impotence, and Who's Got It?" Here, the author explicates the curious findings of Dr. George Ginsberg, Associate Director of Psychiatric Service at New York University Hospital, who hypothesizes that "the male invariably perceives himself a mere sex object in the eyes of his liberated mate" (95), adding that "unconscious transmissions of feminine revenge by an aggressive manner and over-assertiveness may enhance a man's castration anxiety with consequent fear of the vagina" (96). Ginsberg attentively qualifies that it is the individual male's perception of the women's liberation movement's increasing demands and pressures regarding his sexual performance, and not the women's liberation movement itself, that serves as the catalyst here, yet Nobile remains intent upon exploiting male anxiety in the face of gender equality, alerting his male readership to the realities of the penis's fall from primacy in the domain of heterosexual relations: "When the vagina and adjacent areas are engorged to the gills, watch out. A woman's orgasm is longer and more intense than any man's. Since the clitoris is the seat of her sensation, she can have not one but multiple orgasms with or without the penis and before or after the male organ has done its singular duty. Thus the penis is dropped from its super-starring role in the sex act" (98).

Such discourse sets the stage for Hollywood's treatment of sexual dysfunction by the end of the decade. With the focus on male anxiety in mainstream popular discourse, most cinematic treatments of sexual block in the late 1960s and early 1970s accordingly focused upon male impotence rather than female sexual dysfunction. While themes and representations of "frigidity" did not disappear, the disorder did not dovetail effectively with a burgeoning women's revolutionary spirit discovering new sources of empowerment through better and more frequent orgasmic responses. Taking its cues from the field of research on therapies of the sexual block, a film industry that had finally earned the freedom to explore more explicit subject matter now elected to invest so much of its energies in the investigating "problem" of sex rather than celebrating any benefits of sexual equity across gender lines.

A cultural investment in forms of behavior modification that integrate social context also underscores a number of films of the late 1960s and early 1970s that thematize male and female sexual block. If the celebrated 1969 film *Midnight Cowboy* represents an "advance" in the industry's representation of male sexual dysfunction over its practices only two years earlier with *Reflections on a Golden Eye*, it is certainly not because its perspectives or representations of either impotence or homosexuality were more progressive. In fact, this X-rated film features a surplus of fag jokes exchanged between its protagonists Ratso Rizzo (Dustin Hoffman) and hustler Joe Buck (Jon Voight), with Joe clarifying near the beginning of the film that "the men [in New York City] are mostly tutti-fruttis, and I'm gonna cash in on it." Joe's two "blatantly" homosexual clients are depicted as pathetic perverts. One of the encounters finds Joe being jerked off in a movie theater balcony by a teenager who ends up not having brought the cash to pay his client—that the boy's oversight seems entirely planned becomes evident as he responds excitedly to Joe's rage, eagerly awaiting his punishment by exclaiming, "What are you gonna do to me?" The incident that frames Joe's "situational dysfunction" serves mainly to affirm that the cowboy is *neither* impotent nor homosexual: after taking too many drugs at the Warhol-esque party that he and Ratso attended, Joe fails to get an erection with his first paying client Shirley (Brenda Vaccaro). When he protests that this has never happened to him before, Shirley's playful suggestion that "Gay, fay—is that your problem, baby?" provides the requisite provocation that immediately resolves Joe's performance issue. As in *Three in the Attic* (Richard Wilson, 1968) and other dramatizations of impotence during this era, homosexuality functions as the presumed explanation for lack of male erotic response.[10]

Midnight Cowboy does indicate that Joe was traumatized earlier in his life, as he experiences brief, decontextualized flashbacks referencing an incident in which both he and his girlfriend appear to have been sexually violated by a group of teenage men before his move to New York City. In its depiction of sexual dysfunction, however, the film is more noteworthy for its particular social framing of the notion of sexual "performance" through nuanced character development: if Joe's sexual afflictions are situational ones, the process of overcoming them is linked to the broader issue of his becoming a centered, functioning human being who ultimately reconsiders the questionable and unpredictable profession whose prospects of wealth brought him to New York City. He begins to cure himself by reprioritizing needs and desires that redirect his energies into helping his new friend Ratso, caring for him as his health deteriorates, and earning the money that will take Ratso to the Florida of his dreams, in the process deciding to set aside his own immediate needs just as his client base was about to expand.[11] Indeed, two costume changes during the final bus ride sequence show Joe finally taking control over the course of his own life: the first finds him giving Ratso a clean pair of pants and underwear after he has soiled himself in his bus seat; the second witnesses Joe once and for all shedding the veneer of his cowboy hustler persona, disposing of his cowboy boots in a trash can. As it turns out, it has been not only that single occurrence of impotence, but also a series of uncomfortable and awkward sexual encounters and transactions in a city whose fortunes he has miscalculated, that have rendered his life dysfunctional; and just as Ratso has ultimately run out of time, Joe's own time to face the unknown in another new place has come. Unlike Major Penderton in *Reflections of a Golden Eye*, whose enforced, non-communicative reclusion has abandoned him as victim to a host of pathologies, Joe finds the remedy for solitude and isolation through an unpredicted and fortuitous sense of human connectedness that ends his flashbacks and uneasy dreams. Not so surprisingly in this prototype for the buddy film, *Midnight Cowboy* also ends up addressing Ratso's own performance issues: through his relationship with Joe, the physically disabled Ratso comes to perceive himself as something other than a lonely, destitute, and pathetic loser, finding occasion for an embrace of human dignity by welcoming this stranger into his makeshift home, providing him with a means of shelter, and offering companionship.

Written by Paddy Chayefsky, the 1971 black comedy *The Hospital* anchors the issue of impotence yet more securely within the realm of challenging yet addressable problems of human connection, as it directly links male sexual impotence with the contemporary social issues of the era, including civil rights and the generation gap. As the chief of medicine at an inner-city hospital, Dr. Herbert Beck's (George C. Scott) sexual dysfunction is emblematic of a much larger, worsening problem of communication: at the institutional level, several hospital patients have recently been misidentified, resulting in treatments and procedures administered for the wrong ailments and diseases, along with the mysterious demise of several doctors on staff. Making matters worse, a growing crowd of protesters has been gathering outside the hospital, expressing their anger over medical and civil rights issues. Closer to home, Beck's wife has left him, his daughter has been arrested for drug pushing, and his anarchist, bomb-building son has branded him an "old fink" who "can't get it up anymore." These problems never link back to any physiological origin of Beck's impotence, however, and Beck's brief exchanges with a psychiatric colleague are much less therapeutic than his conversations with Barbara Drummond (Diana Rigg), the daughter of the hospital patient who, as we later learn, has been secretly orchestrating the disarray that has led to the hospital's state of administrative chaos. Barbara finds opportunity to engage Beck in a deeper discussion about his growing sense of ineffectuality. "When I say 'impotent,'" he explains, "I mean I've lost even my desire to work. That's a hell of a lot more prime a passion than sex. I've lost my reason for being. My purpose. The only thing I ever truly loved." Beck subsequently concludes that "the only admissible matter is death," and after inadvertently rescuing him from a suicide attempt by potassium injection, Barbara successfully administers her "cure" for his impotence problem and pleads with him to leave his stressful job and escape with her family to the west. "I'm offering green, silence, and solitude," she argues, "the natural order of things," in contrast with the sense of professional disorder that his protestors' occupation of the hospital is now exacerbating. Ultimately, however, the unlikely yet profound connection that he has managed to make with this much younger woman precipitates a cure for the doctor that extends beyond sexual dysfunction, and that turns out to be less situational than symptomatic of a broader sense of disconnection from his calling as a healer. After making an impulsive decision to flee from the hospital with Barbara as the disarray around him rises to a crescendo, however, he just as abruptly reconsiders, realizing that he has now gained a renewed sense of purpose regarding his job, and a stronger commitment to confront what he describes as "the whole wounded madhouse of our times." More determined than ever to face the chaos ensuing before him, the film's final scene finds Beck returning to work.

While Barbara clearly serves as the catalyst for Beck's redemption in *The Hospital*, early 1970s American cinema more often witnesses cases in which women themselves—newly liberated or otherwise—are paradoxically constructed as both the object of male desire and the cause of male sexual dysfunction, with a contemporary discourse of women's liberation constantly threatening to encroach upon previously safe and protected territories of male freedom. If *The Hospital*, despite its reliance upon cognitive therapy, behavior modification, and the foregrounding of factors of environmental stress, occasionally lapses into self-congratulatory martyrdom by identifying with an "older" generation struggling to come to terms with the demands of a new era, Mike Nichols's 1971 *Carnal Knowledge* offers a more harsh and unforgiving indictment of contemporary masculinity and its discontents—one just as extensively informed by the social and political developments of its time, and one that even more intensively articulates the connection between sexual and communicative dysfunction. Indeed, at times the film directly correlates with Masters and Johnson's repeated pronouncement in *Human Sexual Inadequacy* that historically shifting notions of gender identity and empowerment inevitably inform such sexual problems. In the opening scenes of the first of the film's three sections, set in the late 1940s, the sexual problem of Amherst college student Jonathan (Jack Nicholson) appears to be rooted in the fact that he is not performing as often as he would like. His insatiable appetite for sex, and especially for sex talk with his dormitory roommate Sandy (Art Garfunkel), soon frames him as someone destined to pursue only those sexual partners who will inevitably fail to conform with his ideal image of the desirable woman—one with sufficiently ample breasts or buttocks as well as entirely flawless physical proportions. Through his interactions with Susan (Candice Bergen), however, there emerges another, more menacing aspect of Jonathan's sexual pathology: a tendency to be more comfortable with and excited by his sexual fantasies than with the always imperfect realities of his interactions with women. "I'll give her to you," Jonathan tells Sandy at the college mixer where the roommates first encounter Susan, his generosity motivated, he later admits, by the physical imperfections that render her undesirable to him. As the connection that Sandy establishes with her progresses through various stages of sexual intimacy—each of which he compels Sandy to relate and reveal in detail—Jonathan's generosity dissipates. He wants her all for himself not because her body has changed, but because, by demonstrating her sexual accessibility through her relationship with Sandy, she has also become accessible to Jonathan as an object of fantasy. Ultimately indifferent to his betrayal of his best friend, he starts having sex with Susan while she is still dating Sandy, and Jonathan both pressures her into ending the relationship with Sandy and berates her for not responding to him emotionally in the same way that he does with Sandy.[12]

By the film's middle segment, set in New York City in the early 1960s, Jonathan admits to Sandy (who is now married to Susan) that the only reason for his decision to remain in a turbulent relationship with ex-model Bobbie (Ann-Margret) is that her ideal body type relieves the erectile dysfunction problem that has begun to plague him. Constituting a rare moment of insight, his admission also comprises a strictly one-way communication: Jonathan neither solicits nor tolerates suggestions or advice offered by friends or lovers (see fig. 2.2). He abruptly changes the subject or flees the bedroom in fear and rage whenever the unfulfilled Bobbie mentions marriage or children. Not even when his mistreatment leads to her suicide attempt does he consider her as anything but a manipulative shrew hell bent on destroying the sexual freedoms that he has so insistently maintained.[13] And by the closing section of the film (set in present-day Manhattan), his relationship with Bobbie having now ended, the entirely isolated protagonist appears to have nothing

Figure 2.2. "I've been having—a little trouble." Jonathan (Jack Nicholson) confides in an off-screen Sandy (Art Garfunkel) about his problems with erectile dysfunction in *Carnal Knowledge* (Mike Nichols, Embassy Pictures, 1971). Digital frame enlargement.

left to relate of himself but a comprehensive, chronologically structured account of his complete victimization by the women in his life, itemizing their consistently unreasonable demands in the narration of a slide show entitled "Ballbusters on Parade" that he screens for Sandy and his new partner Jennifer (Carol Kane). Bobbie has earned a central position in this chronology by her character path during the first months of their relationship, evolving from shapely, self-assured sex goddess to a case study in excess—eating, sleeping, and whining too much about the lack of fulfillment in her life.

The film's final sequence dramatizes the extent of Jonathan's sexual isolation, as he reprimands the prostitute Louise (Rita Moreno) for failing to remember the exact lines of a seduction narrative that has now become the only therapeutic remedy for erectile dysfunction for what she describes as "a man who has no need for any woman, because he has himself." By giving its audience such uncomfortably close access to the character of Jonathan, *Carnal Knowledge* ultimately frames the pathos of contemporary female emasculation as a tragedy brought about by male intransigence, and by a self-imposed failure to communicate increasingly perceived as pathological in a culture steeped in a therapeutic context that offered such a vivid discourse of sexual dysfunction and remained so fully invested in resolving this problem. Indeed, Jonathan's retreat into the confines of his own fantasy becomes the ultimate act of denying the world around him, a redefinition of social space as personal space. What distinguishes *Carnal Knowledge*'s critical perspective on dysfunction is that while the film clearly responds to the developments of the sexual revolution and the women's liberation movement, it also provides the requisite historical and developmental contexts to demonstrate that male sexual anxiety of the type that Jonathan exhibits predates the advent of these contemporary phenomena, and that, accordingly, the temptation to cite the women's liberation movement as a "cause" of his dysfunction is entirely misguided. Sandy has certainly experienced his own problems with failed relationships over the years, but unlike Jonathan, he remains committed to acknowledging them and learning from his own mistakes. Since the beginning of the film's story twenty-five years earlier, however, and well before he ever argues that women have started to become so sexually demanding, Jonathan has maintained the same unwavering fantasy about women. So what has changed? A new discourse of sexual dysfunction has now rendered his "women-as-ballbuster" philosophy a worn, obsolete relic of another era. Able to respond to his own desires only when they are narrated by a specific woman whose designated, submissive role signals his dominance and empowerment, requiring a delicate and carefully managed script that allows for no deviations or substitutions, by the end of the film Jonathan is effectively reduced to a passive yet willing victim of his own narrowly conceived fantasies.[14]

If the desire to learn—and learn more—about the wonders of a sexual realm that American culture had long appeared to confine to mystery and silence becomes both Jonathan and Sandy's driving motivation in their often competitive college-age experimentation with the intricacies of kissing, touching, and "going all the way," as well as in the equally intimate late-night tales detailing their most recent sexual escapades, this same compulsion to know, and to draw back the curtain of secrecy for the benefit of an ever more curious American public, propelled Dr. David Reuben's manual *Everything You Always Wanted to Know About Sex* (*But Were Afraid to Ask)* to the bestseller list for fifty-five consecutive weeks upon its publication in 1969.[15] Structured as a series of questions and answers designed to satisfy its readers' myriad curiosities, and written in an accessible style largely antithetical to the alienating, scientific jargon that characterized Masters and Johnson's writing (especially in *Human Sexual Response*, their first volume), the book nonetheless embraced the notion of clinical, scientific authority and authenticity to justify pronouncements that were sometimes puzzlingly ambiguous and not always based upon rigorously conducted sexual research. Commenting on the subject of "Male Sexual Inadequacy" for *McCall's* magazine the year after the book's release, for example, Reuben states that "the man who is impotent is desperately trying to say—with his sexual equipment—something he cannot express in words" (*McCall's*, 1970, 26), and in the author's elaborately conceived responses to twenty-two questions about male impotence over the course of the multi-page article, Reuben rarely progresses beyond a restatement of Masters and Johnson's fundamental findings on the subject.

With the Hollywood film industry confining its version of the advancements in the understanding of the physiology and psychology of sexual block primarily to the vehicle of male sexual problem films like *Carnal Knowledge*, *The Marriage of a Young Stockbroker* (Lawrence Turman, 1971, discussed in chapter 3) and *Portnoy's Complaint* (Ernest Lehman, 1972, discussed in chapter 5), Woody Allen's 1972 film "version" of Reuben's sex manual comprised one of the era's only attempts at tackling the subject of sexual science and symptomatology head on, using the book's iconic question and answer format in episodes with titles such as "What Are Sex Perverts?," which replicates the structure and style of the popular game show *What's My Line?* (1950–1967) in a series entitled "What's My Perversion?"; to "What Is Sodomy?," where a physician (Gene Wilder) is called upon to help an Armenian shepherd (Lou Jacobi) who has fallen in love with his sheep Daisy, with whom the physician himself proceeds to develop an amorous relationship that results in his being too tired to have sex with his own wife. Rex Reed argues that the film "exposes the best-seller's foolishness by using seven of Dr. Reuben's most sophomoric textbook headings . . . to illustrate parables containing answers that have nothing to do with the questions, proving how silly the questions were to begin with" ("Woody Allen's Sex Satire Is Inspired Lunacy," 54), yet it would be inaccurate to label Allen's film as a "parody" of Reuben's book, even though the film certainly both plays upon and plays with the culture's contemporary fascination with transforming sex into discourse, and the compiled short-form narrative structure relies less upon conveying revelatory information about sex than upon transforming earnest and "serious" written discourse into surreal and absurd sexual scenarios. Indeed, in his original 1972 *Chicago Tribune* review, Gene Siskel praised the film for providing American audiences with a needed "chance to laugh at sex" at a time when so many manuals seemed more intent upon disavowing the association of sex with pleasure through scientific analysis. While some of Allen's scenarios are aligned with themes and concerns upon which he was already establishing his reputation in its early stages in both cinema and stand-up comedy—especially a playful fascination with the intricacies of Jewish culture and heritage (one of the guests of "What's My Perversion?" is a rabbi with a fetish for silk stockings who longs to be tied up by one woman while another woman voraciously eats pork in his presence)—much of the humor relies upon an adolescent fascination with sex that sometimes only barely manages to mask a sense of anxiety over the potentially unnerving effects of the sexual revolution upon a culture struggling to secure a common ground to establish new parameters of "normal" sexual behavior.

Released as Allen's only "R"-rated film of the early 1970s, its ventures into the territory of adult-oriented subject matter often find the director reveling in the freedom to express a more pronounced disdain for such forms of "aberrant" sexual behavior as homosexuality than for over-the-top fetishes involving sex with rye bread and sex research analyzing premature ejaculation in the hippopotamus. Indeed, homophobic humor finds its way into at least three of the seven segments: a commercial in the "What's My Perversion?" segment for "Lancer Conditioner" depicting two jocks aggressively locking tongues in a locker room; the focus in the "Are Transvestites Homosexuals?" episode upon an obese, hirsute man who politely excuses himself from a formal dinner gathering so that he can try on women's clothes in the host's bedroom upstairs; and perhaps most emphatically in the concluding segment "What Happens During Ejaculation?," in which Allen, portraying one of several sperm cells readying himself for an incipient upstream voyage, elicits the winces and grimaces of his fellow cells when he raises the dreaded question, "what if it's a homosexual encounter?" Despite these tendencies, however, Allen's hyperbolic approach to the contemporary issues of sex research and its advancements in the understanding of sexual dysfunction often registers as remarkably astute and in touch with the spirit of the era. The anthropomorphizing of specific body parts and regulatory systems required to successfully collaborate to produce erections—a group of sperm cells clad in rotund, white costumes, a team of overtaxed erector workers whose coordinated efforts recall the slave teams propelling the movement of ships in biblical epics, a priest residing in the cerebral cortex commissioned to induce the guilt that stifles the erectors' progress— produces a more lucid narrative visualization of psycho-physiological processes than any of the often confusing graphic illustrations featured in sex and marriage manuals of the era. And in the penultimate segment, entitled "Are the findings of doctors and clinics who do sexual research and experiments accurate?," Allen elects to model the era's signature representative of sexual science not according to the obvious choices of Kinsey or Masters and Johnson (or, for that matter, David Reuben, who had established himself as an iconic figure in American media by the time of the film's release), but instead as insane Dr. Bernardo, portrayed by deep-voiced John Carradine, whose credentials as a mad scientist in recent cinematic history were established through his horror films along with his notorious, recent portrayal of the sex-change surgeon in *Myra Breckenridge* (Michael Sarne, 1970). In fact, Allen discreetly distances this portrayal of the scientist from the well-known historical masterminds of contemporary sexual research by portraying Bernardo as a Masters and Johnson reject, thereby establishing a safer critical and (a)historical groundwork for relating the accomplishments of a scientific "genius" whose credits include being the first man ever to measure the soundwaves generated by an erection, writing a groundbreaking work entitled "Advanced Sexual Positions: How To Achieve Them Without Laughing," and designing his magnum opus, a gigantic female breast unleashed from the scientist's mansion, terrorizing the countryside by squirting gallons of milk at its pursuers before being captured by a massive bra.

The primary segment of the film that addresses the issue of orgasmic dysfunction around which Masters and Johnson had developed their groundbreaking therapeutic approach, and to which the popularity of Reuben's own work largely owed its existence, is entitled, "Why Do Some Women Have Trouble Reaching an Orgasm?." Here, Allen offers a subtitled, Italian-language parody/homage to the work of Michelangelo Antonioni, whose own extensive exploration of female characters with conflicted psycho-physiological sexual responses to the men in their lives were well known to art cinema audiences through such works as *L'eclisse* (*The Eclipse*, 1963) and *Il deserto rosso* (*Red Desert*, 1964). Picking up on a theme of male sexual inadequacy that had informed Allen's work since *What's New, Pussycat?* and that would continue at least through *Love and Death* (1975), the segment plays out as an almost exhaustive laundry list of mostly ineffective remedies to the problem of female orgasmic dysfunction as perceived from a male perspective. On his honeymoon with Gina (Louise Lasser), Italian celebrity Fabrizio (Allen, attempting to look like a dead ringer for Marcelo Mastroianni in sunglasses) is dismayed to discover that his newlywed wife is entirely passive in bed. Soliciting advice from a photographer friend whose wife experiences none of Gina's issues with sexual pleasure only exacerbates Fabrizio's anxiety, as he is advised that "It's always the man's fault. Any woman can be made to feel ecstasy." Fabrizio is directed to engage her in extensive seduction foreplay that does little more than lull her to sleep. A cursory attempt to stimulate all of her erogenous zones (a "road map" of which Fabrizio has received from Gina's father) produces no better results. Having ruled out the possibility that inadequate male sexual equipment might be to blame (Fabrizio describes his penis as a "pane francese"), subsequent treatment options ranging from the use of a vibrator (which short circuits before insertion) to a consultation with a priest are attempted before the problem's resolution suddenly reveals itself: Gina's only means of sexual arousal comes from the fear, tension, and ultimate thrill of public display, and her desire for immediate sexual fulfillment manifests itself in the setting of a furniture store, an art gallery, underneath a table occupied by another couple in a restaurant, and even near a confessional booth (we are told, but not shown) in church. As it turns out, the treatment of Gina's sexual "problem" comprises an inversion of the notion of the sexual act as something to be considered and carried out only in the intimate, private realm of the bedroom—an inversion of the very principle of sexual secrecy that the efforts of sex researchers of the early 1970s were attempting to counteract.

The couple continues to carry out their sexual escapades in public settings at the end of the episode, thereby prolonging Gina's sexual satisfaction, but as the public incidents accumulate they must contend with the pressing possibility of being discovered. Unlike the "What Is Sodomy?" episode, in which the doctor's bestial predilections become the basis of scandal and the destruction of his reputation, Fabrizio and Gina's "secret" is never exposed to the world within the confines of the diegesis. As a transgressive model, however, their therapeutic sexual exhibitionism is configured as a dynamic that is impossible to sustain indefinitely, making the prospect of discovery the source of both the couple's (or at least Gina's) sexual pleasure and the audience's own laughter strategically contained by the parameters of the short-form narrative episode.

Instances of male erectile dysfunction far outnumber cases of female "frigidity" in early 1970s Hollywood cinema, and as we will see in the next chapter with the exploration of marital therapies, the advancements of the sexual revolution sometimes did little more than bring into sharper focus prevailing misogynistic tendencies of American culture. If the case of Fabrizio and Gina's sexual secret in *Everything You Always Wanted to Know About Sex* ends up supporting the popular conviction that in the contemporary era women's sexual needs were too quickly transforming into demands whose fulfillment was unsustainable from both a personal and social perspective, the narrative of Gerard Damiano's *Deep Throat*, a much more popular, more financially successful, and controversial exploration of female sexual pleasure produced outside the Hollywood studio system and released two months prior to Allen's film in the summer of 1972, evidences a much more radical take on the matter of sexual dysfunction. Here, distinctions between sexual normality and abnormality immediately transcend notions of secrecy and privacy, since the conventions of hardcore pornographic production and exhibition are such that excessive sexual display becomes a formal expectation rather than a transgression of societal norms and discretions designed to elicit what Foucault might describe as a form of laughter that congratulates the viewer due to the subject matter's outrageousness, as evidence of overcoming the strictures of "bourgeois" sexual repression. Not that the film wasn't "outrageous" in a number of ways: as the 2004 documentary *Inside Deep Throat* suggests, the boldness of its money shots and close-ups of sexual organs caught in the act of "performance" were certainly startling for unaccustomed audiences, and as several critics have speculated, legal issues of obscenity surrounding the film in its first year of release certainly augmented its notoriety and popularity. *Deep Throat* was also distinctive in its attempt to entice audiences as a feature-length (61 minutes) pornographic film that shared several attributes of traditional narrative structure. Yet its unique treatment of sexual block is what makes the film noteworthy in the context of the present study.

One could certainly cite the fact that *Deep Throat* was released less than a decade after *The Chapman Report* and *Marnie*—two of the most provocative and controversial treatments of female sexual dysfunction of their own era—as a sign of the extreme representational transformations in cinema that occurred during the sexual revolution. In the present context, however, even more remarkable are the drastically different ways in which these films of different eras articulate the pathology of female sexual dysfunction. As we have seen, *The Chapman Report* and especially

Marnie configure their heroine's "frigidity" in terms of trauma: both Kathleen and Marnie struggle to acknowledge, understand, and overcome problems rooted in their past histories as part of a psychoanalytic process that will ultimately result in a cathartic cure. And in each case, men in their lives have precipitated the traumatic event, leaving the women helpless in a seemingly endless rehearsal of symptomatology that they remain unable to articulate or communicate, until another man comes along to bring about a disruption of the pattern, as he does by the end of both films. A 1969 *Redbook* article on "frigidity" suggests that "Too often unsatisfactory relations are automatically attributed to the wife; she is described as responding inadequately when in fact she is being inadequately stimulated" (149). Regarding human agency, the role of the woman in these earlier films is to stand and wait for the psychoanalytic therapeutic process to take its course. While *Deep Throat*'s notorious extra-cinematic history reveals an actress whose husband forced her to commit explicit sexual acts in front of the camera against her will, what distinguishes the narrative of the film itself, in relation to its precursor, mainstream representations of female dysfunction, is the agency that it ultimately affords the female subject—agency that originates from a psychotherapeutic community that was turning away from psychoanalysis in favor of behavioral and humanistic approaches to the problem of sex. By the late 1960s and early 1970s, the new psychotherapeutic methods and perspectives had begun to dovetail with the women's movement.

Linda's (Linda Lovelace) anatomical difference becomes amenable to therapeutic treatment by behavioral adjustment. Her clitoris may not be located where it "should" be, yet the sexual block "problem" with which she contends is not the result of something that a man has done to her—she is not attempting to disavow a trauma, and indeed, there turns out not to be any trauma to disavow. What Linda Williams describes as the film's "perverse implantation of the clitoris" (114) also functions as a manifestation of contemporary advancements in the understanding of female orgasm brought to light by Kinsey, Masters and Johnson, and other sex researchers, who verified the specific anatomical location where stimulation produces the sexual excitement required to bring the subject to climax, while also discounting myths about the centrality of the vaginal orgasm. In one sense, then, this sex research corrected a previous "misidentification" of an anatomical site, and the relocation of the clitoris deep inside Linda's throat constitutes more of a pinpointing of sexual pleasure than a physiological aberration.

What is most noteworthy about this relocation is the process leading to its discovery, as well as the process *of* discovery itself. For a brief moment, after Dr. Young (Harry Reems) carries out his gynecological exam of Linda and exclaims that the problem is "you don't have one," the narrative threatens to rehearse a psychoanalytic prescription of female lack. Consonant with the simplified, causal narrative construction of pornography, however, almost immediately afterwards this "lack" is revealed to be simply a physiological relocation of the pleasure center. In the course of a single visit to the appropriate specialist, the patient describes a complex sexual "problem" that is then immediately diagnosed, all by knowing how and where to look. And all that is required to test the validity of the diagnosis is an "experiment" that can readily be conducted at the doctor's office—the act of fellatio that ultimately confirms that Linda's clitoris is located where the doctor said it was, and that the problem can be resolved by the readily available "substitution" of fellatio for intercourse. The problem now defined and its solution tested, what remains is a "practice" stage which, as a requisite aspect of her therapy, comprises an easily learned form of behavior modification. Fellatio need not replace intercourse (or even masturbation) in Linda's sexual regimen: in fact, as she has explained in an earlier discussion with her friend Helen (Dolly Sharp), the act of intercourse was never wholly unpleasurable for her; it only failed to produce the "bombs bursting in air" sensation that she always expected or hoped for in orgasmic release. The behavior modification primarily comprises her understanding that she should not expect the same pleasure from one sexual act as the other. Unlike Damiano's follow-up heroine Justine Jones (Georgina Spelvin), who is sent to hell after committing suicide, and where, after a brief period in which she is permitted to fulfill all of her sexual fantasies, she is confined to an eternity devoid of sexual fulfillment and release in *The Devil in Miss Jones* (1973), Linda's evolution constitutes a discovery of sexual pleasure that immediately follows the discovery of the source of ailment that has been denying her this pleasure. And contrary to the sexual discourse of *Midnight Cowboy, Carnal Knowledge*, or *Everything You Always Wanted to Know About* Sex, where the therapeutic process requires learning—or failing to learn—how to "do" sex the right way, *Deep Throat* articulates, as Williams suggests, "a phallic economy's highly ambivalent and contradictory attempt to count beyond the number one, to recognize, as the proliferating discourses of sexuality take hold, that there can no longer be any such thing as a fixed sexuality—male, female, or otherwise—that now there are proliferating sexual*ties*" (114, emphasis in the original). If Masters and Johnson had defined sexual intercourse as the ultimate form of communication, then the fellatio-based relationship between patient and doctor in *Deep Throa*t becomes an elegantly constructed pornographic "dialect" of such communication—one that exchanges problems for resolutions in a network of mutual fulfillment that recognizes the unique nature of sexual needs and desires. As an exercise in effective, communicative problem solving, the strategies of *Deep Throat* require no extended course of psychoanalytic treatment; instead, the accessibility of Linda's cure makes her more eligible for an immediate promotion to the position of "physiotherapist," in which her newly discovered talent is put to the service of helping others, including Wilbur, the man of her dreams, whom Dr. Young graciously "fits" with a penis of sufficient size so that she may help herself to limitless pleasure.

What the example of *Deep Throat* ultimately suggests is that therapies offering such readily accessible resolutions to problems may actually be best suited to narrative forms which, like pornography, are structurally tailored to diagnose and cure the "problem" of sex without curtailing or disrupting the fantasy of perfectly realized and infinitely sustainable pleasure. Offering the sense of what Linda Williams describes as always being "on time," pornography neither demands nor tolerates psychopathologically complex characterizations or narrative emplotments ("Film Bodies"). Unlike the therapeutically critical case of Jonathan in *Carnal Knowledge*, a victim of the sexual revolution who is required to suffer endlessly through a series of sexual experiences that are never quite right, that progressively fail to excite him, and that always anticipate a better "next time" that will never come, Linda in *Deep Throat* is immersed in the luxurious embrace of a perpetual present, demonstrating the versatility and adaptability of the early 1970s woman who, much like Daisy in *On a Clear Day You Can See Forever*, is finally ready to liberate herself from a lifelong history of misdiagnosis.

3

Marriage Therapies and Women's Liberation

IN A SPEECH DELIVERED AT COLORADO Women's College in Denver on March 2, 1961, Lt. Colonel Gabriel D. Ofiesh assessed the roots of the "problem" with the modern woman. First and foremost, she spent too much time wanting to be like men, mostly because she secretly wanted to *be* a man, while realizing, of course, that she could not. This peculiar position of women resulted—in the psychoanalytic discourse prevalent in American culture of the era—in a "reaction formation" triggered by an inferiority complex. As Lt. Colonel Ofiesh suggested, these feelings of inferiority were most regrettable and ill-founded, given that they resulted in her disavowing an actual superiority to men—one that manifested itself most profoundly in her nurturing roles of wife and mother. "Modern women cannot stand their children and they cannot stand their husbands," Ofiesh proclaimed. "Although they all want to get married they have rejected marriage in its essential meaning" (473). Only the acceptance of "her self-actualization as a WOMAN" would help her to counteract this false perception of inferiority and render her more attuned to the natural, "creative" societal functions for which she was responsible. "We are convinced," Ofiesh concluded, "that women cannot adequately fulfill these roles unless they are healthy women proud of their 'femininity'—rather than 'feminists'" (475).

While Ofiesh's oratory predated the release of Betty Friedan's *The Feminine Mystique* by only one year, his perspective on women's destiny had been prevalent in America's cultural consciousness long before 1961. Friedan exposed this perspective as a false, debilitating myth that had for too long remained unquestioned:

> The feminine mystique says that the highest value and the only commitment for women is the fulfillment of their own femininity. . . . The mistake, says the mystique, the root of women's troubles in the past is that women envied men, women tried to be like men, instead of accepting their own nature, which can find fulfillment only in sexual passivity, male domination, and nurturing maternal love. (43)

Based upon research revealing the prevalent dissatisfaction among married American women, Friedan's cogent response to the all too familiar male perspective held by Ofiesh and so many others constituted an empowering acknowledgment and politicized articulation of the "problem that has no name." The complex, archaic laws regulating the requisite circumstances for couples to officially curtail a marriage notwithstanding, American society in the early 1960s was already experiencing a changing attitude toward institutionally enforced monogamy. Having declined sharply after the end of the World War II and then remaining steady throughout most of the 1950s, the number of divorces and annulments began to climb by 1960, increasing by an average of 4.5 percent each year until 1968, when the annual rate of percentage increase often rose to the double digits. Indeed, in 1971 twice as many marriages ended as in 1960, with the figure soaring to over 1.1 million cases annually by 1980 (Swanson). Under these circumstances, Lt. Colonel Ofiesh's pronouncements evidenced a justifiable anxiety regarding the fate of a longstanding social, religious, and legal institution, even while Friedan, Simone de Beauvoir, and other women were laying the groundwork for a radical rethinking of what it meant for women to submit to a ritual that would leave them legally bound to their spouses for life.

The controversies surrounding the past, present, and future of marriage in the 1960s and 1970s place the examination of therapeutic interventions into the plight of suffering marital partners in a context quite different from the therapies of sexual block discussed in the previous chapter. The causes of sexual dysfunction are both physiological and psychological, but it would seem illogical to recommend that the man who is consistently unable to gain or maintain an erection, or the woman who finds herself sexually disaffected, find resolution to their problems by curtailing altogether their attempts to have and enjoy sex. The increasingly controversial and unstable position of marriage, however, situates the institution in a sociopolitical context that renders both problems and solutions more diverse, complex, and sometimes opaque. From the married clients' perspective, many questions arose at the start of the sexual revolution: Should couples address their problem by agreeing to talk it out in private? Is it preferable to consult a therapist, and if so, which kind? How long will it take to resolve disagreements, and at what expense? At what point should one decide to seek a more suitable partner? When is one too old to find such a partner? Is discord in the present relationship a sign that marriage is a stifling institution best abandoned altogether? Consonant with the perspectives of noted marriage psychotherapists, Hollywood would begin to frame marital problems as communication problems that it would represent as resolvable with the right tools and strategies, even while Hollywood cinema remained clearly skeptical about the efficacy of psychotherapeutic discourse itself. Through the use of irony and satire, however, the industry largely evaded the problem of rendering the marriage institution susceptible to ideological inquiry.

This chapter explores the prevailing and emerging perspectives and recommendations of marital therapies in the 1960s and early 1970s in light of the accumulating evidence that married couples were both expressing more displeasure with the institution and also finding themselves unable to resolve interpersonal disagreement on their own. Considering the statistical evidence on failing marriages, the fact that both men and women were continuing to marry earlier, and that the notion of romantic love as the basis for marriage remained prevalent attested to the complexity of the tasks that psychotherapists and marriage counselors were facing in an era where therapeutic supply was becoming increasingly inadequate to meet the demand for service. As both context and counterpoint, the chapter continues with an overview of perspectives on the purpose and fate of marriage, and on the efficacy of martial therapies that were circulating in the popular press. Following this overview, the chapter turns to the American film industry's treatment of marital discord from the mid-1960s into the early 1970s, by which time alternatives to traditional marriage were being proposed.

The chapter continues with a brief overview of political positions on marriage articulated by Friedan, Germaine Greer, and proponents of the radical feminist movement of the late 1960s, as a backdrop to the analysis of three Hollywood films from the late 1960s and early 1970s that actually did address, either overtly or obliquely, many of the concerns and perspectives of the women's liberation movement regarding the institution of marriage. Curiously, in these films Hollywood acknowledged the value of feminist discourse while most often simultaneously containing and managing it ideologically, through strategies prominent in a refined psychotherapeutic discourse that was emerging by the start of the 1970s. Both Hollywood cinema and these new therapies foregrounded "communication" dysfunction as an addressable and resolvable problem in the midst of a burgeoning human potential movement that sidelined the goal of restructuring issues of gender and power relations that were originally central to second-wave feminism. As such, the chapter traces a set of alliances and divisions circulating around perceptions of the institution of marriage, showing how the film industry strategically (though not always seamlessly or successfully) reconfigured its position in relation to a longstanding social institution and the emerging sociopolitical groups that were intent upon its disruption. Even as a struggling Hollywood attempted to redefine itself by overhauling its content regulation system and lending more authority to "adult"-oriented subject matter, the industry hesitated to embrace any revolutionary position of its own.

Marriage Therapies of the 1960s

Among the most profound developments in the field of marital psychotherapy occurred with its transformed methods and client/patient dynamics. As was also the case in the treatment of sexual dysfunction, marital therapies increasingly focused upon what Gurman and Snyder describe as the patients' "conscious present" behavior rather than mining the psychopathological past (486). A related and equally important shift, however, was the progressively broader movement away from the familiar one-on-one treatment model, and toward therapeutic dynamics that were more interactive, culminating in the encounter group therapy movement that emerged later in the 1960s. Among the developments used in marital therapies were the *collaborative* model, in which husband and wife were seen by separate therapists who communicated with one another; *concurrent* situations, where husband and wife were treated in separate sessions by a single therapist; and most notably in *conjoint* therapies, where both husband and wife participated in sessions together (Gurman & Snyder). The collaborative model was used prevalently in therapies rooted in the psychoanalytically based object relations theory, which foregrounded problems of transference and counter-transference and focused upon recognizing and modifying married patients' predisposition to generate distorted perceptions of one another. In what Peter A. Martin identifies as the "stereoscopic technique" within collaborative therapy, the management of counter-transference becomes central, with the two psychiatrists forced to confront their own assumptions and projections on their separate clients in order to make them more attentive to recognizing their patients' perspectival distortions. Indeed, in 1965 Martin argues that "the therapists' countertransference occupies a position of significance second to no other component, including the patient's transference" (97).

As Gurman and Snyder explain, the use of psychoanalytic approaches—and the collaborative model as well—significantly declined by the mid-1960s, largely because psychoanalytic therapy's focus upon transference and counter-transference ultimately proved to be less effective in providing couples with relief to their symptoms. Additionally, even proponents of the psychoanalytic models admitted that their methods tended to be time-consuming (Martin 100). As early as 1964, Gerald R. Leslie was promoting the advantages of conjoint therapy over the collaborative model, not only because it freed the therapists from contending with two distinct sets of patient/therapist dynamics, but also because it significantly "streamlined" the process of identifying patients' distortions while lessening transference and counter-transference: "Each spouse's tendencies to maneuver the counselor into private roles runs head up against the counselor's relationship with the other partner" (68).

The new therapeutic methods of the mid-1960s did not entirely abandon the central tenets of psychoanalytic therapy; indeed, couples' projection of distorted images of one another in marital relationships remained a central focus (Satir 11). At the same time, in emerging marital therapies the debilitating tendency to project such images was recontextualized as a broader problem of interpersonal communication. "As a therapist," explained Virginia Satir in her 1964 study *Conjoint Family Therapy*, "I have found that the more covertly and indirectly people communicate, the more dysfunctional they are likely to be" (21). Accordingly, the matter of living to please one's partner, and of projecting the image of a person whom one believes one's partner would want, came to be considered as a symptom of low self-esteem, one reflecting a reticence to accept the inherent "different-ness" of the other. Satir and others asserted that such behavior traps partners in dysfunctional communication practices based upon unfounded assumptions and unquestioned generalizations. While Satir, along with William J. Lederer and Don D. Jackson, co-authors of the popular and influential 1968 study *The Mirages of Marriage*, recognized that maladaptive communication habits were rooted in the individual's past, their therapies focused upon replacing acquired, dysfunctional interpersonal behavioral traits with new, functional strategies of communication. Lederer and Jackson assessed marital strength (and weakness) according to the variables of functionality, "temporal compatibility," and "vector relations," or mutual adaptability to the direction and speed of change in a relationship (127). Additionally, fully functional marital relationships were those whose participants managed and contextualized these variables effectively, maintaining an "emotional and psychic balance" (92) attainable only if both partners were dedicated to sustaining effective communication, committed to constructing and reshaping a set of workable relationship rules and guidelines, and then abiding by them. The therapists also stressed that workable relationships require intensive *work*: therapeutic sessions emphasized the open expression of one's views and the formulation of summative responses by interacting partners in the interests of maintaining explicit and open communication. At every juncture, the conjoint therapists of the 1960s acknowledged the statistical evidence that marriages were failing at an alarming rate—a third of these marriages resulted in divorce before their tenth anniversary, according to Lederer and Jackson (13)—and they also stressed that marriage practices in their current, dysfunctional form were ancestors of outworn institutional models that could never survive the changes of contemporary American society. Although therapists rarely made promises about success rates, they remained adamant in their conviction that, using the strategies that they prescribed, the institution of marriage could be saved, and that it was indeed worth saving.

From a contemporary sociological perspective, however, the conviction that marriage could be rescued from obscurity and irrelevance was weaker. While Satir was suggesting that couples were deciding to marry in order to enhance self-esteem and secure qualities in their partners that they lacked in themselves, and Lederer and Jackson were arguing that individuals often mistook a desire for sex for a sign of romantic love that compelled them to marry,[1] sociologist Sidney M. Greenfeld asserted that the search for a romantic partner was functionally related to materialism, mass production, and the American tendency to equate financial wealth with success. In this system, marriage played the crucial role of stabilizing husband and wife in their respective socioeconomic roles of provider and user. From Greenfeld's perspective, in fact, the entire system of commodity distribution and consumption was intricately tied to the structure of marriage and the nuclear family. "Our social system depends upon marriage and cannot work without it," he argued, adding that romantic love served only as an impetus to motivate individuals to secure their positions in this sociocultural system (374). As early as 1962, in an *Atlantic Monthly* piece entitled "A Marriage on the Rocks," Nora Johnson expresses bewilderment about the nation's still "innocent" perspective on marriage ("our uncritical enthusiasm for playing house"), as well as skepticism about contemporary marital psychotherapists' insistence that working at marriage might yield positive results. "Making a project of marriage seldom works," Johnson argues. "It presupposes a failure of communications between two people and suggests that they are simply running out, are not facing the problem, and are being generally irresponsible" (48). Bemoaning the anxious compulsion to marry at increasingly younger ages, a 1965 *Saturday Evening Post* article protests that Americans must at least start entertaining the proposition that marriage does not provide the vehicle for universal happiness for all, and that we must stop submitting the marriage institution to ever more elaborate regimens of improvement (Koempel 10). And in a controversial 1966 *Atlantic Monthly* piece entitled "Marriage Is a Wretched Institution," Dr. Mervyn Cadawallader expresses regret that an adolescent culture so intent upon rejecting "square" and antiquated notions of maturity and responsibility was still placing such a high cultural value on romance and marriage. Given the escalating rate of relationship failure, Cadawallader proposed as a corrective the creation of "a flexible contract perhaps for one or two years, with periodic options to renew" (65).[2]

With this plethora of authoritative prescriptions and marriage fixes—and disagreements regarding whether or not the institution could indeed *be* fixed—the topic of marital crisis also became prominent in popular cultural discourse of the early to mid-1960s. A "healthy" marriage was difficult to maintain, but ending an unhealthy marital relationship was not necessarily any easier, given that the legal grounds for divorce were so complicated and inconsistent from state to state. As a 1966 article by Donald J. Cantor in *Atlantic Monthly* indicated, the only grounds for divorce universally acknowledged by all states in the nation was adultery, with individual states including other grounds such as desertion, cruelty, imprisonment, alcoholism, impotence, nonsupport, and insanity. The concept of no-fault divorce did not yet exist. Cantor argues that the current status of the legal system fails to recognize the fact that in many instances marriages simply do not work, and that couples themselves should be the only ones with the power to decide if and when to curtail their legal bond: "No explanation of why the divorce is desired should be required by this notice" (Cantor, "The Right of Divorce," 67). Yet such perspectives conflicted with the regulations imposed by both the legal system and the Catholic Church, under whose precepts divorce was still not permitted.

Marriage Problems in 1960s Cinema

If rising divorce rates and controversies surrounding marriage would have already made the subject of marital discord ripe for exploitation by Hollywood during this period, the success of two Italian film imports of the early 1960s offered the American film industry ample assurance that marriage problems could be sold to the American public. On the heels of Federico Fellini's 1960 international phenomenon *La Dolce Vita*, Italian cinema was enjoying a surge of popularity in America, and it was especially notable for its more frank treatments of sexual subject matter that remained relatively insusceptible to the regulations of the Production Code.³ Two highly successful international releases directly influenced the structure and content of Hollywood's comedic depictions of marriage and divorce. *Divorzio all'italiana* (*Divorce Italian Style*, Pietro Germi, 1961) and *Matrimonio all'italiana* (*Marriage Italian Style*, Vittorio De Sica, 1964) followed the tradition of the popular *commedia all'italiana* tradition, which derived its humor from the interaction of "characters from different social classes" along with the continued presence of outworn social and institutional practices (especially in Italy's less industrially developed south) in the rapidly modernizing country (Celli & Cottino-Jones 88–92). Relying upon exaggeration and hyperbole, and intent upon exposing and criticizing the sociocultural contradictions of Italy's historical present, these films embrace the tradition of satire. Peter Bondanella associates the satirical vein with a focus on "social customs [that] may be described as the reduction ad absurdum type" (151), and that targeted "ruling elites and established institutions, uncovering social problems demanding attention, thus opening up Italian culture to a wider range of social and political alternatives" (157). *Divorce Italian Style* directs its satire at a Catholic Church that forbade divorce at all costs and an antiquated national legal system that did not yet permit civil dissolution of marriage. Enamored of his cousin Angelina (Stefania Sandrelli), the suave Sicilian aristocrat Ferdinando (Fefe) Cefalu (Marcello Mastroanni) seeks legal justification for curtailing his twelve-year marriage to Rosalia (Daniela Rocca) by prompting her to commit adultery with the also married Carmelo (Leopoldo Trieste).⁴ By such means, Fefe hopes to secure justifiable grounds for him to murder his wife and marry Angelina. His inspiration for this strategy is a local criminal case, for which the 16-year-old female plaintiff received a reduced prison sentence after the murder of her 37-year-old adulterous husband was determined to qualify as an "honor" killing. After a number of mismanaged attempts to carry out his plan, Fefe eventually gets his wish, shooting his wife (who has succumbed to his plan to make her fall in love with another man) and reuniting in marriage with Angelina. The film ends, however, with the new couple jetting off on a yacht while Angelina, unbeknownst to Fefe, proceeds to seduce the handsome sea captain on board, creating new grounds for future marital discord.

Marriage Italian Style makes its satirical commentary by strategically juxtaposing social classes in a postwar Italy still deeply entrenched in the philosophy of the "miracle" of the nation's postwar economic resurgence, yet blind to the social and political effects of this philosophy. If *Divorce* maintains the male Cefalu's perspective throughout, *Marriage* plays with restricted narration to form strategic alliances between its characters and the audience. In the opening sequences of the film, the audience more closely aligns with the wealthy business owner Domenico (Mastroianni again), as he receives an emergency call to come home to attend to the severely ill Filumena (Sophia Loren). In a series of extended flashbacks it is revealed that the couple met during the war years, when destitute and homeless Filumena was forced to work as a prostitute, encountering Domenico as a brothel client during an air raid. Over the next twenty years, the couple shares a complicated relationship convenient only to Domenico, who enjoys his sexual encounters with Filumena whenever he happens not to be away on one of his long business trips, who also attempts to make a "lady" of her by granting her accommodation and various provisions, but who consistently refuses to marry her. He eventually sets her up as a live-in caretaker for his ailing mother, even though Filumena's lower class standing leads him to sequester her in the kitchen and away from the guests during the elderly woman's funeral. Once it is revealed that Filumena has been feigning her present illness, pretending to be on her deathbed in order to secure Domenico's hand in marriage, the narrative starts to embrace her perspective on the relationship, where it remains for the duration of the film. Having succumbed unlawfully and deceitfully to the marriage (a particularly inconvenient situation, given that he is engaged to another woman), Domenico reacts vehemently to the deception and vows to have the fraudulent marriage annulled; from Filumena's point-of-view, however, marriage provides the only means of securing financial stability in a society tailored to protect the sexual "freedom" of its male citizens exclusively. "The problem is our hearts used to be so big," Filomena explains. "Look how small they are now," referencing how extensively the thriving economic "miracle" brought about by capitalism has ended up reshaping their priorities. After she reveals that Domenico is the biological father of one of Filumena's three sons—all of whom she has been supporting although they live apart from her and have never been informed of their parents' identity—her goal of validating her social standing through marriage is further secured. Her revelation also lays the groundwork for Domenico's ultimate redemption and the restoring of his sense of compassion and responsibility, as the film concludes rather predictably with the "official" validation of Domenico, Filumena, and their relationship in an elaborate marriage ceremony and a reunited family.

Taken together, the satirical humor of *Divorce Italian Style* and *Marriage Italian Style* derives from its ability to frame the compulsion to marry—and to end marriage—in relation to customs and longstanding social practices that fail to offer alternatives to Italian citizens, since these practices are rooted in a capitalist system that "naturally" favors male power and female submissiveness. The process of exposing the strategies that maintain this system of gender imbalance involves the narratives' foregrounding of character perspective. Aside from occasionally doting upon her husband too overtly, Rosalia never really does anything to provoke the type of extreme negative reaction that might compel Fefe to contemplate her murder, and *Divorce Italian Style* uses this disconnect between motive and response to force the audience into a critical assessment of his behavior. *Marriage Italian Style* reveals this strategy more overtly by validating a female perspective, one that ultimately justifies (in this specific social context, at least) the measures to which Filumena resorts in her efforts to secure the marriage contract, and that simultaneously questions Domenico's similarly extreme attempts to maintain his "freedom."

"Bring the little woman . . . maybe she'll die laughing!" reads one of the taglines of Richard Quine's popular 1965 Hollywood domestic comedy *How to Murder Your Wife*, which bases its theme and structure on both of these Italian marriage comedies. While hyperbole dominates the humor here even more than in the film's two European antecedents, however, this Americanized version of marital discord adopts a more troubling and sinister tone that problematizes its clearly satirical intent. *Murder* finds celebrated cartoonist and committed Manhattan playboy bachelor Stanley Ford (Jack Lemmon) not realizing until it is too late that he has married the woman (Virna Lisi) who popped out of the cake the night before at the mournful bachelor party of Stanley's close male friend—mournful, that is, until the honoree rejoices that his fiancée has just called off the wedding. In a direct parallel with *Divorce Italian Style*, the film incorporates contemporary legal issues by failing to provide Stanley with justifiable grounds for divorce, and subsequently compels him to consider the logistics of arranging for her murder. Unlike the Italian film, however, the Hollywood version stops short of suggesting that Stanley is actually *planning* to kill his wife, while fully indulging in his fantasy of doing so. This ambiguity is arranged by shifting the source of premeditation from Stanley to the persona of his celebrated comicstrip, autobiographical character creation Brannigan, by which means Stanley communicates his devious plans to the public. When the (unnamed) bride suddenly disappears after happening upon the murder "plot" in comicstrip form prior to its publication, however, Stanley is forced to stand trial for murder.

The comedic strategy of *How to Murder Your Wife* is rooted in contemporary American social anxieties about marriage, gender roles, and commitment in the emerging sexual revolution. Characteristic of Hollywood cinema of the decade at least until the late 1960s, and consonant with developments in films about sexual block discussed in chapter 2, however, the focus of the revolution is its effects upon *men*. The film plays upon the conviction, sustained over the course of the previous decade in culture and media, that marriage—desirable and inevitable though it may have been—was a "trap" that signaled the end of male sexual freedom. Indeed, similar narratives were rehearsed to wide audience appeal in many comedies from the late 1950s and the mid-1960s, including *Pillow Talk* (Michael Gordon, 1959) and *A Very Special Favor*, discussed in chapter 1. When Stanley's lawyer is informed about the marriage, he refers to the bride delightedly as "the little lady that finally nailed Stan." That such a fate could be so insidiously sealed for someone like Stanley Ford, a man committed to remaining single and enjoying the rewards of bachelorhood, on the basis of a single night's "indiscretion" under an irrational, alcoholic stupor, exacerbates the film's sense of anxiety as well as the humor that defuses it. As the above-mentioned tagline suggests, the narrative aligns entirely with a male perspective, but unlike the Italian *Divorce*, the American *Murder* takes on the entire institution of marriage, rather than marriage to the "wrong" woman, as the culprit of anxiety. The narrative establishes its communication network as strictly man-to-man from its outset, as Charles (Terry-Thomas), Stanley's meticulous live-in servant, breaks the fourth wall to address the viewer directly, guiding him room-by-room through the wonders of his master's luxurious bachelor pad, virtually taunting the envious and regretful viewer with the repeated refrain that "this could have been your life" if you had never married. Indeed, unlike *Marriage Italian Style*, the interjections of the female characters are ingeniously designed to affirm this closed male discourse. "A woman is never really free until she is married," explains Edna (Claire Trevor), the wife of Stanley's lawyer Harold Lampson (Eddie Mayehoff). "She's free to enjoy the good things in life. She can spend money. . . . that's why men have to be controlled. It's just a matter of keeping them off balance," reinforcing women's concerted interests in draining the life out of their men. A display ad featured in the United Artists pressbook headlines the following statement, which Stanley utters at his own murder trial: "For too long the American male has permitted himself to be bullied, coddled, mothered and treated by the female of the species as if he were totally feeble-minded!" The most conspicuous element of this conspiracy against men is the woman who becomes Stanley's wife, and who is never granted an identity or a name aside from the moniker "Mrs. Ford" since she can communicate only in Italian, and whose domesticating skills have made her entirely undesirable to him, except for that one night that has escaped from his memory, before they were married. "In Italia, no divorce," she manages to clarify to Stanley early in the film, ironically adding in untranslated Italian that "on the subject of divorce, there's a film with Marcelo Mastroianni, and at the end, he kills his wife."

At once contemporary and retrograde, *How to Murder Your Wife* derives its humor from exaggeration, but if the Italian films qualified as satire on the basis of the constraining institutions that they criticize, to label the very American story of Stanley Ford as satirical becomes problematic: its seeming target is the institution of marriage, but its invective comes to focus more intently upon the overall intolerability of *women*. This is nowhere clearer than in the disturbing courtroom sequence near the film's conclusion: as a strategy for his own defense, Stanley calls Harold to the witness stand and compels him to imagine his life without the constraints of his wife or his marriage. By the end of the interrogation, after Stanley has gotten Harold to admit that he would indeed kill Edna if he could, Stanley asks the judge "to acquit me on the ground of justifiable homicide." His wish is granted, and the jurors and members of the audience salute him! Both of these potentially satirical focuses are, however, conveniently negated in the film's final sequence, which finds Stanley in the arms of the just returned Mrs. Ford, gladly placing the wedding ring back on the finger of the woman whose presence he has mysteriously grown to miss. Indeed, Mrs. Ford's Italian mother has come back with her, amorously eyeing Charles to dispel once and for all any confusion about the desirability of married life.

In her review for the magazine *America*, Moira Walsh argues that in relation to the Italian comedies, *How to Murder Your Wife* lacks "a unified, coherent, satiric point-of-view," later speculating upon "whether satire is genuinely impossible to achieve in a heterogeneous and largely traditionless society . . ." ("Marriage Italian and American Style"). Despite the film's considerable success, the fact that contemporary critics overtly noted such problems and incongruities attests to the workings of a cultural shift in perceptions of gender politics. The *Films and Filming* review cites the grueling familiarity of "the American style in the sex war, with the women treating their men like little children who must be kept feeling as guilty and useless as possible, while all the men hanker after a freedom which is equated with an arrested adolescence" ("Raymond Durgnat finds fun without corpses"). And Bosley Crowther's scathing review of the film looks beyond the protective guise of comedy to reveal a more troubling tendency: "Never have I seen a movie, serious, comic, or otherwise, that so frankly, deliberately and grossly belittled and ridiculed wives" ("Screen: Plotting a Spouse's Demise," 26).

Mid-1960s Hollywood cinema manages to be culturally "contemporary" about marriage and divorce only to the extent that these social institutions were threatening to compromise male sexual freedom. If satire lacked a stable foundation in *How to Murder Your Wife*, the extramarital sex comedy *A Guide for the Married Man* (Gene Kelly, 1967) provides a more grounded satirical attempt to target the contemporary American male's irresistible "temptation" to deviate from monogamous fidelity, revealing the double standard inherent in the focus upon male sexual anxiety. The conflict at the heart of the narrative is fortysomething upper-middle-class suburbanite Paul Manning's (Walter Matthau) unsuccessful attempt to reconcile his love for his wife Ruth (Inger Stevens) with his still strong sexual appetite for other attractive women. Rather than venture into an indictment of monogamous marriage, however, the film entertains the prospect that an occasional taste of adultery might actually *strengthen* a marital relationship as long as the husband finds an experienced "guide" who knows how to keep the situation uncomplicated and keep one's wife "safe" from discovering his indiscretions. Married best friend and experienced casual adulterer Ed Stander (Robert Morse) gladly takes on the responsibilities of this guide, mentoring Paul through the process of meeting women, finding inconspicuous meeting places, and—most important of all—remaining emotionally detached from any possible commitment (see fig. 3.1). What ultimately complicates Paul's plans, however, is the simple fact that he loves his wife. He feels ridiculous and guilty as he orchestrates deceptions to deter her, and in the crucial rendezvous scene that closes the film, after Paul and his extramarital female accomplice narrowly avoid discovery by the authorities at their motel, a fast-motion sequence speeds the would-be adulterer

Figure 3.1. Ed Stander (Robert Morse) advises his friend Paul Manning (Walter Matthau) on the intricacies of no-commitment adultery in *A Guide for the Married Man* (Gene Kelly, 20th Century Fox, 1967). Digital frame enlargement.

back to home base and into the arms of his welcoming wife. Given the absurd accumulation of strategies, complications, and deceptions required to bring the male protagonist to the realization that there is no point in disrupting a marriage that is already working so well, the film manages to valorize the marital institution even as it casts a critical eye at the childish behavior of the bumbling American male.

The improved interpersonal communication that therapists were recommending as the best remedy for a failing marriage did not in itself make for compelling narratives, unless they focused upon communication as a *problem*—one that was inefficiently managed and that might subsequently be corrected. While Hollywood did initiate a more direct engagement with the therapeutic strategies of marital healing by the closing years of the decade, this strategy was entirely ineffective at "rescuing" marriage. This failure occurred largely because the strategies for problematizing marriage were incongruous with the resolutions proposed. In some cases, as in *How to Murder Your Wife*, the ultimate embrace of the marriage institution never made much sense within the narrative—in fact, it served more as an illogical complication appended to the narrative in order to counteract and obscure the logic of misogyny and institutional disruption that the remainder of the film used as the basis for "satire." In other cases, as in *A Guide for the Married Man*, the machinations leading up to the "happy ending" remained so preposterous, and the conditions of marital discord so absurd, that the resolution of the couple's problems seemed like a bland inevitability. In neither case did the return to marital harmony result from a questioning of assumptions or generalizations, nor any commitment to clearer, less dysfunctional communication practices.

As a narrative tracing a married couple's progress from discord, to separation, to divorce, before an ultimate return to a state of harmony (or workable truce), Bud Yorkin's 1967 film *Divorce American Style* qualifies as a provisional milestone on many fronts, and one that reaped the benefits of the contemporary marriage crisis and rising divorce rates. Two of the taglines among Columbia Pictures' display ads attest to the film's relevance to the cultural and historical present: the first identifies the film as "A timely probing look at today's marital dropouts!" (Ad 304); the second reads, "Is Marriage Dead? If you are planning to be married . . . or have been married . . . or know someone who is . . . you must see 'Divorce American Style'!" (Ad 403). In traditional Hollywood fashion, class issues are never addressed, with the central male protagonist Richard (Dick Van Dyke) and his wife Barbara Harmon (Debbie Reynolds) along with their extended community of similarly dysfunctional married couples with children never avowing how much they take their economic standing for granted, while bemoaning their losses exclusively in terms of financial assets and liabilities. The film does sustain its predecessors' emphasis upon how marriage conflicts affect men, as its upper-middle-class, southern California protagonist, along with other male victims of outmoded divorce laws, bears the brunt of personal sacrifice in the divorce proceedings. ("The uranium in our uranium mine to Barbara, and the shaft to me," Richard comments during the legal negotiations.)

Yet the film also attempts a more panoramic approach to its subject matter. Rather than offering *How to Murder Your Wife*'s imposing, intimate, highly personalized effect of an onscreen, diegetic speaker directing his address to an audience, *Divorce American Style*'s opens with a craftily orchestrated series of cuts depicting various married men of the suburban neighborhood performing precisely the same functions in their daily routines—dealing with traffic, and arriving at their respective homes after a long day of work. A judge leaves his car, walks to the top of a steep hill, and begins to conduct an "orchestra" lending rhythm and cadence to a set of cacophonous voices of couples arguing. The cumulative effect is to suggest that these relationship disagreements occur everywhere, every day, with the common thread of these unhappily married couples' arguments resonating, in the spirit of contemporary psychotherapeutic discourse, as a pervasive failure to communicate. The prevalent discourse of this sequence appears to be psychoanalysis. "The problem isn't me, Mildred. It's you," barks one of the husbands in voiceover. "You're split up the middle by your own inner conflicts, so you take your frustrations out on me. You make me your whipping boy, psychologically."

Unlike the virtually exclusive male-to-male discursive strategies of *How to Murder Your Wife* and *A Guide for the Married Man*, then, *Divorce American Style* offers a unique, if briefly maintained, instance of men and women conversing about their own communication problems. Once the film zeroes in on the plight of the Harmons as a "case study," the emphasis on therapeutic discourse becomes yet more pronounced, offering privileged, behind-the-scenes access to their interactions as they shed their facades and attempt, more often than not unsuccessfully, to relate meaningfully to one another. This sense of privileged access facilitates audience identification (with specific characters and the struggles they face) from a comfortable distance—the sense that these problems could indeed be one's own. The lending of a "voice" by turns to both husband and wife effects a mode of interchange in which men and women hold equal footing. If the interpersonal dynamics of the contemporary, popular television series *The Newlywed Game* (ABC, 1966–1971) permitted audiences to witness both the revelation and the questioning of assumptions and generalizations comprising the practice of married life in a humorous context, *Divorce American Style* assumes a somewhat darker perspective on marital miscommunication—one that often shows both married participants to be complicit in hurting one another in ways that often register as more disturbing than funny.[5] "Communication isn't just talking," Barbara reminds Richard after the departure of party guests from their home has resulted in an extended period of uncomfortable silence. "It's feeling the other person. It's making contact. You wouldn't understand."

Divorce American Style does not, however, dramatize marital miscommunication in a way that positions the audience as gapers at a highway accident. While it is among the first of Hollywood's efforts to frame the symptoms of marital discord in terms of contemporary psychotherapeutic approaches that bring husband and wife into a dynamic of mutual exchange, however, the film soon discounts professional psychotherapy altogether as a viable option for couples. Barbara has proven to be more receptive to therapy than Richard, having seen a marriage counselor for two years. After the couple's first extended argument at home following the dinner party—punctuated by scenes in which their two teenage boys listen in from their bedroom, updating a score sheet that they have been keeping on their parents' arguments—Richard takes Barbara's advice about consulting with a professional. What transpires in this therapy only further polarizes the couple, trivializing psychotherapeutic methods in the process. Seeing Richard separately first, the therapist, Dr. Zenwinn (Martin Gabel) compromises his authority and efficacy in his client's eyes by perplexing Richard with extended analogical observations such as "we think of the sex drive as we would a fine violin," and "the ego is a big balloon." Barbara is hopeful about progress when she is called in, and Zenwinn recommends that they proceed with regular conjoint sessions, but the wife's too eager embrace of psychotherapy begins to read as an almost brainwashed indoctrination by popular therapeutic discourse. "There's something wrong," she observes at the end of the visit. "We're choking to death. We're suffocating." Richard's derisively responds, "I'll call the fire department," thereby distancing himself from analogies that register to him as overly dramatic exaggerations.

As the narrative proceeds, with Barbara and Richard filing for divorce after the communication problems intensify, the critique of psychotherapy becomes coupled with invective against a legal system designed to make its professional representatives richer while bleeding their male clients dry. Both Richard and Nelson Downes (Jason Robards), the recent divorcee whom he hesitatingly befriends, are depicted as casualties of a self-serving "system"—one whose victims survive only by tailoring the rules of the game to their own ends. The plot that Nelson and his ex-wife Nancy (Jean Simmons) devise seems ingenious: get Richard to marry Nancy to release Nelson from alimony-induced poverty, and find Barbara a rich husband to get Richard off the hook as well. The extreme measures to which these detaching and realigning couples must resort in order to salvage what remains of their personal, professional, and economic security are depicted to directly result from outmoded divorce laws; indeed, Nelson states overtly that he blames the legal system, and not the woman whom he has recently divorced, for his plight.

If *How to Murder Your Wife*'s mutual disdain for women and marriage taints its attempt at satire with blatant misogyny, *Divorce American Style* strives to be a more humanistic comedy whose focused satirical target is the bureaucratic institution of divorce itself—an institution that victimizes men, women, and contemporary society, even if it does so in conflicting ways. Divorce is offered as a status that should be less regulated, and more immediately attainable for couples who are unable to resolve their differences; at the same time, however, divorce becomes something that can readily be avoided by adopting the communication strategies recommended by psychotherapeutic experts of the mid-1960s, as long as couples are careful to practice such strategies exclusively on a "self-help" basis, *without* the rhetoric of psychotherapy itself or the actual assistance of trained therapists.

Near the ending of the film, when Richard and Barbara finally learn of their assigned roles in Nelson and Nancy's plot, the group converses about the reasons why contemporary marriages are failing. Nelson blames the legislators for making it too easy for couples to marry; Barbara's wealthy fiancé Al Yearling (Van Johnson) suggests that "we've made a sick joke of all the old virtues" of marriage and religion. Expressing their mutual disagreement with these perspectives, Richard and Barbara ultimately find their own viewpoints to be suddenly in alliance, as Barbara agrees with Richard's pronouncement that "It's very simple: marriage is work, and nobody wants to work." Although their subsequent conversation assigns distinct areas of blame to men ("we confuse our jobs with our marriages") and women (who are too often crossing "the line between the sexes"), the discussion focuses upon mutual responsibility. Perhaps the most extended series of pro-social messages in Hollywood cinema of this era plays out as a symphonic communication, culminating in a simple refrain that husband and wife enunciate almost in unison: "The only miracle in marriage is that two people find each other in the first place." Embodying the paradoxical resolution characteristic of so many Hollywood comedies in an era that deemed marriage worth saving even as it exploited marital failure, the Harmons' harmonic communicative system, and the simple, mutual realization that couples must take responsibility for saving their own marriages, are, however, effectively undone in the film's closing moments, when the reunited Richard and Barbara arrive at home only to pick up where they left off, rehearsing the same disagreements, assumptions, and generalizations that got them into so much trouble in the first place. If, as Kreuz and Roberts argue, "the goal of satire is to comment on a state of the world" (102), the film sustains its use of irony while ultimately compromising its effect as social satire: the ending suggests that the institution of marriage warrants no further critical analysis, since Barbara and Richard have become reconciled advocates of the same institution that they (and the narrative) were so intent upon criticizing. Contemporary critics complained that the imposition of a "happy ending" lessened the film's satirical force;[6] just as unsettling, however, is the film's argument for couples to demonstrate effort and responsibility in saving marriage even as it ultimately renders this same effort ineffectual—an especially familiar strategy for Hollywood to adopt, in the waning years of a still influential Production Code Administration, when considerable means to appeal to (and to refrain from offending) a broad spectrum of viewers remained standard practice.

Encounter Groups and Open Marriage

However incoherent this ending makes the film's perspective on marriage and divorce, staging the provisional grounds for better mutual understanding with one's spouse certainly constitutes a major step forward from contemplating her murder, and *Divorce American Style* does evidence a cultural shift in its embrace of potentially productive discussions of marital happiness and fulfillment. In addition to its status as a monument to marriage as a damaged institution that may (or may not) be capable of salvaging, the film's focus upon communication and marital healing aligns it with a contemporary therapeutic discourse that emphasized the importance of interpersonal engagement and the benefits of addressing problems rather than dodging or disavowing them—one that was also a basis of the conjoint therapy model that Richard and Barbara try out briefly. In addition to such therapeutic sessions, the later 1960s witnessed the rise in popularity of the encounter group therapy model—one depending yet more heavily upon strategies of patient socialization within the therapeutic setting as a bridge to the social and interpersonal dynamics of the world outside the controlled group. As psychologist Carl Rogers explains, "the learnings of these group experiences tend to carry over, temporarily or permanently, into the relationships with spouse, children, students, subordinates, peers, and even superiors following the group experience" (6–7).

According to Rogers's description, the encounter group stressed the "personal growth and the development and improvement of interpersonal relationships through an experiential process" (3). With its origins in training groups ("T-groups") for soldiers during and after World War II, the encounter group emerged from a broad subset of humanistic group therapy models, including the gestalt therapy that Fritz Perls developed in the 1940s, and Carl Rogers's client-centered therapy in the 1950s. Rogers's model focused on the immediacy of the present moment, with the group setting offering a safe haven for self-expression, becoming mindful of one's perception by others, and most importantly, nurturing mutual trust. Rogers meticulously outlines the process by which group participants attain these goals, from one's first stages of connection to the group, to a point of "self-acceptance and the beginning of change," to the "basic encounter" comprising intimate contact with group members, to the transformation of the group itself into a more functional microcosm of the world beyond it, and where honesty and respect for difference are nurtured (16–33). The process anticipates interpersonal conflict along the path to attaining workable communication strategies, and by such means the group participant becomes better attuned to an authentic, inner-self distinct from the façade or "outer shell" that he has strived so diligently to project and maintain in his life (8–9). While such efforts often focus upon matters of self-transformation that would come to characterize the human potential movement, the dynamic, interpersonal nature of therapy also prepares the participant to become more receptive to change, leading to increased "willingness to innovate" (11).

As psychologists emphasized at the end of the decade, the need for such groups arose as a counteractive to feelings of social alienation and anonymity fostered by contemporary American society. Rogers attributed the phenomenon to "the increasing dehumanization of our culture, where the person does not count—only his IBM card or Social Security number. This impersonal quality runs through all the institutions in our land" (10). Influential group psychotherapist Irvin D. Yalom suggested that the competitive nature of our culture, along with a "dehumanized, runaway technocracy" that afflicts society as a "disease," leaves people feeling alienated, more inclined to maintain facades, and less willing to risk engaging in authentic interpersonal communication (491-93). A demand for greater intimacy and closeness develops out of this debilitating sense of alienation, manifesting itself as

> a hunger for relationships which are close and real; in which feelings and emotions can be spontaneously expressed without

> first being carefully censored or bottled up; where deep experiences—disappointments and joys—can be shared; where new ways of behaving can be risked and tried out; where, in a word, he approaches the state where all is known and all accepted, and thus further growth becomes possible. (Rogers 11)

The emphasis upon trust, sincerity, and authenticity in social expression and individual identity similarly infused marital therapeutic discourse of the early 1970s. While the future of the institution remained in a state of crisis with divorce rates rising even more sharply by the start of the new decade, the field of psychotherapy became more adamant than ever in protesting not only that marriage itself would survive as long as it developed greater flexibility in an era of change, but also that the troubled institution was still mankind's best suited vehicle for developing human potential to its utmost. Regarding the matter of flexibility, Herbert Otto's 1970 *Saturday Review* article "Has Monogamy Failed?" (a question answered with a definitive "no") explains that our response to "a time of change and rapid social evolution" must be "to provide an atmosphere of sustenance, loving, caring, and adventuring" in order to ensure our continued "growth and unfoldment," and that an "evolving" version of monogamy is essential to this endeavor. The focus on maximizing human potential, and upon the phenomenon of "self-actualization" that permeated marital discourse of this period, similarly deemed legally recognized one-on-one relationships as essential to individual well-being. "New and complex life styles call for a new marriage format," argue Nena and George O'Neill in their influential 1972 study *Open Marriage: A New Life Style for Couples* (22). If "only through knowing another in significant and authentic dimensions can we love, explore the potential of ourselves and others, and fight off the alienation of our time" (26), then marriage remained society's best hope. Some modifications would, however, be necessary in order to guarantee that the institution would indeed expand rather than constrict human potential. Foremost among these was the eradication of an "exclusivity" that forced couples to deny their individual identities, and to ward off intrusion and influence by outside social forces. While the O'Neills never advocated for extramarital sexual relations, they did accommodate the possibility of such relations as long as the married couple had achieved a healthy bond that nurtured "trust, identity, and open communication necessary to the eradication of jealousy" (257).

While Paul Mazursky's *Bob & Carol & Ted & Alice* (1969) never explicates the alienation or anonymity of contemporary American society,[7] it does present at least one of its two eponymous, wealthy southern California couples as wanting something more from themselves and their personal relationships, while also exploring the sexual and emotional boundaries of matrimony. The film's opening sequence finds Bob (Robert Culp) and Carol Sanders (Natalie Wood) driving their sporty convertible to the mountain location of a retreat center named "The Institute," modeled on the Big Sur Esalen Institute where such noted psychologists including Fritz Perls, Virginia Satir, and Carl Rogers had either taken residence or offered programs and seminars in the 1960s. Regarding the therapeutic method itself, *Bob & Carol & Ted & Alice* strives for authenticity: the extended sequence at the Institute depicts stages of a 24-hour marathon session that follows many aspects of Carl Rogers's client-centered encounter group model quite closely. Some group members are uncomfortable with the proceedings at the outset, most notably Bob, who explains that he has come to the Institute to conduct research on a film documentary that he is directing, and Carol, who simply states that she is Bob's wife and has come because of him. When Tim (Greg Mullavey), the group leader, prompts the participants to move about the room and look intently into the eyes of each individual they encounter ("Really try to make contact. Learn something about the other person by just looking."), Carol finds herself breaking into nervous laughter. Shots of group participants screaming and pounding on pillows are followed by a scene that dramatizes the first attempt at more open communication between the central married couple, as Carol denounces her husband's manipulation of her after he bemoans that she never openly shares her feelings with him. Following this revelation, the sequence concludes with the couple confined to a corner, crying in one another's arms as the other participants move toward them and embrace in a massive group hug.

Through this sequence, *Bob & Carol & Ted & Alice* structures a perspective on the human potential movement and encounter group methods that demonstrates the contemporary relevance of the film's subject matter, the relation of the characters to an unexpectedly profound therapeutic experience, and the audience's relation to both the therapy and the development of these two central protagonists. The representation of group therapy dynamics was not itself new to American cinema (as evidenced in chapter 1's discussion of the 1963 film *The Caretakers*), but the similarity of this Institute to the actual, historical Esalen would be sufficient to register to 1969 audiences as authentic and "true-to-life" even if they were unfamiliar with what actually transpired there.[8] That Bob and Carol are initially depicted as curious yet reluctant participants in the proceedings becomes more apparent through the contrast between their reasons for coming to the center and those expressed by some of the other participants: one woman's admission that "I can't say no to any man" and another's assertion that "I came because I want a better orgasm" register as frank, explicit claims that mark the subject matter as intimately adult-oriented in a way that was still relatively unique in the first years of post-Code Hollywood (even for an R-rated film), even if the proliferation of the psychotherapeutic discourse of sexual dysfunction had already become ubiquitous by this time, as we have seen in chapter 2. (Indeed, the frank and potentially controversial subject matter—here the matter of swinging and wife swapping—is also strategically exploited in the film's tagline, "Consider the Possibilities.") Crucially, the frankness of the participants' expression is uncompromised by the judgment of any other group members through the familiar technique of intercutting reaction shots—a device often used to build an alliance between the audience and one character at the expense of another. By eliciting personal and interpersonal intimacy through a process of breaking down psychological and emotional barriers, the sequence constructs a broad array of possible narrative access points for its audience, whether they have come to the film already skeptical about such therapies, entirely resistant to them, curious about them, or ready to engage with them for any of the reasons that the group members themselves specify (see fig. 3.2).

Figure 3.2. Bob (Robert Culp, rear, 3rd from left) and Carol Sanders (rear, 4th from left) share a breakthrough moment during a marathon encounter group therapy session at the Institute, while group leader Tim (Greg Mullavey, rear, 2nd from left) and other group members gather for a group hug in *Bob & Carol & Ted & Alice* (Paul Mazursky, Columbia Pictures, 1969). Digital frame enlargement.

Rather than extending the dramatization of the Sanders's experience at the Institute beyond the point of breakthrough represented in the group hug scene, the narrative shifts to an interpersonal exchange at once intimate but less exotic, as Bob and Carol share a dinner and the details of their transformative experience at the Institute with their best friends Ted (Elliott Gould) and Alice Henderson (Dyan Cannon) at a favorite restaurant. Even at this early point, the film suggests a difficulty upon which founders and advocates of the group encounter movement—like Carl Rogers and harsh critics who later reflected upon its inefficacy would invariably foreground—the problem of fruitfully sustaining the insights gained within the encounter group after the experience itself has concluded. As representatives of the uninitiated and untransformed, Ted and Alice serve as contrasting complements to the Sanders—they listen respectfully yet respond reluctantly to their friends' intimate expressions ("We love you," Bob declares. "We really love you"), and allow the Sanders to stack their accumulated hands on the table in an expression of emotional solidarity. This scene's introduction of the Hendersons offers yet another perspective on the Sanders' sudden psychotherapeutic transformation—one of tender yet restrained admiration tainted by a slight hint of embarrassment, exacerbated especially after Carol's new predisposition to open, honest communication inadvertently embarrasses the maître d'. ("Do you really hope the service is satisfactory?" she asks him.) Heavy handed though the expression of their new perspective occasionally becomes, however, Bob and Carol never lapse into a state of myopic, cult-like embrace of their new, "enlightened" identities; in fact, the entire group responds with laughter to the concluding exchange of the scene, in which Ted, appearing to have embraced the call for openness and honesty, struggles profoundly with something difficult that he would like to express. "I feel I have to say it," he protests to Bob. "I feel that you should pay the check."

Through such means, the film attempts to accommodate both alliances *and* resistances to popular, contemporary therapeutic methods and those whom they have affected. In the process, *Bob & Carol & Ted & Alice* reveals some of the era's conflicting perspectives on marriage and its elasticity in relation to changing social and cultural values. There is some attempt, for example, to align the status of the Sanders's relationship with the requisite trust and respect that the O'Neills would valorize in *Open Marriage*: when Bob reveals to Carol that he has had an affair during a business trip to San Francisco, Carol carefully reflects upon her reaction before stating confidently that she is not jealous; indeed, she even expresses that his revelation of the affair has made her feel closer to him than ever. At the same time, however, Bob's initially angry and aggressive reaction to Carol's disclosure that she is having a sexual encounter with a man in their own home, followed immediately by a realization of his own hypocrisy, conveys the contradictions of human responses to infidelity in an era when one is expected to be more "enlightened." Here, Bob's initial expression of jealousy registers as more authentic than the "insight"-prompted acceptance that follows it, and that resonates like a response from a performer who has momentarily forgotten his "correct" lines.

To complement this sense of discomfort, the narrative clearly frames Alice as uncomfortable with such blurring of the sexual boundaries enforced by monogamy—she is devastated by Carol's news about Bob's sexual affair and is able to reconcile her judgmental feelings only through more traditional, one-on-one sessions with her psychiatrist. The film's crucial, penultimate sequence in a Las Vegas hotel suite brings the forces of acceptance and resistance to changing sexual mores into a state of crisis, as the news that both Carol and Ted have also had sexual affairs compels Alice to propose that the foursome take their own mutual relationship to the next level by having an orgy. The result of this "experiment," however, is less a revolutionary transgression of "square," outdated values than an uncomfortable yet ultimately nonjudgmental litmus test that provides the foursome a clearer sense of their expectations from intimate relationships. After the orgy that never happens, the closing sequence follows the two couples emerging silent and fully clothed from their suite, only to be joined later by a group of strangers outside the hotel—strangers with whom they engage in directed and ambient movements of advance and retreat, of intimate looks and returned glances among smiling faces, all orchestrated to Dionne Warwick singing "What the World Needs Now." Echoing the initial exchanges among the Institute's participants, and valorizing the need for human closeness even if it is not nurtured in radical group therapy marathons, this closing sequence, a welcome application of therapeutic dynamics to the world outside the confines of the encounter group, resonates as a utopic gesture of resolution, one that forgives the loving foursome for not being able to follow through with their impulsively manifested intentions.

The film's ending precipitated controversy and polarity among contemporary critics in the fall of 1969. According to *Variety*, "The ending may be interpreted in different ways. Liberals might say it's a cop-out; conservatives might say, 'see, that's what happens.' The obvious answer to the problems, as always, must fall somewhere in the middle" (Rela 3). Vincent Canby's scathingly negative *New York Times* dismissal of the film led to vehement opposition from Pauline Kael, Hollis Alpert, and other critics who came to its enthusiastic defense, their collective responses featured in a noted October 9, 1969, display ad for the film that the *New York Times* itself published. Hollis Alpert retorted that the failed orgy "ending is not a 'cop-out,'" describing the film as a testament to a human community that is not "quite ready for such ventures in human 'touch sensitivity'" (Oct. 11, 1969). Despite the care it devotes to rendering its characters sympathetic in both their emotional and sexual interactions with one another, that *Bob & Carol & Ted & Alice* should provoke such a spirited and disparate set of responses from both critics and audiences is unsurprising, given that its nonjudgmental tone permits the film to play strategically to both proponents of new therapies and new perspectives on monogamous marriage, and to those skeptical about the restorative potential of the former and the flexibility of the latter. Yet for a film that ends up at least interrogating the efficacy of the changing moral values that it exploits, *Bob & Carol & Ted & Alice* offers a much more narratively coherent response to the challenges that marital partners were facing in the 1960s than what is offered by *How to Murder Your Wife*, *A Guide for the Married Man*, or even *Divorce American Style*, imbuing its four central participants with a keen sense of awareness of the often contradictory signals that guide them in their search for a "revolutionary" sense of intimacy and self-insight.

As such, the satirical aim of *Bob & Carol & Ted & Alice* differs from that of the other films, since the object of satire here is neither an outworn social institution nor the equally outworn legal and religious structures bound to hold it in place. Whether one deems the conclusion of *Bob & Carol & Ted & Alice* to be a "happy ending," the film's closure is distinctive from these forerunners for refraining from negating the logic and value of the entirety of the narrative preceding it; instead, the insights and experimentation that the film dramatizes make its culmination more resonant, "failing" only in the sense that its protagonists do not follow through on the sexual experimentation that they have only minutes ago prematurely convinced themselves that they should want.[9] The lack of dialogue in the final sequence certainly may frustrate viewers who expect a clearer resolution or commentary upon the foursome's fruitless attempt at group sex. At the same time, however, this "silence" permits the film to maintain a consistency of tone absent from most previous Hollywood experiments with dramatizing marital discord. If *Bob & Carol & Ted & Alice* ultimately contends inconclusively with the alternatives to the monogamous marriage contract that the film both opens up and closes off, it does so in a way that strives to be neither condemnatory nor regressive in relation to the "possibilities" it suggests. The film becomes, however, much more consistent regarding the importance of "insight" (a term which at least three of the four central characters exclaim at a breakthrough moment), whether it is gathered within or beyond the therapeutic setting.

Feminist Perspectives on Marriage in the 1960 and 1970s

Both patients and facilitators of encounter group therapy often faced the problem of determining a common starting point for a session, given the broad spectrum of problems that were bringing Americans to Esalen and other such institutes in this era. In the case of the women's movement and the nascent consciousness-raising groups that emerged from it by the end of the 1960s, however, the starting point was the psychological, social, economic, and institutional oppression that women had been facing for so long at the hands of men. The problems were articulated, and brought to the level of active public discourse, in the early 1960s through such works as Simone de Beauvoir's *The Second Sex* and Betty Friedan's *The Feminine Mystique*. Friedan predicated her study upon her observation of the facts: women were dropping out of college at an increasingly alarming rate, marrying at earlier and earlier ages, and incessantly striving to find a proper spouse in order to avoid the risk of being labeled a spinster. As a writer for women's magazines, Friedan had direct experience with the very successful strategies that the popular cultural industries were using to sell an image of the contentedness and fulfillment of the ideal American housewife to millions of women. Friedan was also cognizant of what she would describe as the prevalent "Problem That Has No Name," a growing sense of alienation and dissatisfaction with the realities of "Occupation: Housewife."

The Feminine Mystique articulates the obstacles that women were facing in affirming this sense of disappointment—of attributing their dissatisfaction to something other than personal failure at adapting or adjusting to an ideal. A key goal of Friedan's influential study was to create a broader sense of awareness, to facilitate the validation of women's resistant responses to constraining social and cultural configurations of gender. The forces and agents that were assigning and selling disingenuous identities to women comprised the problem, and not women themselves: "the chains that bind [the suburban housewife] in her trap are chains in her own mind and spirit. They are chains made up of mistaken ideas and misinterpreted facts, or incomplete truths and unreal choices. They are not easily seen and not easily shaken off" (31).

The radical feminist movement of the late 1960s emerged directly from this commitment to helping women come to terms with an awareness of external factors, the set of oppressive conditions that maintained illusory notions of female contentment in the workforce and at home, as a direct cause of the internalized conditions of oppression that women suffered. If this was a primary goal of the method of consciousness-raising, the original proponents of this movement were careful to distinguish consciousness-raising from therapy. "Women are messed over, not messed up!" Carol Hanisch emphasizes in her 1968 document "The Personal Is Political"; in their influential piece "Toward a Female Liberation Movement," Beverly Jones and Judith Brown asserted that "I cannot make it too clear that I am not talking about group therapy or individual catharsis (we aren't sick we are oppressed)." And as Kathie Sarachild clarified during the same year,

> The purpose of hearing from everyone was never to be nice or tolerant or to develop speaking skill or the 'ability to listen.' It was to get closer to the truth. Knowledge and information would make it possible for people to be 'able' to speak. The purpose of hearing people's feelings and experience was not therapy, was not to give someone a chance to get something off her chest . . . that is something for a friendship. It was to hear what she had to say. The importance of listening to a woman's feelings was collectively to analyze the situation of women, not to analyze *her*. The idea was not to change women, was not to make 'internal changes' except in the sense of knowing more. It was and is the conditions women face, it's male supremacy we want to change. ("Consciousness-Raising: A Radical Weapon")

Consciousness-raising was thus conceived as crucial to the process of transforming what were insidiously touted as "personal" problems of women's dissatisfaction with conforming to an externally defined ideal into political awareness that would become the prelude to action and social change. It was also implemented as a system of dedicated communication, requiring an ability both to assert and to listen attentively.

In its commitment to engage rather than to offend large blocks of its viewership, Hollywood cinema's response to the women's liberation movement was ambivalent in many of the same ways that had characterized its response to other controversial subjects of the decade. Still, some films of the late 1960s and early 1970s incorporated the subject of women's "enlightenment" in ways that respected the initial aims of the radical feminist movement, while refraining from situating the process of feminist consciousness-raising as a therapeutic enterprise that directly or inadvertently pathologized women. Couched in the genre of the "thriller," for example, Roman Polanski's controversial 1968 film *Rosemary's Baby* dramatizes a process of enlightenment modeled upon Friedan's insights into the woman's condition, positioning its central female protagonist within a set of marital, social, and institutional contexts that effectively regulate her agency as a woman without revealing to her the operations of such containment. Although it makes no overt reference to contemporary perceptions of gender disparities or the social movement that struggled to bring these problems to the attention of a broader audience, *Rosemary's Baby* serves as a most timely cultural artifact that is aligned with the aims of radical feminism and the initial aims of consciousness-raising.[10] While depictions of marriage earlier in the decade focused upon the institution's oppression of either men (*How to Murder Your Wife* and *A Guide for the Married Man*) or couples (*Divorce American Style* and *Bob & Carol & Ted & Alice*), through devices of restricted and subjective narration *Rosemary's Baby* consistently aligns its audience with Rosemary's (Mia Farrow) perspective, tracing her gradual transformation from a passive and naïve American housewife who defines her identity solely in relation to her husband Guy (John Cassavetes), to an empowered, resilient woman who refuses to capitulate to the demands of the demonic cult that has selected her to bear the child of Satan.

With its release preceding the broad proliferation of radical feminist discourse in the late 1960s, contemporary critical responses to *Rosemary's Baby* largely ignored its place in the women's liberation movement; in fact, most of the controversy surrounding the film centered upon its depiction of Satanism and the issuance of a "C" (condemned) rating by the National Catholic Office of Motion Pictures (NCOMP).[11] Released in 1970, however, Frank and Eleanor Perry's *Diary of a Mad Housewife* carries more distinctive markings of the liberationist discourse to which film critics and Hollywood as a popular cultural institution were already responding, and often in negative terms. The *Hollywood Reporter* review asserts that the married female protagonist Tina Balser's (Carrie Snodgress) "image of herself dramatizes so much of the Women's Lib rhetoric," while reassuring viewers that the film is ultimately "less a piece of Women's Lib propaganda and more an acute study of male and female lifestyles ("U's 'Housewife' a BO Winner").

As a testament to the virtues of consciousness-raising that draws its rhetoric yet more freely from contemporary liberationist discourse, *Diary*'s differences from *Rosemary's Baby* are as illuminating as its similarities. While both films use similar narrative means to align the central female protagonist's perspective with that of the audience, and neither film provides this protagonist with a definitive resolution for her domestic plight or a "way out," *Diary of a Mad Housewife* is more deliberately constructed to provoke a sense of rage in its audience, serving as a call to action that overtly politicizes the process of self-enlightenment. Through restricted narration, we witness Rosemary gradually developing insight into the deception being orchestrated at her expense, and becoming stronger and more confident in the process; the narrational alliance with Tina is at once more intimate, more deliberate and self-conscious. As Stanley Kauffmann observes,

> there is . . . only one credible reason for her acceptance of continual abuse. *Because she knows the camera is there*. She has witnesses (us) who know what she is suffering and how fine she is, who are sitting in judgment on her harassers and will reward her—at least with our sympathy and high opinion—for the reticent courage with which she undergoes her trials. . . . [The film] has the effect of conscious autobiography for those who are watching. This effect [comprises] a sense that the protagonist of a fiction knows that he (or she) is being watched or read or listened to. . . . ("Diary of a Mad Housewife")

While *Rosemary's Baby* draws attention to its eponymous heroine's perception of the increasingly oppressive, stifling world that encompasses her, *Diary of a Mad Housewife*'s narrative strategy tends to focus more intently upon Tina's *reaction* to oppression, upon a confirmation of the intolerability of this oppression that is offered by allowing the audience access to her own remarkable ability both to endure it and to rise above it. "Imagine her unwitnessed," Kauffmann suggests," and the only thing that would be credible is her quick flight or quick breakdown." In the context of consciousness-raising, through her responses to a demanding lawyer-husband Jonathan (Richard Benjamin) and her equally demanding free-spirited writer-lover George (Frank Langella), Tina participates in the intended enlightenment of her audience, seeking to validate their own (perhaps unvoiced or unnarrated) sense of oppression in the process. Such a narrative voice is in fact consonant with the source material serving as the film's basis, Sue Kaufman's 1967 novel of the same name, which is presented as a series of intimate reflections in diary format. In the film version, however, this sense of participation is ultimately revealed to be connected not to an imagined group of empathetic female listeners, but to the context of a group therapy session that is played out in the film's final scene, in which Tina is systematically berated by each of the male (and many of the female) members who accuse her of being spoiled, wonder why she would ever need therapy given her upper-class social status, and denounce her decision for hiding her own affair with George after her husband has admitted his affair with another woman. The establishment of closure with the group therapy scene threatens to reframe Tina's narrative as a solely psychopathological enterprise: having apparently confessed everything that we have just witnessed to a group that appears onscreen only in this final scene, Tina's own process of enlightenment might appear to be compromised, or at least transformed into a vehicle that anticipates a "cure" to an ailment now been reinscribed as personal rather than social or political. Consistent with her characterization, however, Tina's reaction to this heated conflict within the group session is contained by the close-up of her slowly broadening smile, overtly breaking the fourth wall as she makes eye contact with another "group" that is not in the room with her. Dissociated from the heated argument playing out within the group session, Tina reiterates her alliance with the audience even as she reaffirms her conviction that she is *not* the source of the problem that we have been witnessing over the course of this narrative.[12]

But for this sense of witnessing that Tina strives to elicit, Charles Champlin's observation that "you quickly feel that she has got to be some sort of a nut to put up with all she puts up with" might seem a valid assessment ("Carrie Snodgress Star Rises"). That Tina, as the presiding narrative voice, needs to demonstrate to us the lunacy of her sense of endurance attests to the film's rootedness in liberationist discourse; indeed, the film's perspective is aligned with the strategy of publications of the feminist Redstockings group such as Pat Mainardi's "The Politics of Housework," which includes pronouncements from a *male* viewpoint such as "I don't like the dull, stupid, boring jobs, so you should do them," and "oppression is built into the system and I, as the white American male, receive the benefits of this system. I don't want to give them up." In both cases, the narratives offer scenarios structured as presentations of evidence designed to confirm the workings of the tyrannical, and in both cases, we are presented with a "seasoned" perspective on marriage that has already moved well beyond Rosemary's initial innocence and blind idealism. The "world" that Tina and Jonathan have created for one another, within a massive and opulent apartment in central Manhattan, is characterized from the outset by mutual disdain, by ideals long ago abandoned. Jonathan is unrelenting in his demands and criticism of his wife, and Tina is rarely surprised by the invective that her husband unleashes upon her. When he does take matters too far, by inviting the children to join in his mockery of her, she immediately condemns him, yet these confrontations have no effect upon the course of their interactions, and they remain at a stand-off, at least until the closing scenes, in which the combined effect of the recklessness of Jonathan's social climbing, his failing job performance, and his adultery—none of it at all surprising to Tina—compels him into a confession and a desperate, pathetic plea for his wife's forgiveness.

In this confessional scene, Jonathan infers that the disconnection and loneliness plaguing their marriage derives from the lost sense of shared idealism that initially brought them together as activists committed to social change, long before capitalist concerns insidiously rerouted his priorities toward the present state of disaster that he has precipitated. While his argument seems more convenient than persuasive in the context of the Balsers's present circumstances, the sense of dissatisfaction arising from outworn middle-class values is certainly a pervasive trope of this era, often linked to a condition of alienation and anonymity which, as noted earlier, was recognized as a symptom of a troubled marriage within psychotherapeutic discourse. In their popular study of marital conflict, *The Intimate Enemy: How to Fight Fair in Love and Marriage* (1969), psychologist George Bach and *Ladies Home Journal* executive editor Peter Wyden explicate the destructive manifestations of this loneliness, describing a class of marital loners as pathological cowards who are "trying to exist psychologically alone and bear the stress of isolation rather than live as authentic twosomes and bear the stress of intimacy. Most loners are nominally attached to someone. . . . But they cannot abide by being emotionally dependent. They don't get truly involved. They detest tension and personal hostilities. The true loner would rather split than fight" (32).

This always looming prospect of marital loneliness, and the often desperate means that Americans in the early 1970s would take in order to evade or overcome it, forms the foundation of Cy Howard's successful summer of 1970 romantic comedy *Lovers and Other Strangers*. The film puts Bach and Wyden's therapeutic strategies to the test by applying them across generations in an assembly of couples (all either married or marriage-seeking) drawn together to celebrate the marriage of Susan Henderson (Bonnie Bedelia) to Mike Vecchio (Michael Brandon). The older, parental generation's obsession with wanting their children to be "happy" is soon revealed as a pretext for their expectation that, once married, couples be willing to forego their search for happiness for the sake of preserving the marriage institution, no matter what the emotional cost. *Lovers and Other Strangers* counterposes such expectations with the more "liberated" perspectives of a sexual revolution that confronts them with a quite different set of demands involving the ready accessibility of divorce, the prevalence of sexual performance anxiety, and especially, the negotiation of gender difference inflected by a pervasive attentiveness to the women's liberation movement. In an effort to address the concerns of both ends of the broad age spectrum comprising the parameters of the film's target audience, and consonant with the generic demands of romantic comedy, the film is devoted to preserving the notion that marriages can still work in the early 1970s—a notion which, as we have seen, was also pervasive within the broader psychotherapeutic community.

Lovers and Other Strangers's comedic exploration of gender discord within contemporary marital relations becomes most resonant as it adopts the strategies of popular contemporary marriage therapies to address the problems of couples whose age and experience situate them ambivalently, somewhere between the traditional and "revolutionary" generations and their respective mindsets, firmly clinging to the stability of the former while recognizing the increasing prominence of the latter. As soon as the film introduces the twelve-year marriage veterans Johnny (Harry Guardino) and Wilma (Anne Meara), the tensions emerging from a sense of togetherness grown stale are already manifest: the couple has taken a hotel room for the wedding weekend, and Wilma perceives the getaway setting as the ideal place to renew expressions of a sexual intimacy about which Harry seems less than enthusiastic. It soon becomes clear that, according to the terminology of Bach and Wyden, instead of risking conflict or momentary discord, Wilma and Harry have been resorting to seething silently in a communication-averse, "fight-phobic household" where the penalty of "emotional divorce" has already taken hold (6). In the inescapably intimate confines of the hotel room, such behavior readily fosters a "gunny-sacking" in which man and woman secretly accumulate grievances that must eventually erupt in a vengeful "Vesuvius" ("Fight Together, Stay Together," 64).

The eruption centers upon frustrations about gender identity inflected by women's liberationist discourse. After his withholding of affection prompts Wilma to remind him about how infrequently they have sex, Harry retorts that such reminders compromise his masculinity and his libido. "Out of all the women in the world, I had to go and marry an equal time orgasm fanatic," Harry laments, transforming the situation into a problem of containing women's excessive—and therefore unnatural and menacing—female desire. "You read a couple of Ladies Home Journals, and all you can think of is 'me too, me too.'" As Harry continues to travesty Wilma's familiarity with contemporary therapies of sexual intimacy among married couples, however, he unknowingly guides the argument toward a broader problem of how to define— and how to perform—masculinity and femininity in a historical era so intent upon challenging and destabilizing the sustained norms of gender identity. After asserting that Wilma has become "butch," she vehemently retorts that her ex-marine husband's seemingly invulnerable macho guise puts him in a class of "latent fags" who are "not real men." These desperate attempts to inflict pain upon one another by referencing "extremes" of sexuality that American culture still perceived as aberrant only exacerbate the couple's confusion as they struggle to navigate their ill-defined expectations of proper gender behavior. Ultimately, Wilma and Harry's free exchange of accusations—an exchange that Bach and Wyden would certainly categorize as "unproductive fighting"—evidences the troubling, unavoidable realization that the prospect of eliminating or even obscuring normative gender roles in marital relationships is sufficient to trigger anxiety.

But perhaps this fighting is not so "unproductive" after all. Curiously, the paradoxes regarding contemporary perspectives on gender difference with which Wilma and Harry contend are directly addressed and even "resolved" in Nena and George O'Neill's explication of "'open marriage": in the spirit of an era that celebrates the value of connection and communication, the O'Neills's manifesto bemoans easy recourse to any form of "rigid role behavior" in marriage (44), arguing that "the hackneyed role stereotypes in our society (the male as aggressive and dominant, the female as passive and submissive) actually inhibit men and women from expressing the full range of sexual and sensual pleasure natural to human beings" (138). The solution, as the O'Neills frame it, is not for couples to bind themselves to the categories of "man" and "woman"—and indeed, to reject the notion of equality in *gender*—but instead to embrace the concept of an "equality of personhood for both wife and husband" that emerges from "the equality of responsibility for the self," a responsibility that ultimately resituates married couples as gender-agonistic "peers" (186). When the couple returns to their hotel room that night, they both seem to have made a breakthrough that facilitates such an embrace—"We're equals," Wilma proclaims, as the partners pause to count their blessings.

Yet this notion of "equivalence" between marital partners flourishes only for less than a minute before Wilma and Harry reiterate the already articulated terms of their gender-based conflict, ultimately (and tacitly) reaching a most unlikely compromise: Wilma will permit her husband to play the role of the stronger, decision-making marital partner on the condition that she be able to remind his that she is *permitting* him to do so. As was the case with *Divorce American Style* three years earlier, *Lovers and Other Strangers* effects a paradoxical yet workable "resolution" to contemporary marital issues—one that does not require a commitment of time and financial resources to benefit from the professional institution of marriage counseling—by briefly entertaining the prospect of abandoning gender hierarchies in order to teach couples a lesson, thereby prompting them to foster a renewed respect for the necessary limits of such play.

While *Lovers and Other Strangers*'s therapeutic strategy hypothesizes the elimination of gender difference, Lawrence Turman's *The Marriage of a Young Stockbroker* (1971) takes its therapeutic propositions a step further by toying with the prospect of entirely eliminating the marital institution itself. This contemporary domestic comedy-drama engages with problems of alienation in a study of a husband and wife whose mutual isolation correlates with their inability to express their own needs and desires. The opening scenes of the film suggest that "the system" noted by Jonathan in *Diary of a Mad Housewife* is also at fault here, as the figure of stockbroker William Alren (also played by Richard Benjamin) gradually emerges in an extended, slow, high-angle tracking shot at his Los Angeles brokerage firm, seeming small and insignificant in the context of the visual clutter of tickertapes and a distracting cacophony of competing voices. His feet are up on his desk as he doodles on a notepad, re-engaging only when his boss perceives his inactivity, at which time Jonathan pretends to contact customers from his client list. Mr. Franklin (Ed Prentiss), the successful senior broker in the neighboring cubicle reassures Jonathan that "One of these days you'll be telling [the clients] what you want them to hear without even knowing that you're doing it. Then you'll be home free." William takes Franklin's subsequent death by heart attack as a sign that his own professional path is meaningless. For him, the brokerage firm is a place of alienation, incapable of producing a sense of "fulfillment" that he has yet to define. The primary manifestation of William's "loner" status is his voyeurism, a condition that was officially classified as a deviant or perverted sexual behavior described most often in psychoanalytic terms in relation to fetishism and castration anxiety, but which by the 1970s was being treated as a learned form of behavior susceptible to such behavioral therapies as systematic desensitization, aversive conditioning of undesired behavior, and even hypnosis.[13] When his wife Lisa (Joanna Shimkus) catches him spying on a group of women at the beach one night and then decides to leave him, his reluctance to articulate his loneliness comes to a crisis point.

Unlike *Diary of a Mad Housewife*, whose narrative strategy depends upon a female perspective, a testimonial witnessing of endured and resisted injustices, with *The Marriage of a Young Stockbroker* the voice that tells the tale of marital discord in an era of changing gender relations once again becomes a primarily male voice, as the audience is granted access to William's thoughts, his anxieties, and his fantasies through restricted narration. During a visit to a porno theater and later in conjunction with a brief sexual encounter with a stranger after his wife Lisa leaves him, the intimacy of the narration increases through voiceover. In addition to forging an alliance with the audience, the narration serves the purpose of dramatizing William's isolation, providing the requisite context for his consistent inability to communicate his feelings to Lisa. What distinguishes the film's narrative strategy is its simultaneous attempt to dramatize Lisa's own struggle to explain the roots of her loneliness and marital dissatisfaction. Throughout the first half of the film, she is silent, complacent, and largely affectless, complementing William's own communicative problems. When William and Lisa's "fight-phobic household" erupts in its "Vesuvius" moment, however, she comes as close as any Hollywood film of the era to articulating the plight of the contemporary married woman, attributing her silence to power imbalances that have denied her ability to speak:

> I have no power with you. It's that simple. . . . If you could find some way of giving me power, I'd stay with you, but you can't. . . . Over myself. I want the feeling that I can make things happen. I can't take it anymore. You sit over in your office all day; I sit at home. As long as you're over there, I can kid myself. I can sit there staring out the window kidding myself into thinking that sometime, things will change. Then you come home, all hostile and sullen and making idiotic small talk and I say to myself "it's because he's tired, it's because he's worked hard all day, making money so that one day, our lives will change." . . . But it won't Bill. It can't.

If Lisa's enlightened expression resonates in contemporary feminist discourse, *The Marriage of a Young Stockbroker* immediately undermines the agency and authenticity of her voice by attributing these thoughts to underhanded feminist indoctrination by her sister Nan (Jessica Walter). Indeed, Nan is stereotyped as a manipulative, man-hating feminist, constructed to provoke male anxiety over a future in which the goals of the liberation movement have been achieved. Nan does her best to convince Lisa that William's voyeurism is pathological and incurable; she even arranges to make herself the object of his "peeping" in order to prove her point. As it plays out, then, Nan's ability to dictate Lisa's future makes Nan just another person intent upon disempowering her. Indeed, the only deviations from the film's restricted narration occur when Lisa is alone with Nan, and in this way the film manages to correlate the oppression that Lisa endures as a wife with manipulation she endures through feminist "enlightenment." "It's the old story: male oppression of the female," Nan tells William, the irony clearly marked by the fact that she has compelled her own husband Chester (Adam West) to undergo professional therapy so that she can dominate him. When Nan arranges for an extended family group session to be conducted at their home (without informing William) under the guise of "helping" the couple with their marital problems, the therapist, Dr. Sadler (Patricia Barry), turns out to be so entirely inept ("So, what did you do today, William?" "How do you feel about that, Lisa?") that William seems justified in accusing her of being a fraud as he storms off.

The preposterous encounter with the therapist marks the apex of a cynical, reductive depiction of contemporary psychotherapeutic practice that presents an overwhelming number of unnecessarily complicated solutions to "simple" problems. In response, *The Marriage of a Young Stockbroker* proposes a strategy by which troubled married couples might simply reinvent themselves from the ground up, maximizing their prospects of (inter)personal fulfillment by spontaneously self-actualizing in ways that mirror the ideals of the contemporary human potential movement. In its closing minutes, the film aims to resolve the couple's problems by summarily neutralizing the "square" values and institutions that have conspired to "help" them. Foremost among these is capitalism: William quits his job, and Lisa gives up on her goal of attending modeling school as a means of providing for herself (realizing that she never really wanted to do this anyway). Next on the list are consultations with therapeutic professionals, whose maneuvers are rendered indistinguishable from the oppressive form of jargon-ridden, feminist consciousness-raising tactics that Nan has been practicing on her sister—tactics whose radical nature has now been effectively neutralized. And finally, apparently, is the marriage contract itself, which William informs Lisa that he has negated through a quickie Mexican divorce. No longer concerned with power imbalances, decisions about what they want from life, or even William's continued tendency to "peep" at attractive women—a tendency that they are now able to laugh about—they emerge in the film's closing moments as a fully "liberated" couple, awaiting new adventures.

The Marriage of a Young Stockbroker's resolution reveals the drastic measures to which Hollywood narratives resorted in order to render the happy ending as a "logically" formulated outcome for married couples experiencing communication problems and power imbalances in the early 1970s. Responding to the previous cinematic strategy of plaguing a central female, unhappily married protagonist with the debilitating tendency to interiorize—to mistake an inability to confront oppressive social and institutional conditions as a personal inability to cope and adapt—*Marriage* offers an extreme version of exteriorization by which all social and institutional influences, including those that have emerged in efforts to combat oppression, have united in conspiracy against the couple's inalienable right to happiness and personal fulfillment. By highlighting the feminist challenges to gender/power relations within the plot itself—here, through a character tailored to emblematize the potentially catastrophic outcome of such challenges, at least as they are considered from a reactionary, retrograde perspective that disempowers consciousness-raising efforts—both the future of marriage and the perpetuation of gender disparities can be acknowledged while remaining unchallenged. With *The Marriage of a Young Stockbroker*, irony no longer becomes necessary in a narrative trajectory that posits ambiguous narrative closure as the opening up of infinite possibilities, and that leaves entirely open the matter of what will be left to compel the happily (un)married couple to stay together now that they are "free."

4

Psychedelic Therapies

IF HOLLYWOOD WAS ATTEMPTING TO "have it both ways" with marriage therapies in the context of the burgeoning women's liberation movement—exploiting the emergence of feminism as a phenomenon while limiting liberation's potential to inspire alternatives to the traditional marriage contract—the industry also played to both ends of the audience spectrum in its treatment of the therapeutic potential of hallucinogenic drugs (mescaline, psilocybin, and most notably, LSD) that by the early 1960s had exceeded their original applications in professional psychotherapy to more broad-based "recreational" vehicles for introspection, insight, and reflection. Despite their clear differences, the parallels between the advances sought through feminism and hallucinogenic drugs are noteworthy. The second-wave feminist movement promoted freedom from the constraints of traditional institution of marriage, while LSD use came to be recognized as a component of a liberating act of rejection—one that targeted the larger set of traditional American cultural values upheld by an "older" generation that remained out of touch with the needs, interests, and anxieties of modern youth culture. A common therapeutic feature of both movements was the struggle to express the human agency required to realize the prospect of living on one's own terms outside of the rules and expectations imposed by traditional culture. And both movements also gained strength and momentum from discrete versions of consciousness-raising: for the women's movement, the enlightenment and affirmation to be gained through the political and social interaction of the encounter group setting; in hallucinogenic drug culture, the ability to secure the requisite perceptual distance from one's current mindset to reflect upon it, transform it, or even reject it outright.

On a broad scale, this search for new or renewed perception was rooted in a desire for connection and communication correlating with the goals of other revolutionary movements of the decade. As therapeutic agent, hallucinogenic drug use promised to counteract feelings of isolation and alienation that characterized postwar American society—an issue around which youth cultural values coalesced. As Theodore Roszak explains in his influential 1968 study *The Making of a Counter Culture*, American culture of the early to mid-1960s was "fatally and contagiously diseased" by its impossible-to-disavow commitment to bring about its own destruction through "thermonuclear annihilation":

> And how viciously we ravage our sense of humanity to pretend, even for a day, that such horror can be accepted as 'normal,' as 'necessary'! Whenever we feel inclined to qualify, to modify, to offer a cautions 'yes . . . *but*' to the protests of the young, let us return to this fact as the decisive measure of the technocracy's essential criminality: the extent to which it insists, in the name of progress, in the name of reason, that the unthinkable become thinkable and the intolerable become tolerable. (47)

Daniel Binchbeck argues that the prospect of broad-based Cold War annihilation, which reached its apex for Americans during the 1962 Cuban Missile Crisis, also ultimately intensified the countercultural need for meaning, "self-knowledge, and spiritual illumination" (*The Psychedelic Experience*, xiv). By the mid-1960s, the escalation of the war in Vietnam would keep America's preoccupation with world dominance and destruction close to home.

Precipitating the need for a countercultural, therapeutic restorative was the ascendancy of technocracy, of what Roszak described as "that social form in which an industrial society reaches the peak of its organizational integration" (5), and that derives its momentum from the professional expertise that dictates its indisputable authority in all matters of personal and social life. "With such a society, the citizen, confronted by bewildering bigness and complexity, finds it necessary to defer on all matters to those who know better" (7), Rozsak argues, identifying the cumulative effect of this deferral as an alienation that serves "as the deadening of man's sensitivity to man" (57–58), and that threatens to shape a world where humanity has become subservient to the forces of "conventional scientific respectability" presiding over our access to knowledge. Roszak identifies a restorative to this process of deadening in R. D. Laing's model of ego-loss and rebirth, in a commitment to the "non-intellective capacities of the personality" (49), and ultimately in a challenge to the logic of conventional scientific inquiry—one that refuses to frame human difference in terms of negativity and otherness (49–53). In their very different ways, countercultural factions from the advocates of the radical New Left to the followers of the hippie movement pursued a common goal that Roznak recognizes as an "absurdity" from the perspective of technocratic, expertise-driven, conventional wisdom—"to assert that the essence of human sociability is . . . the communal opening up of man to man" (54). Asserting that the counterculture's common tactical strategy "is grounded in an intense examination of the self, of the buried wealth of personal consciousness" (63), Roszak argues for the political pursuit of radical social change that hinges upon the personal transformation of consciousness, resulting in the development of a humanitarian and empathic relationship between self and other, "therapeutic" in the sense that it facilitates compassion, empathy, and understanding, celebrating the human potential to value multiple perspectives and human difference. Although it was often portrayed as a form of hedonistic self-indulgence, for many the act of ideological rejection and refusal associated with the use of hallucinogenic drugs in the 1960s signaled a reflective, contemplative movement inward that served as a prerequisite to interpersonal, social, and political engagement.[1]

Countercultural movements of the 1960s remained susceptible to hegemonic co-opting by institutions that upheld mainstream cultural values—by stereotyping, and by the peculiar capitalistic process that insidiously transforms a potentially radical force into a marketable, brand-able lifestyle. As discussed in the previous chapter, the American film industry certainly participated in this commodification of whatever was radical about the women's movement and its views of traditional marriage. By the mid-1960s, however, the industry's own transformative process might have accommodated a different set of cinematic products that were more attuned to the box-office dynamics dictated by the widening generation gap, or that less clearly aligned with mainstream cultural ideologies. In this context, it might seem that the cinematic treatment of hallucinogenic drug use would be better positioned to benefit from the contemporary changes in the Hollywood film industry. After all, box-office receipts were dwindling throughout the decade, especially for those big-budgeted releases that continued to attempt (usually unsuccessfully) to appeal to "general" audiences. By 1967, a seemingly more permissive system of self-regulation had been devised, one that differentiated levels of content suitability according to age-based categories and the principle of parental guidance. As it turned out, however, this new permissiveness in cinematic content rarely correlated with any broadening of perspectives on controversial subject matter that challenged the dominant ideology; instead, the new rating system more often provided studios with more opportunities to define expressions of political difference as problematic or aberrant. In its treatment of the potential therapeutic value of youth culture's "illicit" drug use, Hollywood continued to adhere to an outworn model of universal appeal, seeking through both its promotional efforts and its cinematic narratives to subscribe to opposing, incongruous perspectives on a controversial issue.

This chapter focuses upon the cultural confluences, tensions, and contradictions that informed Hollywood's treatment of hallucinogenic drug therapy in the 1960s. The chapter begins with an overview of the psychological, social, political, and cultural factors informing contemporary perspectives on hallucinogenic drug therapy's potential value, setting a context for American cinema's treatment of this issue beginning in 1966, when LSD became classified as an illegal substance, and ending in 1969, when LSD's association with the "cult" behavior of the hippie movement veered the drug's popular perception more directly toward the psychopathological. The industry's tendency to keep seeking universal audience appeal initially resulted in ideologically conflicted productions that appeared to empathize and identify with the concerns of youth culture, while maintaining a condemnatory and judgmental stance aligned with more politically conservative perspectives. By differing means, however, a small set of film releases—some of them mainstream studio products engaging in an almost self-conscious parody of Old Hollywood practices—ultimately intervened in these paradoxical approaches to the matter of drug use and its therapeutic value.

Governmental and Military Applications of LSD Use

As Martin A. Lee and Bruce Shlain assert in *Acid Dreams*, "the central irony of LSD is that it has been used both as a weapon and a sacrament, a mind control drug and a mind-expanding chemical" (xxiii). The hallucinogenic properties of LSD were first recognized in 1943 by the Albert Hofmann, a Swiss pharmaceutical specialist who developed the LSD chemical compound in 1938 in his work for Sandoz Laboratories. By 1951, the CIA began to experiment with LSD as a mind-control or "truth" drug for political interrogation (4), in reaction to anxieties in the early years of the Cold War that China and the Soviet Union might be exploring LSD's potential as an "espionage weapon" (16). Gathering its information from commissioned research scientists, the CIA was receptive to reports that LSD induced and disrupted the user's ability to manage anxiety. In 1953 the Agency mass-purchased the drug from

Sandoz, and by 1954 the American pharmaceutical company Eli Lilly had managed to replicate the substance's formula (26). By the mid-1950s, LSD had become a key instrument in the CIA's Project MKUltra, which experimented with in mind-control techniques during the height of the Cold War; justified as an act of competition with the Soviet Union, the program's reach soon expanded to the point where the CIA conducted random dosing of its own staff and others in an investigation of the drug's effects upon human behavior (27–34). LSD was frequently used in interrogation and torture tactics throughout the late 1950s and early 1960s (19). The military subsequently continued with the CIA's experimentation until the pharmaceutical giant Hoffmann-La Roche provided the United States Army with the drug named BZ, a military weapon much more powerful than LSD, one that entirely incapacitated its subjects and disrupted recollection of their experiences under the drug's influence. The military ultimately preferred BZ also because it was much cheaper to manufacture (41).

Psychotherapeutic Uses of Hallucinogens

The psychiatric community engaged in a number of forms of hallucinogenic drug therapy in the 1950s. LSD was first used in clinical attempts to reproduce psychotic states in "healthy" patients (as well as psychiatrists themselves), especially after noted research scientists such as Dr. Paul Hoch postulated that the chemical substance was "psychomimetic," capable of reproducing many of the same effects as schizophrenia. A 1955 *Saturday Evening Post* article entitled "Help for the Living Dead" affirms the research value of a drug that permits "experimenters . . . to explore the terrible country of the insane on a round-trip ticket which gets them back to normal in a few hours" (Yoder 43). In conjunction with new research into the biochemical bases of human behavior, LSD was used to recreate the sensations and the experience of "madness" in order to lend insight into potential psychopathological cures. As Lee and Shlain suggest, the psychomimetic model, with its pathological basis of "negative states of mind" (54), would later yield to a "psycholytic" approach, in which the psychiatrist administered LSD to the patient as an accelerant to the psychoanalytic process, since the drug facilitated the release of "repressed memories and traumatic experiences" while also making them accessible to recall by the patient and examination by both doctor and patient after the hallucinogen's effects had worn off (Lee 55–56).

Coterminously, the era witnessed the emergence of "psychedelic" therapies that required much higher doses of LSD to help patients to reach the altered states of consciousness required for "healing deep-rooted psychological wounds" (Lee 56). High-dose therapies were subsequently administered successfully to treat alcohol and narcotic addictions (57). Popular press reports in the early 1960s disseminated the potentially therapeutic value of LSD use in professionally monitored settings, often marveling at related scientific advances, and viewing as scientifically progressive the synthetic replication of organic chemical substances that affect human behavior in such positive ways. In a 1963 *Life* magazine article entitled "The Chemical Mind-Changers," for example, Robert Couglan acknowledges the sinister potential of such drugs in mind-control experiments, yet he also advocates for the reflective component of new drug therapies that permit the patient to become a "lucid observer of his own situation" (92), that increase the patient's ability to communicate with his therapist, and that promote "cheerfulness" and human "productivity" (92).

The work of Dr. Timothy Leary would greatly expand the nation's awareness of LSD's therapeutic value even while his notoriety ultimately rendered the government, the psychiatric community, and the popular press more anxious about the drug's potential for abuse. Beginning with his work as a professor at Harvard with Richard Alpert in the early 1960s, Leary's methods were in sync with group psychotherapeutic approaches of the era that emphasized the importance of relationships of collaboration and trust, with doctor and patient sharing decision-making and problem-solving responsibilities. Such features are evident in an experiment that his research team conducted at the Concord State Prison in Massachusetts between 1963 and 1965. Assessing the potential value of hallucinogens in reducing rates of recidivism, the team administered doses of psilocybin to the prisoners, and the experiment was designed according to a group psychotherapeutic model that valued "observation and understanding of the 'here-and-now' experience and behavior" ("A New Behavior Change Program," 61). Leary stressed the importance of objectivity in the therapeutic setting, insisting that "group leaders carefully avoid imposing *their* expectation" (63). A professional decision that many psychiatrists perceived more skeptically was Leary's directive that group leaders take a low dosage of the drug in the first sessions "in order to minimize suspicion on the part of the inmates and to increase the sense of collaborative trust" (63). At the same time, Leary always insisted that "our approach is outside of a medical framework" (64), and that a primary goal of the therapeutic process was to help the patient to attain the requisite psychological distance to observe his own patterns of behavior in an optimal "state of dissociation and detachment." Using the terminology of psychologist Thomas Szasz, Leary describes these behavioral patterns as the "game-quality of human conduct," where the "game" is defined as "any learned behavior sequence with roles, rules, rituals, values, specialized languages and limited goals" (64). Rather than considering his therapeutic subjects as victims of medical illness or psychopathology, Leary emphasized psychedelic therapy's goal of making patients aware of the self-destructive behavioral patterns that were determined by forces outside of their own psyches, and that patients might endlessly repeat unless they were introduced to more workable behavioral patterns, developing alternatives that might correct the subject's lack of agency and feelings of helplessness (64).

The favorable decrease in instances of recidivism that Leary's research team reported was ultimately challenged because of research design flaws,[2] but this did not disrupt the team's determination to create the optimal circumstances for patient success. Leary emphasized the crucial role of "set" and "setting" in determining the outcome of psychedelic therapy, where "set" refers to the therapeutic subject's attitude and perspective in preparation for the psychedelic experience itself, and "setting" refers to the actual physical environment in which the drug is administered. As Lee and Shlain assert, set and setting play such crucial roles in psychedelic drug therapies because "LSD has no standard effects that are purely pharmacological in nature"; indeed, as they explain, this also accounts for the fact that the ego loss and depersonalization effects of the same drug that the CIA and U.S. military were using to increase anxiety in mind-control situations could also be successfully deployed to promote insight, self-reflection, and individual enlightenment (58).

If the success of the Concord Prison Experiment was compromised in part because the researchers had to conduct their work in the less-than-ideal conditions of the prison setting where participants would return to their confinement after a given session, what became known as the "Good Friday Experiment," conducted by Harvard graduate student Walter Pahnke under Leary's direction as advisor in 1962, supported the prospect of more sustained behavioral change under more favorable conditions of setting. According to Rick Doblin, Pahnke hypothesized that the hallucinogen psilocybin could facilitate a "mystical" experience in religiously inclined volunteers who took the drug in a religious setting, and that such experiences could initiate "persisting positive changes in attitudes and behavior" (Doblin, "Pahnke's 'Good Friday Experiment,'" 2). The results of this double-blind experiment, in which psilocybin was administered to a group of divinity students in Boston University's Marsh Chapel, seemed to confirm Pahnke's hypothesis that optimal set and setting were crucial to attaining the desired result of the mystical experience, and a 1991 follow-up study with the original participants further supported Pahnke's hypothesis. Here, participants regularly reported that the hallucinogenic experience had offered them a sense of unity and connectedess that would continue to affect them deeply throughout their lives. As Doblin indicates, some of the self-reports also noted the ways in which the experiment ultimately forged connections between desirable, transcendent psychological states and increased political awareness and sensitivity. "Feelings of unity led many of the subjects to identify with and feel compassion for minorities, women and the environment," Doblin suggests (15). "The feelings of timelessness and eternity reduced their fear of death and empowered the subjects to take more risks in their lives and to participate more fully in political struggles." Self-reports such as the following support his assertions:

> I got very involved with civil rights after that and spent some time in the South. I remember this unity business, I thought there was some link there. . . . There could have been. People certainly don't write about it. They write about it the opposite way, that drugs are an escape from social obligations. That is the popular view. . . . (15)

Leary has been criticized for the apolitical, individual-centered nature of his work in a culture that valued revolutionary and socially active responses to an oppressive cultural climate; indeed, his familiar motto, "turn on, tune in, drop out," became a stereotypical emblem of this insularity. This "either-or" tension between self-reflection and political action also emerges in the relationship between the more overtly political advocates of the New Left and the era's hippies, whose connection to Leary and the "turn on" hallucinogenic drug culture did not dispel their commitment to social values. "They challenged the formidable Western tradition of setting the individual on a pedestal," Timothy Miller asserts, adding that "for the hippies, communal values stood over the rights and privileges of individual persons" (xiv). While the hippies and the New Left held opposing views on the place of hallucinogenic drug use in revolutionary efforts, Roszak asserts that both groups prioritized humanity over doctrine, and that reflection and introspection were inherent in their respective belief systems, which were "grounded in an intensive examination of the self, of the buried wealth of personal consciousness" (63). Indeed, Roszak notes a complementary relationship between the two groups, with the hippies practicing the ideals of what the New Left had conceptualized (96).

LSD in the Popular Press

The historically specific oppositions and tensions at play—CIA instrument of mind control vs. psychotherapeutic agent of insight, technocracy vs. counterculture, inward reflection vs. social and political action—offered the popular news media of the 1960s seemingly limitless options for framing the "issue" of the therapeutic value of hallucinogenic drug use. It was, however, Timothy Leary's 1963 resignation and Richard Alpert's dismissal from Harvard after close CIA scrutiny that ultimately provided the foundation for the media's depiction of LSD and related hallucinogens.[3] Until the early 1960s it was relatively easy for researchers, research universities, and psychiatrists to access quantities of LSD for experimental and psychotherapeutic purposes, yet regulations were progressively imposed thereafter: first, the designation of LSD as an "experimental" drug, thereby revoking its availability to psychiatrists; Congress's 1965 Drug Abuse Control Amendments that resulted in harsh restrictions on psychedelic drug research; the illegalization of the substance in 1966 after Sandoz ceased marketing efforts because of negative publicity; and finally, the reclassification of LSD possession as a felony in 1968 (Lee & Shlain 90–95).

Before the Harvard scandal, the popular press had sought to balance the negative with the potentially positive aspects of LSD therapy, or at least to conditionally accept the value of continuing research on the drug despite an awareness of its potentially sinister use as an instrument of mind control (as documented in "The Chemical Mind-Changers") or the younger generation's growing interest in using the drug recreationally (as expressed in the 1962 *Newsweek* piece "Hallucinations," 56). Almost immediately after the scandal, however, drastic changes began to occur. Some acknowledgment of the therapeutic aspects of LSD certainly continued: a 1965 *New York Times* article discusses its use as an effective pain killer, an accelerant to the psychotherapeutic process in the treatment of neuroses, and a proven treatment for alcoholism (Robinson 50, 57); a 1966 piece in *Life* magazine even suggests that some mathematicians found that the drug lent them insight in their work with abstract theoretical concepts, due to LSD's capacity to alter perspective (Farrell 31). During this aftermath, however, even these occasional affirmations of the drug's benefits were contextualized within larger narratives of disapprobation.

LSD's turn from prospective agent of psychological healing to insidious instrument of mass destruction was orchestrated by an appeal to the absolute, indisputable value of "real" science over what could now be perceived as the pseudo-science of psychedelic studies. As such, the national discourse of LSD therapy came to reflect a distrust of any agent that promoted an altering of the "given" reality that countercultural forces found to be alienating. One prevalent strategy in popular news media was to play upon the anxieties surrounding the very real and already proven science of mind control—one in which the CIA and the military had already been engaging for several years. A late 1963 *Saturday Evening Post* article entitled "The Dangerous Magic of LSD" was one of several sources to provoke the fear that in the wrong hands, LSD could be—and may already have been—used by hostile foreign governments against the interests of the United States: "In the hallucinated state the mind is so suggestible that a skilled psychological manipulator could make black look white. The brainwashed American soldiers in Korea, the political captives of Communism in Europe who confessed to crimes they never committed, may have been mentally altered by hallucinogens" (39). Inherent in this strategy was a concern about the scientifically infinitesimal, micro-minute amount that comprised a potent dosage of the substance lysergic acid diethylamide, set against a seemingly infinite set of potential effects that remained beyond control or predictability. The recent disaster surrounding the "miracle" drug Thalidomide, a medication for morning sickness that resulted in thousands of birth deformities before being taken off the pharmaceutical market in 1961, only exacerbated the skepticism and concern for the as yet unknown side effects of new, complex chemical substances; indeed, the Thalidomide debacle compelled the FDA to start requiring scientists to submit drug research for review in advance, no longer permitting them to interface directly with drug manufacturers to obtain their products (35). In this context, the news media would reference the correlation of LSD use with chromosomal damage (Baumeister & Placidi 37)—a widely circulated myth whose validity was scientifically refuted by the early 1970s—in order to alert the public to yet another increasingly popular chemical substance capable of an irreversible degree of harm that might remain undetectable indefinitely before its results were made manifest. As *Time* magazine suggested, "though 250 micrograms of LSD can be had for $2.50 . . . its cost in potential chromosomal damage and long-lasting psychotic aftereffects is much higher" ("The Hippies," P7). And a 1963 article in *Time* criticizes the recently dismissed Leary and Alpert for their reckless experimentation with a substance so powerful that "as little as four-millionths of an ounce is sometimes enough to throw an emotionally wobbly individual into a mental hospital" ("LSD," 96). Proclaiming that "one pound would be enough to render 4 million people at least temporarily deranged mentally," in 1965 another source's warning that the military operations of unnamed governments (including, perhaps, the

United States) may be "stockpiling" LSD exacerbated public concern to the level of panic about mass destruction in a cultural climate already entrenched in Cold War dynamics and polarities (Robinson 14).

Aligned with Roszak's assertions about the workings of technocracy, the broadening distinction between real science and pseudo-science would compel news sources to differentiate between levels of "authoritative" professional expertise within the larger professional psychotherapeutic community. *Time* deployed this strategy of hierarchizing professionals in 1963 in the same article that announced Leary and Alpert's departure from Harvard, proclaiming that "Now the cosmic ball is over" (96), decrying the researchers' unprofessional misbehavior, and further undermining their authority by stating that "Psychiatrists and other physicians in general" agree about the dangers of LSD usage, while conceding that clinical psychologists are more on the "borderline." Three months later, *Newsweek* reiterated the strategy by suggesting that "Leary's and Alpert's use of hallucinatory drugs is embarrassing to other researchers" ("No Illusions," 93); three years later, the strategy was picked up once again in a *Time* piece published on the occasion of Leary's arrest at the Mexican–U.S. border for marijuana possession, referencing the scientist's continuing "wave of irresponsible experimentation" and announcing that Leary had opened "a sort of Hallucination Hilton" near Acapulco after being evicted from the Millbrook, New York, estate where he had relocated after leaving Cambridge ("The Silver Snuffbox," 97).

This dichotomization of "real" science and pseudo-science also promoted a distrust of any inward-directed, reflective, or spiritual exploration, despite its claims of therapeutic potential. Accordingly, it was not only the case that, as Lee and Shlain suggest, "psychedelics were out of kilter with the basic assumptions of Western medicine" (89), but also that, as Baumeister and Placidi argue, "the contemplative approach to life has never flourished in America," and that especially after the Great Depression, drug use resonated as antithetical to a national ethos of "productive" behavior (44). It consequently became convenient to mock or travesty any cultural practice that praised or elevated self-enlightenment as a life goal. "Eastern mysticism vastly attracts the LSD set because their ideal drugged state, a passive, egoless union with the infinite, resembles that sought by yogis, lamas, and the like," the *Saturday Evening Post* proclaimed, adding that "With their junkie jargon [Leary's followers] mingle the terminology of the Oriental sects" (Kobler 35). With the publication of the highly influential *The Psychedelic Experience: A Manual Based on the Tibetan Book of the Dead* in 1964, in which Leary, Alpert, and Ralph Metzner reconfigured the original Buddhist treatise as an instructional resource guide to assist LSD users to attain a state of "liberation, illumination, or enlightenment" (3), the press's denigration of the group's spiritualist endeavors only proliferated.[4]

The citation of scientific authorities within the medical and psychotherapeutic communities often accentuated this distrust in spiritual enlightenment by polarizing those forms of human endeavor that directed individuals toward recognizable and tangible goals, and those acts of introspection that by contrast were depicted as senseless, pointless activities discouraged by a society that prevails upon its citizens to be productive and to focus upon and better themselves. An article in 1966 quotes noted psychiatrist Sidney Cohen to lend credence to the perspective that LSD users constitute "life's losers—dissatisfied, restless people, afflicted with problems they can't handle," adding that "a lot of them wallow in self-pity and denigrate those who have made it in the 'square' world" ("An Epidemic of Acid Heads," 56). As the decade progressed, it became more common within the popular news media industries to develop vivid scenarios detailing the harrowing transformation of drug users who may have initially decided to pursue self-insight, but that ultimately became representatives of an impressionable, immature youth generation prone to bad decision-making. A 1966 piece in *Life* magazine explains that

> No matter how thrilling and illuminating a trip may be, only a good mind can return from it without some serious re-entry problems. Many perceive their past life as the pathetic, surrendering performance of an absurd cosmic clown, and they change it accordingly: get divorced, quit work, read aloud from *The Book of the Dead*. They discover that life is only a game, then begin playing it with less and less skill. Their vision becomes a beguiling scrim drawn over a life of deepening failure. (Farrell 30)

Instead of ameliorating public concern about the effects of the drug, the popular press transformed the criminalization of LSD in 1966 into yet another opportunity to heighten anxieties. Concern now re-focused upon the likelihood that those individuals who would risk incarceration to use the drug were precisely those who were most likely to threaten the helpless and the innocent. Reports alerted Americans that "the Humane Society is picking up disoriented dogs," and that married couples were dosing their children, leaving them on their own to "spend the day freaking out in the woods" so that husband and wife could take their own LSD trips in private (Farrell 32).

In 1966 and after, media coverage of the LSD "crisis" would alert parents to remain vigilant in the face of an insidious chemical substance that threatened to destroy their children. With LSD's potentially therapeutic functions within and beyond the professional psychotherapeutic community largely cast aside, the popular press exacerbated this threat with suggestions that hallucinogenic drug use was now prevalent in high schools, and that youth culture's obsession with drug experimentation readily progressed from seemingly less harmful substances to LSD: "most have tried marijuana, then the amphetamines, before 'graduating' to what they regard as the ultimate in kicks" ("An Epidemic of Acid Heads," 56).

If the identities of the sordid assembly of individuals who epitomized "typical" LSD users remained unspecified for some time except for the frightening possibility that they might include "your children," the emerging hippie culture offered popular news media a convenient prototype of the ultimate offender. After swiftly enumerating the praiseworthy values of a subculture committed to happiness, honesty, altruism, and nonviolence, *Time* magazine's 1967 cover story exposé on hippies proceeds to place the pursuit of these values in the domain of the abnormal, decrying "the unreality that permeates hippiedom, a cult whose mystique derives essentially from the influence of hallucinogenic drugs" ("The Hippies," P1). With his connections to communes, spiritual ancestors, and ego loss, the figure of the hippie, as *Time* would depict him, provided America with the composite face of, and scapegoat for, America's "drug problem." They chose to tune out because they are "unable to reconcile themselves to the stated values and implicit contradictions of contemporary Western society" ("The Hippies," P1), and what the news media would portray as a symptom of weakness was precisely what Roszak asserted to be the ultimate sign of the counterculture's remarkable strength—a conscious decision to refute the values and disavow the power of the prevailing technocracy. As punishment for this refusal, the hippie would bear the national stigma of social, psychological, and ideological dysfunction. If, as Lee and Shlain suggest, introspective approaches to human experience in the 1960s correlated with an ethic of pleasure that ran counter to the "Protestant Ethic mentality [that] tends to maintained a strict dichotomy between what 'feels good' and what is 'good for you'" (43-44), hippies embodied a hedonistic pleasure ethic correlated with unproductive inertia. Like much of the decade's counterculture, they were criticized not only for "condemning virtually every aspect of the American scene," but also for failing to devise any "debatable alternatives" to the world they rejected ("The Hippies," P8).[5] And as the embodiment of all that was threatening about hallucinogenic drug culture, the hippies and LSD became less an emblem of therapeutically expanded consciousness than a rapidly spreading pathology; indeed, the *Time* magazine exposé secures this link to illness by noting that the unsanitary participants in the 1967 "Summer of Love" left the city of San Francisco with outbreaks of hepatitis, venereal disease, typhus, and malnutrition.

Cinematic Perspectives on Countercultural LSD Use

A ribbon-cutting ceremony is disrupted when Mickey Dolenz jumps off a bridge and propels himself underwater, guided by mermaids. Later, shirtless in the desert, Mickey climbs a sand dune where he encounters a gigantic Coca-Cola vending machine that takes his change but never dispenses his selected beverage. Mickey, Mike, Davy, and Peter lie engulfed in a massive mound of human hair that is being sucked up by a vacuum cleaner. After Victor Mature appears as a giant on a Western movie set, shots of cartoon violence are intercut with newsreel footage of the war in Vietnam. A journey traces a pattern transporting the foursome through various surreal states, only to reveal its trajectory as an infinite loop leading back to the opening scene of Mickey once again jumping off of the same bridge, with all four Monkees now shown to be trapped in an oversized fish tank.

With its radical cuts, liberation from the constraints of time and space, recursively embedded self-references, non-linear narrative, stirring superimpositions, and emphasis upon bold, saturated colors, Bob Rafelson's 1968 odyssey *Head* might—in an alternate universe or some other cinematic marketplace—have provided a suitable model for a psychedelic, countercultural American cinema that celebrated the hallucinogenic drug experience as therapeutic perceptual liberation, replete with incisive cultural and political commentary on the prevailing contradictions of the "straight world" and its hypocritical preoccupations with order, authority, and mass destruction. And it might have done so, as *Head* did, without ever representing or referencing the actual experience of using a hallucinogenic drug. With the notable exception of the bold, saturated colors that had become a staple of psychedelic cinema by this time, *Head* instead materialized more as a brazen yet solipsistic anomaly in a cinematic mode of production that imposed the moralistic logic of cause-and-effect—of symptom diagnosis and treatment—upon any countercultural attempt to radically re-envision the contemporary world. It would, however, be inaccurate to label even the early years of psychedelic cinema's brief run in the late 1960s as ideologically monolithic. As the following discussion suggests, the film industry's course did indeed run parallel with the popular news media in its depiction of hallucinogenic drug use as an insidious, pathological phenomenon, even while exploiting the potential for sensationalistic treatment of the phenomenon itself. Paradoxically, the film industry also diverged from the popular news media—to varying degrees of effectiveness, and often with unexpected results—by attempting not to align with either side of the generation gap, thereby reiterating its struggle to target multiple sectors of a broader audience whose perspectives on hallucinogenic drug use were largely out of sync.

As Harry Benshoff explains in his illuminating study, the LSD film originated in the sexploitation, social problem, and horror genres, as early as 1959, with William Castle's *The Tingler* (34). Another key factor influencing the industry's subsequent attempts to address hallucinogenic drug culture was that they did not occur until the start of 1967, shortly after the criminalization of LSD, by which time the government had curtailed most of the psychopharmaceutical community's research on related drug therapies. This sense of the illegal, of the criminal, frames the release of *Hallucination Generation* (Edward Mann, released in December 1966), *Riot on Sunset Strip* (Arthur Dreifuss, released in March 1967) and *The Love-Ins* (Arthur Dreifuss, released in July 1967), all of which entirely disavow the previous psychotherapeutic history of the drug. Both media and governmental efforts were by this time primarily devoted to alerting the public to its dangers, and accordingly, most of these early films advance a blatantly conservative pro-social agenda. After a prologue that contrasts recent advances in the nation's space program with drug-induced, equally "far out" experiences that "often turned out to be one way trips," *Hallucination Generation* proceeds with the voiceover of central protagonist Bill (Danny Stone), who previews the plot trajectory of a "trip" that will take us "step by stupid step" from mistake, to failure, to crime, to madness. The film delivers on its promise: to repay his gambling debts, this Ibiza drifter agrees to commit a robbery organized by the criminal mastermind Eric (George Montgomery), who overdoses Bill with LSD to release him from any ethical inhibitions. A freaked-out Bill convinces himself that he has committed murder during the botched robbery attempt, and by the ending he has isolated himself in a Barcelona monastery, nervously awaiting his apprehension by the local authorities. Indeed, all trips are bad trips in these films: the dose administered to southern California high school student Andy (Mimsy Farmer) in *Riot on Sunset Strip* becomes the prelude to a gang rape; *The Love-Ins* finds one freaked-out hippy leaping from a window to his death, while another user who can never get enough LSD in her system participates in a psychedelic ballet/stage production of *Alice in Wonderland*, endlessly repeating that "I'm Alice—I'm really Alice."

While *Hallucination Generation* sustains a constant high-pitched state of alert to its undifferentiated audiences, *The Love-Ins* stages interpersonal conflicts that purport to acknowledge the generation gap, and to enable viewers to appear to come to their own conclusions about the dangers of LSD. Rather than ultimately designating a parent or other "square" authority figure as the voice of reason, *The Love-Ins* strategically shifts alliances in mid-narrative. After a sympathetic initial portrayal of Dr. Jonathan Barnett (Richard Todd), a college professor who resigns from his position in alliance with students Larry (James MacArthur) and Susan (Patricia Cross) after the university expels them for publishing an underground newspaper, the narrative proceeds to cast doubt upon Barnett's motives when it is revealed that years earlier he had written an academic paper extolling the use of LSD "to explore the inner self." After the ex-professor attracts a devoted coterie of hippie followers in Haight-Ashbury, ex-student James confronts the now megalomaniacal Barnett over his mindless devotion to LSD (see fig. 4.1). In the process James reveals the corrupt nature of this middle-aged advocate of reflection and self-exploration who manipulates others to serve his will—a "healer" even more hypocritical than the "square" representatives of the older generation. Contemporary critics were attuned to such manipulations: the *Motion Picture Herald*'s review of *The Love-Ins* notes that "while seeming

Figure 4.1. At a psychedelic party, Guru Dr. Jonathan Barnett (Richard Todd, far right) presides on his throne with followers Larry Osborne (James MacArthur, 2nd from right), Patricia Cross (Susan Oliver, 2nd from left) and Elliott (Mark Goddard, far left) in *The Love-Ins* (Arthur Dreifuss, Columbia Pictures/Four-Leaf Productions, 1967). Digital frame enlargement.

to take a stand that those who 'tune out' on our conformist society are engaging in a legitimate form of social protest, the film changes course at about the midway to preach the evils and dangers of 'mind-expanding' drugs, purportedly the staff of life for the hippie community" (Oshinsky).[6]

Despite such attempts to appeal to both sides of the generation gap, however, the early films ultimately align morally and moralistically with the anti-drug perspective of the older generation, even as they exploit youth culture's exotic excursions into the unpredictable world of hallucinogens. This alliance is especially apparent in the films' promotional strategies. In conjunction with a series of taglines featuring the terms "maryjane," "grass," and "acid," one of the display ads for *Riot on Sunset Strip* reads, "PARENT'S NOTE: If you don't dig the following, ask your kids . . . They can explain it to you" (*Riot on Sunset Strip* Pressbook, Ad Mat 206). And if the films themselves comprise voyeuristic explorations of something "different" and unfamiliar to the older generation, while retaining the guise of objective presentation, publicity discourse serves to enhance a sense of the countercultural, exploitatively summoning the uninitiated to a shocking encounter with the other[7]: "Meet the Teenyboppers—with their too-tight capris," reads another advertisement for *Riot on Sunset Strip*, "The Pot-Partyers . . . The Hippies . . . out for a New Thrill and a New Kick! The Most Shocking Film of Our Generation" (*Riot on Sunset Strip* Pressbook, Ad Mat 310).

The early films condemn any reference to the therapeutic dimension of the hallucinatory experience, with the guiding human agent of therapeutic change taking on the identity of a false prophet in ways that echo the popular press's contemporaneous treatment of the fallen intellectual Timothy Leary. If Leary himself emphasized the crucial role of the guide who was charged with arranging the proper set and setting for the hallucinogenic experience, in *Hallucination Generation* the guide is transformed into a corrupt, menacing, self-serving figure, audiotaping Bill's slurred, incoherent speech during the acid trip ("I come from an ancient people. I have blue blood.") so that he can later threaten him with blackmail. When Eric's group intentionally overdoses Bill, Eric tells them that "You'll have to keep him that way or he'll never go through with [the robbery]." In *Riot on Sunset Strip*, after Andy politely refuses the dose of LSD that Herby (Schuyler Haydn) offers her, he drops a dose in her drink without telling her, before leading her up the stairs of an old Hollywood mansion to be gang raped. *The Love-Ins* offers the most exaggerated version of the corrupt guide in Barnett, whose communitarian values and advocacy for peace and love gradually degenerate into the pronouncements of a fame-obsessed, self-proclaimed messiah figure, a false idol who literally sits at a throne above his tripping subjects, directing them to "Be more, sense more, love more," and barking orders at the technicians arranging the acoustics for his stadium rally: "When I speak, give me all the volume you can." Barnett is equally insensitive to those who remain closest to him, including Patty, whom he commands to "get rid of it" when she reveals that she is pregnant with his child, since family life would taint the desired image that he seeks to project.

"I created a martyr," Larry realizes, after confessing to the police that he is the person who has just shot and killed Barnett, as he witnesses the immediate ascendency of Barnett's successor-idol at the rally—an idol to which the followers respond with the same maniacal devotion they had offered the just-dethroned Barnett. The realization of the corrupt LSD figurehead's irresistibly seductive power and charisma—attributes that would take their most menacing context in media reports of the Charles Manson murders in 1969—served as a stern warning to parents who were being bombarded by news of the dangers that hallucinogenic drugs captivating a younger generation that was desperate to try almost anything to be different from their elders. All that parents might offer were vigilance and an openness to communication, as police lieutenant Walt Lorimer (Aldo Ray) learns, almost too late, after being informed of his daughter's gang rape in *Riot on Sunset Strip*. "I got sick and tired of being alone," Andy confesses to him after the brutal incident at the mansion, and the film clarifies that her victimization under the influence of the "wrong crowd" resulted directly from failed parental guidance—an alcoholic mother, and a father devoted only to his job, and whose hypocritical proclamation in a broadcast interview about today's youth that "these are our sons, our daughters" compels his own daughter to turn off her television in disgust. Indeed, it is only Walt's success as a professional mediator between disaffected youth and Sunset Strip business owners that ultimately forces his awareness of how inept he has been as a father to Andy.

Breakthrough Efforts of American International Pictures

"I was afraid of getting the LSDT's," confesses Bill in the throes of his very bad trip in *Hallucination Generation*. "I thought a drink might help." While these early hallucinogenic narratives disseminated misinformation about LSD—which research had already proven not to be habit forming, unlike the chemically addictive properties of legal substances like alcohol and tobacco—American International Pictures (AIP) would achieve something of a breakthrough in the therapeutic perspective on LSD with its 1967 late summer release of Roger Corman's *The Trip*. The film clearly qualifies as exploitation cinema, but in this case the filmmakers attempt a more "authentic" version of hallucinogenic drug use, one in which the therapeutic value of the drug experience itself was not automatically negated by judgment or condemnation. Rather than suggesting that the film lends support to personal experimentation with LSD, however, it would be more accurate to assert that *The Trip* is unique in its willingness to accommodate a tension between the therapeutic and the pro-social, and also in its escape from the logic of either/or binaries that pervaded the representation of LSD-centered experiences up to this point.

If previous AIP releases had been promoted as "realistic" depictions of LSD experiences, *The Trip* extended this notion of authenticity into the circumstances of its production. As Mark Thomas McGee notes, as part of the research for the film, Corman and his initial screenwriter accompanied the crew to Big Sur, where each took his turn with an acid trip while the other observed and notated the experience (253–54); in a 1967 review in *Films and Filming*, Corman indicated that he also discussed hallucinogenic experiences with over fifty LSD users (41). After two of the resulting versions of the screenplay were scrapped, AIP commissioned Jack Nicholson as screenwriter because of his own experience with LSD.[8] The film's commitment to authenticity, as well as its therapeutic dimension, extended to the representation of its central tripping protagonist, television commercial director Paul Groves (Peter Fonda). Introduced to Max (Dennis Hopper) at the Psychedelic Temple, Groves admits that he is drawn to LSD out of curiosity and a desire for insight and reflection. The ensuing drug experience offers a fascinating series of representations of the tripper's thoughts and fears, as he confronts his own death, conflicting sexual desires in light of his impending divorce, and the lack of personal fulfillment he derives from his professional identity. When Max asks, "what's the first word that comes into your mind about TV commercials?" Paul's instantaneous response is "Lies." Compared with the earlier films, *The Trip* is also devoted to an authentic and unsensationalized portrayal of the figure of the guide, closely following the detailed prescriptions that Leary had outlined for this important role. John (Bruce Dern) is established early on as Paul's devoted friend, meticulously preparing his subject for the drug experience by showing him the drug capsules, explaining that a supply of Thorazine is on hand in case of a "bad trip," soliciting his musical preferences, and ensuring him that "You must have absolute confidence and faith in me. . . . Turn off your mind, relax, and just float downstream." While Paul's trip leads him to dark places and paranoiac hallucinations (including his unshakable conviction at one point that John has been killed), the film balances the profoundly negative aspects of the journey with moments of celebration and insight. Early on, Paul describes the feeling of his trip in terms of energy, caressing a round paperweight as he exclaims, "That's the sun in my hands, man"; peering at his mirrored reflection in a later scene, he proclaims that "I can see right into my brain."

Aligned with this emphasis upon authenticity, realism and balance, the film's ending—at least as Corman originally conceived it—retains ambiguity regarding the extent to which the protagonist's trip has fulfilled the promise of providing Paul a renewed perspective. His final conversation with Glenn (Sally Sachse), with whom he has just had sex at a beachside residence, remains inconclusive:

SALLY: Did you find what you were looking for? The insight?
PAUL: I think I love you.
SALLY: And everybody else.
PAUL: Yeah, and everybody else.
SALLY: It's easy now. Wait till tomorrow.
PAUL: Yeah. I'll think about that tomorrow.

In one sense, the lack of resolution only enhances the authenticity of Paul's experience, since it demonstrates an acknowledged reality specific to the therapeutic dynamic—that the insights experienced in the immediate moment provide no guarantee of sustained future change. Discussing the film after its showing on Turner Classic Movies, however, Corman indicates that the film's final shot—a zoom in to a freeze frame of Paul's face overlaid by a panel of cracked glass—was inserted at AIP's insistence, to ensure audiences that Paul's trip was a bad trip. Additionally, as McGee indicates, producers James Nicholson and Samuel Arkoff "got an attack of cold feet when it came to the release of the film," adding a forward "warning that drug experimentation was dangerous" (256).

The pro-social nature of this ideological framing device informs the studio's ideas for advertising slogans.[9] Some of these resemble the exploitation strategies used to promote the earlier films, with references to the "newest cult of the sicknik generation" and promises that *The Trip* will provide "a shocking inside view of the weird world of pills and parties." There are also various clever acronyms, including the tagline "This is the pill they call a Lovely Sort of Death," which was eventually adopted in display advertisements. Most curious, however, is the appearance of a slogan idea that aligns with the original intention to retain ambiguity and dispel binaries in judgment of the hallucinatory drug experience: "Is it Love Sex Delight or Lonliness [sic] Sorrow Depravity. Find the answer for you.... To some of you it may open new doors of perception. To others it may shock—even as it fascinates." In the context of the studio's imposed additions and changes, the highlighting of such ambiguities might resonate as just another exploitation strategy, a way of feigning an objectivity in representation that the narrative ultimately undermines. At the same time, the framing of opposing interpretive options as equally accessible to the viewer ("Find the answer for you") underscores the integrity of Leary's emphasis upon the important roles that set and setting play in determining the "course" of the hallucinogenic drug experience—of explaining how the same chemical substance can, under different circumstances, produce a good or a bad trip. Despite AIP's last-minute manipulations, *The Trip* remains among the first psychedelic films to overtly honor differences of perspective among viewers. In the AIP liner notes to the film, Corman clarifies that "Although we will not attempt to delve into the pros and cons of the use of LSD in *The Trip*, we will provide the audience with more experience than anyone has yet dared to show on the subject. Then if anyone wishes to make a judgment on LSD they'll have something on which to base their decision" (Liner Notes, Margaret Herrick Library). The critical community largely acknowledged the sincerity of Corman's conviction to objectivity. A reviewer for the *Los Angeles Free Press* commented that "Corman is wise enough . . . not to harangue against LSD usage," and he continues by describing the addition of the "disclaimer" and the shot of the cracked glass as "obviously forced gimmicks" that do not controvert the fact that "Corman takes no overt position on the subject" of LSD use (Youngblood 13).[10]

AIP's subsequent 1968 release, *Wild in the Streets*, continues in this vein of accommodating opposing audience perspectives, even as it also adopts a unique stance that overtly *embraces* the inherent contradictions of attempting to appeal to disparate viewpoints on LSD use. The sense of contradiction also informs the film's handling of the hallucinogen's therapeutic potential. While the narrative elaborates a hyperbolic, deeply satirical, yet ultimately nightmarish vision of establishment culture's fears regarding the atrocities that a politically empowered youth culture might carry out, the film also remains grounded in historical circumstances more realistic and topically current than *The Trip* or any of its antecedents, interacting with the social and political tensions of the present moment. Released in an election year and shortly before the National Democratic Convention in Chicago (the city where the film would also premiere),[11] *Wild in the Streets* is prescient regarding the police violence that would characterize that event, while harshly criticizing the hypocrisies of a federal government that was willing to send teenagers to die overseas in an undeclared war even as it denied them the right to vote.[12]

Wild in the Streets reworks and upends the moralistic conventions of the hallucinogenic drug film that earlier AIP narratives had established, and in its initially heroic yet ultimately megalomaniacal leader Max Frost (Christopher Jones) the film finds a suitable vehicle for critically examining the insidious ideological forces that threaten to silence an increasingly rebellious youth culture. If earlier films thematizing hallucinogenic drug use blamed inattentive or uncaring parents for their children's corruption, the high-pitched invective launched at the older generation in *Wild in the Streets* denigrates the notion of parental "guidance" altogether. Before Max ever appears onscreen, his mother Daphne (Shelley Winters) exclaims that "I never wanted a baby," and in the opening scenes his parents bicker over aspects of child-rearing and parental responsibility that they clearly abhor. Daphne is intrigued rather than concerned when she discovers her son distilling LSD in a homemade lab in their basement, and throughout the film she clings to the shield of Max's growing notoriety for her own public recognition. The veneer of respectability covering the "normalized" family life of presidential candidate Johnny Fergus (Hal Holbrook) begins to crumble when a swift slap to his son's face echoes the physical abuse that the child Max had suffered at the film's beginning, and the tainting of Fergus's preferred image as ideal father soon extends to his ineffectiveness as a prospective national leader. Lacking a sound, viable platform of his own, Johnny becomes more and more dependent upon Max's support to bolster his chances to win the election.

At the same time, *Wild in the Streets* constructs no heroic role model in Max, nor even a profound or logical thinker. Charismatic as he initially seems, Max is framed by extremes and contradictions, insisting that the voting age be lowered to fourteen only because his brain-child accountant has just reached that age, and brazenly shouting "down with experience" to the cheering masses after he is accused of lacking the requisite preparation for the presidency. Still, compared to the empty megalomaniacal ambitions of Professor Barnett in *The Love-Ins*, Max remains politically passionate and focused. He energizes the younger generation by successfully reversing the corrupt power dynamics of the ruling government, promising liberation with his pronouncement that "They won't draft us; we'll draft them!" Yet the sense of reversal specific to Max's revolutionary strategy replays the same power dynamics that he finds so oppressive in his parents' generation, and rather than developing communication strategies to bridge the generation gap, he instigates more divisions and rifts. "I don't want to live to be thirty," he announces early in the film. "Thirty's death, baby." Accordingly, once he is elected as president, Max creates a law that forces all citizens to retire at this "death" age, and by age thirty-five to be relocated to concentration camps where they will be rendered interminably harmless through massive, compulsory doses of LSD. Max's own susceptibility to the realities of chronological progression remains hidden to him until the closing scenes, when he is finally forced to confront the inherent paradox of the revolutionary, age-based political dynamic he has set in motion: haunted by the implications of Fergus's youngest son's biting proclamation that the twenty-four-year-old president is already "old," Max ultimately finds cause for self-reflection, yet he actively resists this insight through pathetic displays that reassert his own power and influence. In the film's final sequence, Max mercilessly crushes a crawfish that a group of children have adopted as a pet, daring his young victims to challenge him in this brazen display of his authority. Ultimately, Max's "revolution" amounts to little more than the tenuous substitution of one seemingly outworn power dynamic with the next.

Strategies of reversal similarly inform the film's treatment of LSD's psychotherapeutic value. Rather than serving as an advocate for the American public's unregulated, universal access to a drug noted for its potential to yield self-insight, and that segments of the counterculture have adopted as a sign of their rejection of "straight" values, Max deals with the hallucinogenic substance exclusively on an economic basis, benefitting from his keen understanding of the laws of supply and demand. Although *Wild in the Streets* never explains how Max has become a Beverly Hills millionaire and savvy business mogul by the age of twenty-two, the film implies that he has amassed his fortune through the success of his rock band and the large-scale manufacture, distribution, and sale of the same LSD whose formula he was perfecting in his parents' basement; this also explains his access to the gallons of the hallucinogenic drug that his crew dumps into the DC water supply to make members of Congress bend to their master's will. Max never doses himself, however, and his identity as a savvy hallucinogenic drug entrepreneur distinguishes him from the stereotyped figure of the blissed-out drug guru and false messiah that the mainstream news and culture industries found so revolting. Yet the film's most dramatic reversal comes with Max's savvy decision to reverse and overturn the prevailing therapeutic rhetoric surrounding the same hallucinogenic substance that had caused so much public anxiety among the older generation—and that had also emerged as such a powerful countercultural symbol for imaging and realizing the radical reconfiguration of a senselessly violent, oppressive, society—as a weapon of mind control that harks back to the federal government's own original uses of LSD in the Cold War during the 1950s and early 1960s. While the set and setting may differ, it remains clear that just as the CIA and the military had used the drug as a weapon to break down enemy defenses, Max's band of revolutionaries devises a scheme that relies upon LSD's capacity (at least as mainstream culture understood it) to induce an extended state of disorientation that would render its users docile and compliant. The representation of the concentration camps also alludes to *Shock Corridor* and other films that provided eager viewers with a glimpse of life in the insane asylum, curiously highlighting the connections to schizophrenia that were proposed in psychomimetic applications of the drug, but that by 1968 had largely been abandoned. Rather than seeming retrograde or naïve, the film's references to these elements of LSD's historical past serve as ironic political commentary on "official" uses of the drug that have been sanctioned by "experts" in the intelligence and psychiatric communities—uses that were now being deployed to overturn the same technocracy from which they originated.

"Is this the way the world will end?" reads one of the proposed advertising slogans for the film (Advertising Slogans, Margaret Herrick Library), and AIP's extensive pressbook reads like the transmitted newsfeed of a sci-fi dystopia, with articles headlining Max's "reign of terror" and his directive to send the "elderly" to concentration camps. One article entitled "Prison Camps Over 30!" offers an "eye-witness report" from a desperate citizen currently incarcerated in "Paradise Camp 23," a hellish place resembling an "insane asylum," who struggles to disseminate this urgent, desperate, written plea for salvation before the prison guards detect her (Pressbook, Margaret Herrick Library). These promotional strategies highlight the cultural anxieties that the film was targeting for 1968 audiences, and critical responses to *Wild in the Streets* were wildly mixed. One repeated complaint was that the film attempted to appeal to both sides of the generation gap, fueling adults' fears about youth culture even as it offered teenagers a fantasy vision of control over their own destinies.[13] A perceptive *New York Times* piece on the contemporaneous controversy of lowering the voting age to 18 notes a common contemporary public presumption—one that *Wild in the Streets* exploits—of an overwhelmingly liberal consensus among younger would-be voters (Hacker 6), and indeed, many critics of the era bemoaned the model of polarization that the film supported. *Life* magazine suggested that the film's reliance on stereotyped version of youth and adult culture subverted its political force ("Overpraised Quickie"), while the *Los Angeles Times* recognized a paradox in "a picture that's aimed directly at youthful audiences yet tells them if they ultimately took over the world they'd turn into fascists," adding that the film's exploitation of cultural anxieties about LSD undermined and disavowed the potential for therapeutically beneficial uses of the drug that scientific research had explored prior to the drug's criminalization (Thomas, "'Wild in the Streets' Opens").

If the outrageous, anxiety-inducing elements of *Wild in the Streets* emerge from the film's insistence upon an unbreachable communicative divide between generations, two notable, subsequent releases of 1968 embraced a less ominous and more accommodating perspective on the countercultural spirit of what Theodore Roszak would call "the communal opening up of man to man" (54) by linking the values of respect, connection, compassion, and mutual understanding to the countercultural use of mind-altering drugs. Even though marijuana rather than LSD serves as the agent of personal transformation in the first of these, the fall 1968 release *I Love You, Alice B. Toklas* (Hy Averback, 1968), the film's perspective on hippie culture and the therapeutic value of mind-altering drugs remains noteworthy. Released by Warner Bros-Seven Arts, the film reiterates the trend of playing to both sides of the generation gap, but in a way that is antithetical to the polarizing approach of *Wild in the Streets*. *Toklas* traces the central protagonist's experience in a personal journey of self-discovery that yields its insights through his active engagement in his own decision-making process. The opening section of the film places its representative of establishment culture, Los Angeles attorney Harold Fine (Peter Sellers), in various situations of confinement that reflect his sense of personal and social disconnection. In one scene, as his fiancée Joyce (Joyce Van Patten) compels him to agree upon a wedding date, Harold expresses neither enthusiasm for the forthcoming ritual nor any pronounced resistance to it, partly because he is more preoccupied at the moment with the fact that his car has been hemmed in at the parking garage. With no way out, his immediate predicament is "resolved" only by a car crash, which results in the straight-laced attorney being issued a "flower power" loaner car at his auto body repair shop.

Thus begins Harold's unlikely introduction to a hippie counterculture whose fascination for the protagonist the film conveys through an opening up of both physical space and alternative ideological possibilities. Commissioned by his wealthy mother (Jo Van Vleet) to track down hippie brother Herbie (David Arkin) at his Venice Beach shack, Harold becomes intrigued at the concept of a free clothes market, even while remaining troubled by what his mother calls Herbie's "LSD clothes." Harold becomes more connected with the countercultural community through Herbie's hippie friend Nancy (Leigh Taylor-Young) who later bakes him a batch of her "magic brownies" as an expression of gratitude for his hospitality. His drug experience is catalytic, and before long he has left Joyce at the altar, shed most of his possessions, sported a long-haired wig, and invited Nancy to move in with him.

As a major studio release, *I Love You, Alice B. Toklas*'s take on the counterculture and its agents of spiritual transformation is often touristic, yet its commitment to a central protagonist who learns directly from experience in unfamiliar cultural territory marks the film as unique, even if this countercultural immersion soon leaves Harold feeling just as alienated as he did as a dispassionate advocate of the traditional marriage institution and the dubious accomplishments of his law career. As it turns out, Harold's ultimate rejection of the hippie scene stems from new insights about boundaries and possessions: after his apartment transforms into a hippie hangout inhabited by too many uninvited dropouts who never wash the dishes or dispose of the trash, Harold finds himself longing for something else. When Nancy begins to read his affection for her as possessive, she warns him that "you're making a marriage scene out of it," and that his attitude is "very unhip." As he discovers, living in a boundary-free culture turns out not to be what Harold wants after all, and the film's closing scenes find Harold first escaping his home to return to Joyce, next leaving her at the altar yet again (!), and ultimately choosing to proceed directionless on his own. When a stranger on the street asks where he is headed, Harold replies, "I don't know, and I don't care. But there's got to be something beautiful out there. There's got to be, I know it."

This ending might be perceived as equivocal, as it refrains from routing Harold on either of the paths before him, yet it also marks *I Love You, Alice B. Toklas* as a distinctive film that occasionally trivializes and typecasts both the technocratic "establishment" and the resistant counterculture, but that also points out the merits and pratfalls of both paths without vilifying either of them, all while valuing the process of its protagonist's personal discovery over any unsolicited advice. Even though the film strives to address both sides of the generation gap, contemporary critics found its sense of balance and even its lack of resolution to be refreshing. *Newsweek* exclaimed that "the movie displays all the virtues and vices of a pot trip itself, at once giggly, marvelously wild and freewheeling, pointless and directionless" ("Forbidden Fruitcake"), while *The Hollywood Reporter* commented that the film "panders to no group, and exploits none" (Mahoney, "Alice B. Toklas").

Consonant with its focus upon marketing and box-office potential, *Variety*'s review of the film illuminates not only *Toklas*'s strategies of audience address, but also a broader issue of how the film industry was promoting such "adult" subject matter pertaining to the counterculture and the sexual revolution after the mid-decade demise of the Production Code:

> Whether this [box-office] potential will be realized will depend on the sales campaign. Film is not heavy-handed in its approach

either to hippie life, or to what is considered 'normal' modes of behavior. Instead, there is a sympathetic look at the advantages and disadvantages of each. Thus a campaign which aims too exclusively for the mod market may alienate older, squarer patrons, many of whom should enjoy the pic immensely. Film is too good to be impaired by a one-sided sales pitch. (*Variety*)

The "problem" inherent in *Variety*'s assessment involves the matter of how film marketing strategies might *in themselves* resolve the generation gap, and also how Hollywood might start making counterculture-based films for which marketing strategies to attract both older and younger viewers might be devised. This is paradoxical, however, since the notion of a "counterculture" is *itself* inseparable from an association with the generation gap. As in cases such as *The Trip*, the only way in which the film industry was imagining a bridging of the generation gap was by overlaying a template of judgment upon a therapeutic countercultural practice of mind expansion whose aims were either indifferent or antithetical to such judgment. Accordingly, making one appeal to a youth culture receptive to seeking self-insight through the use of LSD, while making a separate appeal to an establishment culture intent upon condemning such drug experimentation, rarely resulted in the capturing of both audiences as box-office targets, marking a difference from the industry's already distant Golden Age, when securing such broad-based appeal was a key to a film's success. Indeed, even such progressive films as *I Love You, Alice B. Toklas* ultimately address both traditional and countercultural audiences as separate entities, relegated to different parts of the narrative according to Harold's own sequential experience of the two lifestyles, despite his ultimate rejection of each. And as *The Trip* demonstrates, exclusively targeting an audience that was receptive to the notion of LSD's potential as a therapeutic agent also remained problematic, since studios were wary of being perceived as favoring a long vilified and quite recently criminalized drug.

Otto Preminger's Paramount-produced, 1968 holiday season release *Skidoo* directly addresses but never fully resolves these problems of audience address and target marketing to the studio's benefit—the film was a critical and commercial flop—yet *Skidoo* remains among the decade's most progressive and unconventional experiments with the collision of cultures on opposite sides of the generation gap. And if what emerges from this confrontation remains too easy to label or dismiss as "incoherent," this late-stage work of an industry-changing filmmaker reveals an attentiveness to the therapeutic potential of LSD unrivaled in the film industry. Even in the context of the long series of Preminger films that challenged the restrictions of the Production Code Administration throughout the 1950s and 1960s in narratives with such controversial subject matter as heroin addiction (*The Man with the Golden Arm*, 1955), graphic discussion of sexual intercourse (*Anatomy of a Murder*, 1959), and homosexuality (*Advise and Consent*, 1962), *Skidoo*'s post-Code testament to the therapeutic value of hallucinogens for personal enlightenment and political communication—resulting in what J. Hoberman has called "the most LSD-tolerant movie ever made" ("Head Trips")[14]—still seems radical. Having worked in Hollywood since 1935, Preminger was already 63 years old when the film was released, and earlier in the 1960s both he and his screenwriter Doran William Cannon had experimented with LSD.[15]

Where *Wild in the Streets* addresses the generation gap through reversals and oppositions, *Skidoo* orchestrates clashes, incongruities, and anachronisms that become evident even at the level of casting. The younger actors are all relative newcomers to Hollywood, but the film's starring cast assembles performers from the industry's Golden Age (Groucho Marx, Fred Clark, and Mickey Rooney), a musical actress (Carol Channing), an actor who initially achieved celebrity status in the television industry (Jackie Gleason), an aging teen idol (Frankie Avalon), and three older actors most familiar to 1968 audiences for their recent portrayals of villains in the 1966–1967 series *Batman* (Burgess Meredith, Frank Gorshin, and Cesar Romero). Unlike the casting of yesteryear's celebrities that would be a staple in films of the still forthcoming disaster genre from *Airport* (1970) to *The Towering Inferno* (1974), however, *Skidoo* becomes confrontational through its unlikely yet strategic use of such stars in a narrative that ultimately validates the ideals of a counterculture that remained interested in going to the cinema, but that since the 1950s had become increasingly indifferent to the traditional products of Old Hollywood.

Yet *Skidoo* is less invested in positioning readymade oppositions between youth and age than in facilitating new crosscultural connections and subverting audience expectations. The film adamantly critiques technocratic authority and notions of professional expertise against which counterculture was rebelling: the opening sequence comprises a series of televisual images and prompts that American society has generated to keep its citizens in line—commercials proclaiming that "blondes have more fun," "you'll never lose your man if you drink fat cola," and "for family fun, get your gun"—all chaotically orchestrated by a married couple's prolonged battle over access to the remote control. The film extends its critique in a later sequence where Angie's (Avalon) malfunctioning remote control keeps shifting the layout and setting of his apartment between drably designed professional office and mood-lit bachelor pad complete with a round, sunken bed. Arriving at a penitentiary, new prisoner Fred the Professor (Austin Pendleton) is baffled by an automated "check-in" system with a wealth of nonsensical selection options, prompting the prisoner to respond exasperatedly that "I've dropped out of your gadget civilization. I've renounced all science and technocracy."

The plot centers upon a comfortably retired gangster, Tough Tony Banks (Gleason) who is summoned by organized crime leader "God" (Marx) to pose as an Alcatraz prisoner so that he can murder the incarcerated former gangster friend George "Blue Chips" Packard (Rooney) to prevent him from turning state's evidence against the entire crime organization. The "hippie" contingent of the counterculture first connects with this central plot trajectory in a strategy typical of the era's generation-gap cinema, through Tony's rage at his daughter Darlene's (Alexandra Hay) sexual relationship with the hippie Stash (John Philip Law), who reminds Tony that "violence is the sign language of the inarticulate" after Tony hits him on the head, proclaiming that "no daughter of mine is gonna marry a hippie." ("Hippies don't even get married," Darlene reminds her father.) Once Tony inadvertently doses himself in prison with the LSD that his bunkmate Fred the Professor has covertly affixed to his own envelope seals, however, Tony's—and *Skidoo*'s—attitude about drugs, hippies, and the counterculture's dedication to nontraditional values shifts dramatically. While Tony's wife Flo (Channing) reaches out to Darlene, Stash, and a displaced group of hippies and invites them to stay at her home, Tony begins a process of insight and self-enlightenment that initiates social transformation in precisely the way that Roszak describes as a primary aim of the counterculture. Yet Tony is no hippie, nor is he an advocate to the resistance; indeed, moments before his accidental dosing, he berates Fred the Professor for his draft dodging ("Don't you believe in America?"). Once he is under the influence of the hallucinogen, assisted by Fred as the quintessential Leary-esque guide ("Tony has high ego retention," he comments at the start of the trip), Tony gains new perspective on the "game" playing involved in maintaining his identity in the role of gangster, and he publicly renounces violence and reneges on his mission to execute Packard. In the therapeutic transformation of the LSD user, Tony's hallucinogenic experience mirrors the ideal goal and purpose of Leary's Concord Prison Experiment, devised to inspire prisoners to evade the patterns of recidivism through hallucinogenically induced insight into their behavior.

What follows this personal transformation is yet more radical. With a representative of traditional, "square" cultural values initiating this bridging of the generation gap, *Skidoo* proceeds to complete its countercultural therapeutic enterprise as the LSD user and his trusted guide mastermind a process that will not only get both of them out of prison, but that also neutralizes the workings of an entire ideological system that establishment culture uses to "protect" society from criminals and deviants, including those who have chosen to burn their draft cards. The duo's elaborate plan for mass dosing the prison authorities—including its switchboard operators and two armed watchtower guards who hallucinate a ballet of dancing trash cans as Tony and Fred escape the compound by hot-air balloon—registers as both a means of escape and a gleeful expression of political liberation (see fig. 4.2). At the same time, their subversive mass dosing figures as a poignant reversal of the CIA and the military's longstanding establishment-sanctioned practice of administering LSD for the purposes of mind control. Once Tony and Fred have airsailed their way to the yacht where "God" is holding Darlene prisoner, the liberation becomes complete. Reunited with Tony, sporting a pirate hat and accompanied by her gang of hippie followers, Flo leads a final musical number that affirms the film's commitment to use "the power of the flower and the power of the dove" to keep steering society's values toward a countercultural ideal of harmony, connection, and communication. Indeed, *Skidoo*'s final shot reiterates this commitment, as Fred the Professor and the flower-clad "God" smoke pot together in a life raft.

Tough Tony Banks's hallucinogen-induced, therapeutic transformation references Hollywood's increasing tendency to shift away from outworn models of narrative construction and audience marketing—models that either attempted to capture "mature" viewers by appealing to an undifferentiated, "general" audience that no longer existed, or that para-

Figure 4.2. After dosing the entire prison administration with LSD, Tony Banks (Jackie Gleason, right) and Fred the Professor (Austin Pendleton, left) escape by hot air balloon in *Skidoo* (Otto Preminger, Otto Preminger Films/Sigma Productions, 1968). Digital frame enlargement.

doxically strived both to reconcile and invalidate politically incongruous perspectives by branding attempts to imagine alternative configurations of the human psyche or nontraditional social values as politically suspect or pathological. Yet *Skidoo* also marked the ending of Hollywood's briefly sustained period of experimentation with the therapeutic, transformative possibilities of hallucinogenic drugs in an America that would continue to bear the label of "sick society."[16] By June of 1969, the film industry would witness the release of a financially successful countercultural film that refreshingly demonstrated an indifference to its own indecipherability by establishment culture, as *Easy Rider* traced the cross-country journey of two enterprising hippies made instantly rich by a south-of-the-border drug deal. Instead of comprising a therapeutic act, their experimentation with LSD in an New Orleans cemetery during Mardi Gras would yield only the expression of enlightenment that "We blew it," shortly before rednecks shoot both hippies on a lonely southern highway. Only six weeks after its release, the national perception of LSD would once again shift—and this time more drastically—as the slaying by Charles Manson and his followers of pregnant actress Sharon Tate and four of her guests, and the murder of Tony and Rosemary LaBianca the following night, once again cemented the drug's association with pathology and mind control.

5

Therapy and Confession

THE PREVIOUS CHAPTERS HAVE TIED therapy in the 1960 and early 1970s to the process of facilitating interpersonal connection and communication, whether the context is the dynamic between patient and psychotherapist, the relationship (or pathological disconnect) between partners who no longer experience pleasure in the act of sex, the trials that married couples face as they negotiate the demands of traditional and emerging gender roles, or the feelings of transcendence, empathy, and community sought by many psychedelic drug users. The phenomenon of confession, the focus of the present chapter, shares with these other therapies an increasing emphasis upon the process of opening up to the world—here, by transforming an intimate, contemplative practice into a meaningful act of interpersonal and social engagement. As the 1960s progress, confession aligns with psychedelic drug therapies in a mutual focus upon the value of reflection in the restoring of human sensitivity, compassion, and a sense of belonging perceived as lacking in the contemporary world. By examining how the American film industry responded to the cultural transformation of spiritual forgiveness into a psychological construct, consonant with recent changes in attitude in the 1960s toward confession in both the psychotherapeutic community and a Catholic Church that had exerted such profound influence upon Hollywood's system of self-regulation throughout most of the twentieth century, we witness yet another aspect of Hollywood's sometimes uncertain yet consistent attempt to shape popular narrative constructs in ways that might resonate with changing film audiences.

As the disclosure or revelation of a truth, the phenomenon of confession was for some time specific to legal and religious realms, yet the findings of Freud, Jung, and other psychoanalysts in the early twentieth century would ultimately bring confession into the arena of psychology and psychotherapy. For some time, the Catholic Church resisted this co-opting of a redemptive spiritual enterprise; unwilling to relegate the origins of sin to the depths of the unconscious; by the late 1950s, however, the Church was committed to engaging with social scientific disciplines whose perspectives could shed light upon human behavior. This interest in collaborating with disciplines traditionally considered to be outside of the Church's proper sphere grew with Pope John XXIII and the reforms of the Second Ecumenical Council—also known as "Vatican II"—which was held from 1962 to 1965. Although the documents produced in Vatican II addressed the matter of confession only in general terms, through the Council's profound influence the religious and psychological realms of confession would become inextricably intertwined. As psychotherapeutic discourse became increasingly prevalent in descriptions of the religious practice of atonement, the Church's new receptivity to the developments of the contemporary world would enable its connection to social, political, and global matters after an extended period of self-imposed isolation, instilling in its parishioners a more reflective and contemplative perspective on confession, penance, and the seeking of God's forgiveness of sin.

As earlier chapters have demonstrated, from the late 1950s into the 1960s the field of psychotherapy was undergoing its own transformation, branching out from psychoanalytic to behaviorist, humanistic, and self-actualization methods, and embracing and adopting new client-centered therapeutic models that demanded dynamic and interactive forms of communication between patient and therapist, while also valuing communication among patients in group therapy and encounter group settings. Bolstered by the Catholic Church's own transformation, the cooperative relationship between religion and psychology witnessed the emergence of confession as a therapeutic vehicle. With the Church newly committed to addressing the problems of the contemporary world, the auricular confession considered as standard practice since 1215 AD began to migrate from the realm of the dark, secret confines of the private confessional booth to a ritual that could be practiced among a community of parishioners in the context of the mass (O'Toole 176). And as the Church itself began to temper the role of the priest as authoritative intermediary between the penitent and God, the spiritual atonement traditionally provided by auricular confession became more widely accessible through psychotherapeutic outlets offering greater possibilities of interaction between confessor and listener. By the later 1960s, psychotherapeutic discourse had infiltrated religious confessional practice to such an extent that the matter of forgiveness might emerge from within the conscience of the contemplative penitent, with personal reflection gaining agency as an alternative to private, priest-centered confession.

This chapter addresses the phenomenon of confession at the intersection of religious and psychotherapeutic discourses to illuminate commonalities that were emerging in the 1960s after Vatican II, by which time the Catholic Church's once profound influence in defining the parameters of permissible representation in the American film industry had waned significantly, only to weaken further when the MPAA adopted its new rating system later in the decade. After establishing this historical context, the chapter examines a set of confessional narrative films released between 1966 and 1972 that emblematize the shift in both the Catholic Church and the psychotherapeutic community to more open, embracing, and socially collaborative models of confessional practice—models that strive to empower the penitent through a process of reconciliation through disclosure that almost always occurs at the end of the film. None of these films dramatizes an auricular dynamic involving a priest and a penitent in the private, confessional booth. Indeed, while the presence of the Church itself occasionally emerges as a background element, confessional disclosure in these films involves a quite different construction of the confessor/penitent dynamic, as well as a setting almost invariably comprising a group of active and "qualified" listeners who are intimately familiar with the penitent as friends or family members. Conducted in an interpersonal context and framed as a willful response to pressing social issues of the contemporary era, the act of confession in these films very rarely brings about a psychopathological "cure" or spiritual absolution, and it just as rarely effects a strong sense of narrative closure. Derived from reflection and examination of conscience, however, confession within the structure of cinematic narrative remains an integral part of a therapeutic process of avowal, forgiveness, and reconciliation that permits the confessing protagonist to "move on" to subsequent actions and decisions that the narrative suggests but never specifies.

Contexts of Confession

While definitions of the concept of "confession" differ among disciplines, a common element is the verbalized acknowledgment that one has committed an action, the "truth" of which the disclosure verifies. The confession cannot be an "easy" admission, but instead one that requires an intensive reflective process, and a revelation that is difficult or painful to disclose to the intended listener (Taylor 8). With respect to matters of avowal and acknowledgment in the legal realm, another feature distinguishing confession from other forms of verbal discourse is its function as what J. L. Austin defines as a "performative," such that "the issuing of the utterance is the performing of an action—it is not normally thought of as just saying something" (Austin 6). The confession of participation in a crime to a police officer, for instance, serves as a definitive mark of the defendant's guilt in the eyes of the law. If, historically, confessions can carry considerable weight in legal discourse, by the mid-1960s the performative aspect of the confessional utterance had shed some of its association with this invariable equivalence of word and deed, to stress the centrality of the notion of "appropriate circumstances" (Austin 8) in which the confession must be contextualized in order to be viable: the juridical decisions in *Escobedo v. Illinois* (1964) and *Miranda v. Arizona* (1966) invalidated confessions that were exacted before the defendant was given access to legal counsel, specifying also that "when an investigation shifts to accusation, police must tell all suspects of their rights to silence" ("Confession Controversy" 78).

The psychoanalytic school was among the first to elaborate upon the psychotherapeutic dimension of confession. In their articulation of "the talking cure," Freud and Breuer posited that the patient's act of verbalizing a sexual problem in the presence of a psychotherapist, coupled with the analyst's subsequent interpretation of the patient's confession, constituted a cure "of their various psychological and hysterically physiological ailments," although the psychoanalysts later rescinded this conclusion after observing that such verbalizations tended to "repeat rather than heal trauma" (Taylor 71). It was, however, Karl Jung who first illuminated the strong link between religious and psychological confession, identifying the confessional act as a plea for forgiveness that comprised the unearthing of both conscious and repressed unconscious matter—an unearthing that rescues the patient from "moral isolation" (Todd 46) and releases him from "shame and guilt" (42) through the communicative connection that the presence of the listener affords. Noting that "Jung emphasized both the insight-oriented and cathartic value of confessions," Janet Hymer goes on to reaffirm the connection between confession and release, adding that the expression of previously repressed material ultimately stimulates "growth-promoting activities" (131). And regarding the central role of transference in the patient/client dynamic, Carl Rogers's client-centered therapy had also significantly influenced the development of psychotherapeutic notions of confession by the 1960s.

Prior to the reevaluation of Catholic Church's policies on the expiation of sin that were advanced in the late 1950s and that culminated in Vatican II, the parameters of the confessional process were strictly prescribed. As O'Toole asserts, confession adhered to a three-part structure comprising (1) contrition, beginning with the penitent's self-assessment of conscience to identify and quantify committed sins, and culminating in a sincere expression of sorrow or regret to God; (2) the confession itself, including the auricular act and a "straightforward listing of sins"; and (3) satisfaction, involving the priest's prescription of punishment for the sins which the penitent would then enact, thereby reinforcing the sincerity of his regret and his determination not to repeat the sin (Todd 145; O'Toole 151). While it distinguished mortal sin ("a grievous offense against the law of God") from the more pardonable category of venial sin, the Church demanded that sins of both types be disclosed and enumerated in the confessional booth, a space of darkness, confidentiality, and anonymity where "priest and penitent whispered so as not to be heard by the person on the other side or by those waiting—sometimes standing, sometimes moving forward successively in the pews a safe distance away—and all were strictly enjoined not to eavesdrop or overhear what someone else was saying" (O'Toole 151).

Before the late 1950s, the Catholic Church remained suspicious of psychology and psychiatry, with both traditional psychoanalysis and behaviorism setting forth a deterministic perspective on sinful acts and behavior. If the origins of sin were indeed relegated to the unconscious, it followed that one might not necessarily know if or when a sin has been committed, thereby compromising notions of free will and personal responsibility. And if, instead, human behavior is such that one has been "programmed" to commit sinful acts, behaviorist psychotherapeutic approaches suggested that this problem could be corrected through effective reprogramming (Gillespie 2, 84). By the late 1950s, however, many core psychological principles were gradually gaining acceptance by an American Catholic Church that was becoming more actively receptive to sociological and psychological disciplines. As Gillespie explains, a keystone in this changed attitude was the St. John's Summer Institute, formed in 1954 to provide clergymen with the opportunity to interact with psychiatrists to obtain a better, and broader, understanding of mental health and illness. The founders demonstrated their commitment to openness by making the institute ecumenical. The free exchange of ideas and perspectives resulted in "a greater understanding and trust between religious leaders and psychotherapists," and it also offered a "means of collaboration between clergy and psychiatrists that continued long after the workshops" (Gillespie 93).

The field of psychotherapy was progressively embracing new theories and methods of treatment that relied upon productive interpersonal exchange, and through the doctrines of the Second Ecumenical Council, initiated by Pope John XIII between 1962 and 1965, a formerly hermetic

Catholic Church would more directly address issues and concerns of the contemporary world. The Church began to perceive itself as a vehicle for the promotion of social justice through such monumental constitutional documents as *Gaudium et Spes* (*Joy and Hope*, 1965), which Gillespie describes as "a mutual dialogue between the church and the world," with its confirmation of the Church's commitment to political ethics, human dignity, the lessening of world poverty, and the promotion of world peace (96).

Although the Council's call for the reconfiguration of the Church's policies on confession and penance were not specific, through such documents as the *Lumen Gentium* (*Light of the Nations*, 1964) the Council affirmed its recognition of the penitent's increasingly central role in the process of human redemption, and Vatican II impacted perceptions on acknowledgment and absolution that would resonate throughout the Catholic community. While the Council adhered to the hierarchical relationship among the penitent, priest, and God so central to Catholicism's distinction from Protestantism, the *Lumen Gentium* also emphasized the "priestly" status of all penitents in a way that recalled Luther's notion of a "Priesthood of all Believers":

> Christ the Lord, High Priest taken from among (people), made the new people 'a kingdom and priests to God the Father.' The baptized, by regeneration and the anointing of the Holy Spirit, are consecrated as a spiritual house and a holy priesthood, in order that through all those works which are those of the Christian (person) they may offer spiritual sacrifices and proclaim the power of Him who has called them out of darkness into His marvelous light. (*Lumen Gentium* 10, pp. 26–27)

In light of Vatican II reforms, debate within the Catholic community about the efficacy of traditional auricular confession commenced shortly after the Council disbanded. In March of 1966, one Reverend Beaumont Stevenson reasserted his conviction that it was essential to maintain the confessional dynamic's one-on-one penitent-to-priest configuration, because it provided the requisite "painful experience" in which "there is no provision for the penitent to place the blame on anyone else but himself for his failure" ("Confession and Psychotherapy," 10). Stevenson finds what he describes as "general" or "corporate" confession as the "easy way out," since the large-group dynamic fails to guide the individual penitent's attention in contrition as directly to God. Offering an alternative perspective in a publication appearing a month earlier, Agnes Regina Hall of the Congregation of the Sisters of Saint Joseph describes the traditional auricular confession as routinized to the point of meaninglessness, "a mere recital of sins in the framework of a mechanical, memorized formula with its equally mechanical, memorized 'act' of contrition" (97).

In the context of this same article, Hall intimates a perspectival shift that would result in profound changes to the Catholic Church's configuration of the confessional act—a shift in emphasis upon the precise enumeration and categorization of "sins" to a more inherently contemplative process that challenges the penitent to discover, recognize, and understand the underlying causes of "sin" itself, in order to provide him with more effective ammunition to reject it. As Gillespie suggests, "moral life had begun to be understood not as a series of discrete actions judged to be right or wrong, but as a lifelong growth process" (110). Under the terms of this quite different configuration, sin would be considered less as a specific act than as a state of being, and specifically, a state of being cast off or isolated from the "union of love embracing a man, his God, and his neighbor"; indeed, Hall describes sin as an "alienation" (97). Here and elsewhere in post-Vatican II discourse, whether or not to live in sin remains man's own choice; however, the decision to move away from a position of egocentric isolation and toward a re-union with one's social and spiritual community demands forms of contrition and confession more intensive than "an item-by-item cancellation of misdeeds in somewhat the way a person uses a spot remover" (99). Reconnecting to God requires an interactive relationship with the priest as God's advocate; as Hall explains, confession ideally involves [a] genuine, personal communication between confessor and penitent," a "natural, matter-of-fact dialogue" instead of the "two monologues" that traditional auricular confession comprised (100). Yet such new forms of connection and communication are also more firmly grounded in a two-stage process—one that elevates reflection and the examination of conscience as an inward-directed process that ensures genuine contrition, so that this same penitent might then engage in the outward-directed process of establishing a stronger (re-)connection to the fellow Christian community, and to God.

These conceptual shifts would bring about significant changes in confessional practice. Aligned with the new focus on communication and connection, as O'Toole explains, the Catholic mass would now be conducted in English rather than Latin, and "the altar was moved forward and the priest stood behind it, facing the people rather than standing with his back to them as priests had done for generations" (174). Hall's prescient recommendation that confession abandon its emphasis upon the itemization of sins in favor of the penitent's conceptual "summary," and that the confession of venial sins be eliminated entirely ("they only clutter up the confession and divert attention from the main issue") would come to pass by the mid-1960s, and by the mid-1970s the Church would re-label confession as "reconciliation" (Gillespie 107–08). By 1967, *Time* magazine would report that confession could take place outside the confessional booth, or even in conjunction with a couple's joint visit to a priest—one who now functions as "less of a judge, and more of a counselor" ("Confession to Counseling" 60). By 1969, the Church's decision to offer mass on Saturday afternoons and evenings—when penitents had traditionally lined up at the confessional booth so that they might receive the holy sacrament during Sunday mass—and to embed pleas for the forgiveness of sins within the structure of the mass itself, were among the factors contributing to a sharp decline in auricular confession after Vatican II. Largely as a result of the *Lumen Gentium*'s highlighting of the notion of penitent as priest, O'Toole asserts that "many lay Catholics were revising their self-image, seeing themselves as religiously autonomous" (173). When it came to such controversial matters as the Church's insistence that Catholics avoid the use of contraceptive devices—a position that Vatican II reinforced instead of challenged—the renewed empowerment of the individual brought many Catholics, and especially women, to conclude that "they could indeed decide important matters on their own" rather than place themselves hypocritically in the role of a penitent seeking a male priest's forgiveness in the confessional booth. By 1971, O'Toole reports, results of a major survey revealed that 65 percent of the responders "agreed with the statement that 'they can simply confess their sins directly to God and be forgiven,' without going through the traditional form of a priest" (170).

The focus upon the penitent's responsibility for personal reflection and contemplation, coupled with the importance of communicating with others about sin, brought the goals of the Church and the psychotherapeutic community into much closer alignment on the subject of confession. Differences certainly remained, especially surrounding the relationship between the unconscious, which psychotherapy investigated in terms of causality, and religious confession, which focused on the assessment of sin that was consciously accessible to the penitent (Worthen 280). As McConnell pointed out in 1969, however, there emerged more widespread support for the perspective that "in confession, religious and psychological dimensions of life interpenetrate one another in the context of some degree of personal unity" (81). In October 1967, *Time* magazine reported that "the role of the priest has changed. . . . [H]e is less of a judge, and more of counselor" ("Confession to Counseling" 60). Also, especially in the context of Jung's ideas, efficacious confession could be said to involve *both* psychotherapeutic and religious practices, through the process of bringing repressed, unconscious forces to the level of accessible consciousness so that the penitent subject could both understand and meaningfully communicate his own self-perception within the context of the larger human community. Regarding the value of personal reflection in the post-Vatican II period, O'Toole asserts that "since essential parts of confession—the examination of conscience, the feelings of contrition, the purpose of amendment—went on entirely inside the mind of the penitent, the practice was inevitably grounded in psychology" (175). On the matter of outward-directed expression, both disciplines emphasized the central role of verbalization and disclosure. Within or beyond the confines of a darkened booth in a church, confession could not be considered "confession" if it were limited to the stage of contrition, of formulating knowledge of one's behavior and acts on a purely reflective, contemplative basis; similarly, the therapeutic process would be reduced to something other than therapeutic if the patient elected not to express to others—therapists, partners, or participants in group therapy sessions—the gained insights into his own behavior (Hymer 141). The increasing use of psychotherapeutic discourse in articulations of the practice of penitence aligned with the Church's recognition of advancements in the understanding of human behavior accomplished in the field of psychology. Speculations in 1967 that "Christians might be allowed to gather in penitential services to confess their errors to one another in the matter of a group-therapy session" turned out to be well timed rather than far-fetched ("Confession to Counseling" 60).

The connections between psychotherapy and religious confession extended to the conceptual level, with both phenomena described metaphorically in terms of transition, a journey from a state of isolation to connectedness, from confusion to understanding, and most crucially, from internalization to communication. The trajectory of forgiveness, healing, and integration suggested a movement outward which, as discussed earlier, also comprised an essential component of confessional "treatment." Todd suggests that "it is essential that the confession involves another human being who hears, accepts, and pardons"(42), yet in both religious and psychotherapeutic contexts, confession was meant to facilitate a form of communication involving not only the act of speaking to someone else with a reasonable expectation of non-judgmental listening, but also the process of completion, one that suggested that the pre-confessional penitent/patient had been fragmented; accordingly, Worthen describes the attainment of "wholeness" as a goal in psychotherapy and confession (276). The path to this state of wholeness is also framed as a *return*, such that "both disciplines strive to bring the individual back into his true and rightful state of being" (Stevenson 14). Accordingly, the return becomes a journey that one was always meant to take—a recapturing of what was once more familiar, or even more "real," than the sinful or psychopathological state that the subject is currently enduring—and that constitutes an intangible "nowhere" sensible only to the extent that it requires escape. Indeed, consonant with the themes of communication and connection that characterize so many forms of therapeutic discourse in the late 1960s, the unanchored subject finds his place by joining the world that exists beyond the constraining realm of his selfish needs, to experience the joys of investing his energies in the development of the community he will join upon his return. As Worthen explains, the goal of both disciplines becomes "the restitution of community life once sin or egocentrism is re-directed or eliminated" (282).

The Catholic Church in the Hollywood Film Industry

While the discipline of Catholic confession was increasingly aligning with psychotherapy through a shared process of "opening up" to the needs of a larger community, conservative factions of the highly influential Catholic-centered Legion of Decency were undergoing a correlative process of transformation in relation to the Hollywood film industry. The Legion originated in the early 1930s as a group that exerted pressure upon Hollywood to align its products with a prescriptive moral code, adhering to a moralism that limited the range of cinematic representation without attention to narrative context or to the audience's ability to act on its own to formulate moral decisions. The Motion Picture Producers and Distributors Organization of America devised its Production Code in collaboration with the Legion of Decency to fend off the possibility of local and national censorship in an entertainment industry that had been denied the same First Amendment rights afforded to print and theatrical media. After the scandals and exhibitions of immoral behavior that plagued the reputation of the film industry in the 1920s, this collaboration developed in recognition that the Catholic Church was a highly organized force capable of compromising or destroying a film's box-office potential through public protests and boycotts. As Jon Lewis explains, "the inclusion of the church in the operation of the cinematic enterprise was good public relations and it was also a business necessity. . . . The church wielded significant power on Wall Street" (101).

As Lewis suggests, in an era of especially vigorous audience attendance, when "the film industry could afford to make one product for everyone," the industry's collaboration with the Legion of Decency and similar organizations remained sustainable. During the postwar period, however, when box-office receipts began to decline, and when the notion of an unspecified, "general" audience became no longer feasible to maintain, with studios increasingly tailoring their products to those specific market sectors that continued to patronize the cinema regularly, the Production Code became an unduly obtrusive mechanism: "Too much money was at stake with the studios to abide by production guidelines that prevented them from exploiting such potentially lucrative markets" (133–34). The increasing popularity of representationally unrestrictive European cinema, especially among urban audiences, verified the demand for a type of American cinema that confronted the personal, social, and cultural issues to which more educated and informed film enthusiasts would be receptive (Black 132). After the "Miracle" case of 1952, which resulted in the extension of First Amendment rights to the film industry and severely limited the power of local censorship boards to ban individual films, the tensions between the film studios, the Production Code Administration, and the Legion of Decency were exacerbated. During the mid-1950s, filmmakers including Elia Kazan and Otto Preminger tested both the PCA's and the Legion's authority to insist upon cuts and modifications before a film could be exhibited, and while studios had previously yielded to the Legion's recommendations in order to avoid its "C" (Condemned) rating, the success of such C-rated films as Preminger's *The Moon Is Blue* (1953) attested to the Legion's declining influence, demonstrating that condemnation by the Catholic Church might only generate publicity that could translate to stronger box-office receipts.

Especially after Geoffrey Shurlock assumed leadership of the PCA in 1954 following the conservative Joseph Breen's retirement, the PCA and the Legion were more frequently at odds, with the Catholic organization also prone to internal strife in cases where a consensus of judgment on a film classification could not be reached. The same Catholic Church that was becoming receptive to advances in the field of psychotherapy for its insights into human behavior, was also undergoing a process of modernization that would challenge the Church's longstanding position on morality in cinema. Through its participation in a 1957 conference organized by the Office Catholique International du Cinéma (OCIC) and commissioned by Pope Pius XII, the American sector of the Catholic Church was compelled to reevaluate its largely condemnatory stance on immoral representational practices—a stance which theological participants from many other national Catholic churches perceived as retrograde and presumptuous (Black 178–80). Faithful to the spirit of an era that was witnessing America's proliferating interest in world cinema, Pope Pius issued the 1957 encyclical *Miranda Prorsus* (On Entertainment Media), which encouraged Catholics to engage in dialogue about the products of the medium, to study film and appreciate the possibilities of moral redemption that the cinematic form harbored (Black 179–80). In a correlative process that invited fresh and diverse perspectives, Geoffrey Shurlock radically reconfigured the PCA's review board membership to include priests, teachers, professors, media critics, and other professionals whose interaction might make the Association more progressive (Black 182).

Especially in the context of the late 1950s and early 1960s, when the Production Code Administration was gradually relaxing its censorial stance on the representation of "immoral" subject matter, the condemnatory tirades of conservative factions of the Legion of Decency seemed anachronistic. And just as Catholics were growing more confident in their decisions to bypass or eliminate the traditional intermediary role of the priest who issued penance and effected reconciliation with God in the act of auricular confession, sectors of the American Catholic clergy and laity questioned the authority of bishops and Catholic organizations to impose a hierarchical system that compelled them to take a vow during a Sunday mass to refrain from viewing any film that had been designated as "Condemned," and that deemed noncompliance with this directive a mortal sin.[1] Ultimately, by the mid-1960s, the PCA, the Catholic Church, and what remained of the Legion of Decency were yielding their self-granted moral authority to the individual, who accordingly became empowered to make moral evaluations and decisions based upon the workings of his own conscience, just as the penitent availed himself of options for divine absolution outside the confessional booth.

Nowhere is this transfer of authority to the individual more evident than in the film industry's transition to a classification system that distinguished "general" from "adult" subject matter, and that thereby acknowledged the adult audience's distinct interests and evaluative capacities. Ironically, it was the Legion of Decency that took the lead in this effort, with the development of its A-II, A-III, and A-IV rating categories that designated levels of suitability by age group. By 1968, the film industry followed suit by replacing the "yes/no" system governing the Production Code's granting or withholding of its seal of approval, with the Motion Picture Association of America's rating system that aimed to provide a service for parents by differentiating films according to their suitability to "general," "mature," and adult audiences.

Cinematic Confession After Vatican II

That the slow yet steady transition to classification systems acknowledging adult subject matter as a legitimate category of audience interest did not result in the curtailment of the Catholic Church's efforts to alert its congregation to what it considered as morally transgressive cinema in the late 1960s is evident by its strong reprobation of such films as *Rosemary's Baby* (discussed in chapter 3), which received a "C" rating for its depiction of Satanic worship. At the same time, however, changes in the representational practices of the Hollywood film industry, the system of self-regulation to which the industry transitioned, the Catholic Church's role in this system at a time when the Church itself was reevaluating and embracing its relationship to a changing world, and this same Church's increasing empowerment of the individual in matters of contrition and moral redemption, collectively bear witness to a distinctive shift in late 1960s and early 1970s American cinema in its handling of the phenomenon of "confession" as a theme, a style, a narrative device, and an interpersonal dynamic. Aligned with the sharply diminished role of one-on-one priest/penitent auricular confession in the 1960s, the confessional narratives examined in the remainder of this chapter deviate from the setting of the church confessional booth; indeed, corresponding with the emphasis upon the power and integrity of the individual human conscience in the process of absolution, these narratives largely transcend the realm of religion itself, while cultivating the core elements of reflection and contemplation that comprise the confessional act's psychological foundation. While the presence of a psychiatrist occasionally serves as a reference point that grounds the confessional process, the therapeutic dynamic of these cinematic confessions relies less upon the traditional, official markers of the professional psychotherapeutic setting than the inclusion and integration of features essential to the "scene" of the confessional disclosure: the presence of a speaker who is either determined to avow a transgression or no longer able to repress it; the focus on a "secret" whose revelation promises to bring the confessing protagonist to a state of full presence as it reifies or illuminates a covert, undisclosed "truth"; and the co-presence of one or several authorized listeners who bear witness to the speaker's verbalization. As a confessional "breakthrough" within the narrative, the intended purpose of confession is to offer a sense of release or a moment of catharsis, highlighted by the positioning of the central confessional act in a climactic final scene. At the same time, these therapeutic confessions most often fail to offer any sense of definitive resolution or closure; instead, the completion of the act always prefigures a "next" action to be taken or a decision that must be made. Consonant with the spirit of embrace and opening up that both the Catholic Church and the institution of psychotherapy had been experiencing, the aim of confession in 1960s and 1970s American cinema is both relational and interpersonal, marking the penitent's therapeutic attempt to connect with the world around him through an act of reconciliation—of reaching out—that seeks to embrace others in the spirit of social, cultural, or political change.

Especially considering how emphatically the transition from the Production Code to the new rating system brought about new and "liberating" possibilities of incorporating sexually frank and explicit subject matter in the sexual revolution, Foucault's model of confession as a means of transforming sex into discourse seems especially pertinent to the structure of the cinematic confessional narrative in the late 1960s and early 1970s. In Catholic faith, the diminution of traditional auricular confession did not signal the demise of the confessional act itself; rather, as we have seen, other viable options outside the confessional booth—options that were also largely psychotherapeutic—became available to the penitent. These options preserved many essential components of auricular confession while reconfiguring them in contemporary terms—for example, with the painful disclosures among the encounter group participants in the opening sequence of *Bob & Carol & Ted & Alice*. "One confesses one's crimes, one's sins, one's thoughts and desires, one's illnesses and troubles," Foucault proclaims; "one goes about telling with the greatest precision, whatever is most difficult to tell" (59), and the confession of whichever aspect of sex one deems necessary to transform into discourse brings with it the promise of not only an act of "pleasure" and a violation of "law and taboo," but also an ultimate revelation of "truth" readily distinguishable from "falsehood" (56). Religious or psychotherapeutic, the confessional act itself was not unfamiliar to American cinema, which had used it in genres from the domestic melodrama to the suspense thriller, even occasionally incorporating the ethical crisis of the priest's vow to secrecy regarding disclosures in the confessional booth in films such as Hitchcock's *I Confess* (1953). In conjunction with contemporary religious and psychotherapeutic developments, however, and framed as a strategy of transgressive liberation that the abandonment of Production Code representational restrictions might enable—especially, though not exclusively, those centering upon sex—late 1960s American cinema brought an unprecedented sense of urgency to the compulsion to confess, along with an equally unprecedented set of expectations regarding the therapeutic dimension of confession.

Released eleven months before the implementation of the new rating system, *The President's Analyst* (Theodore J. Flicker, 1967) satirically demonstrates the national preoccupation with confession and disclosure, correlating the need for psychotherapy with contemporary cultural anxiety. The story begins much like a laity's version of *I Confess*, with U.S. intelligence agent Don Masters (Godfrey Cambridge) starting a psychiatric session by disclosing his recent murder of an Albanian double agent (an incident that the audience has just witnessed) to psychiatrist Sidney Schaefer (James Coburn), almost casually unburdening himself of the criminal act, because he knows that his therapist cannot disclose what he has confessed. As it turns out, Schaefer's work frequently requires that he too have immediate access to his own psychiatrist (seemingly located adjacent to his office). Masters reveals that through their sessions he has been covertly assessing Schaefer's discretion and integrity—especially important attributes for the position of private analyst to the President of the United States, who complains of being "overstressed, overtired, and overburdened." While Schaefer is initially honored to have been selected for the job, his top-secret work at the White House, where the President calls upon him day and night for emergency therapy sessions—combined with the strain of being constantly placed under surveillance by agents who worry, for example, about what he says when he talks in his sleep—soon plagues him with such fatigue and anxiety that he decides to flee. This "escape" only entangles him more deeply, raising the concern of investigative and intelligence agents, double agents, spies, informers, and snitches about the classified "secrets" that Schaefer has taken with him—or what they suspect or fear that Schaefer knows but cannot repeat.

Schaefer is ultimately discovered by Masters and the Russian counterspy V. I. Kydor Kropotkin (Steven Darden), who agree to help him as long as he agrees to continue to take them on as psychotherapeutic clients. Schaefer accommodates, but now that he has forfeited access to his own therapeutic confessor (a matter of security specified as a condition of his employment), the arrangement leaves him without any outlet for his own mounting anxieties. Indeed, with its diagnoses, analyses, and revelatory disclosures, *The President's Analyst* suggests that the confessional/psychotherapeutic dynamic now provides the only means for interpersonal relationships to foster intimacy, sincerity, and transparency, and for making sense of a world where people have become too afraid to say what they mean, and where they have grown accustomed to using discourse to obfuscate rather than illuminate meaning and intention. In the network of intelligence and counter-intelligence offered to the film's protagonists, "the weekly visit to the psychiatrist is a given" (*CinemaTexas Program Notes*).

Notably, the ultimate entity of human surveillance, deceit, and alienation turns out to be The Phone Company, a pillar of American bureaucracy that has entirely reneged upon its responsibilities as a communication service, that now condemns its customers to being placed eternally on hold or severing their connection entirely, and that also uses hard-sell tactics to persuade Schaefer to bring its latest invention to the president's attention—a revolutionary, intravenous phone technology powered by the human brain (see fig 5.1). As the embodiment of evil, The Phone Company ultimately captures the anxieties of a technocratically dehumanized culture whose citizens are desperate to regain a sense of community and belonging.[2]

If *The President's Analyst* identifies the confessional psychotherapeutic relationship as the only respite from the pervasive alienation and loneliness that contemporary American culture fosters, it is both ironic and most fitting that the film that would become the prototype for the era's confessional dynamic is Mike Nichols's controversial *Who's Afraid of Virginia Woolf* (1966). Based upon Edward Albee's successful, award-winning stage play that premiered on Broadway in 1962, the film's production history comprised the culmination of a series of battles between Hollywood studios and the Production Code Administration, which Warner Bros. ultimately placated by releasing it with the stipulation that it could be seen by adults only, with the caption "No one under 18 will be admitted unless accompanied by his parent" required to appear in all display ads. The fact that the Legion of Decency issued the film an "A-4" rating ("morally objectionable for adults with reservations") rather than the condemnatory "C" provided the studio with leverage,[3] and the

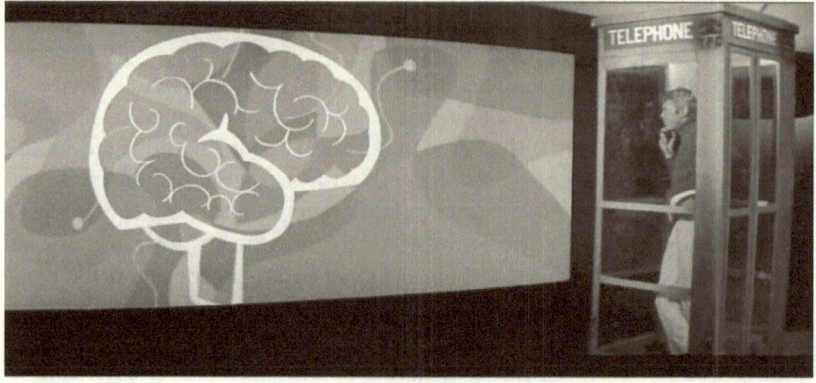

Figure 5.1. The Phone Company forces Dr. Sidney Schaefer (James Coburn) to view a presentation of its new intravenous product in *The President's Analyst* (Theodore J. Flicker, Paramount Pictures., 1967). Digital frame enlargement.

film was granted exemption from Code approval, paving the path to the implementation of the rating system two years later. As Jon Lewis explains, "the code exemption offered an opportunity to see how an age-based, exhibitor-enforced system might work and whether a film targeted at such a narrow demographic could still make money. The answer to the latter question was a resounding yes" (139), with the film earning the third highest box-office revenue of 1966.

Who's Afraid of Virginia Woolf? correlates psychotherapy with absolution, aligning the narrative with its protagonists' compulsion to confess, to disclose long-guarded secrets, and to do so before witnesses. The promise (or threat) of confession comes to dominate a long, painful evening at the home of history professor George (Richard Burton) and his wife Martha (Elizabeth Taylor), the daughter of the college president, with invited guests new biology professor Nick (George Segal) and his wife Honey (Sandy Dennis). The gathering is actually an after-party following the dinner at the president's home that has just concluded as the plot begins. As it turns out, several withheld "truths" are disclosed in the course of the narrative, including the fact that Nick married Honey after she appeared to become pregnant, only to learn soon afterwards that she was actually suffering from a hysterical pregnancy; that he also married her for her money; and that, before the evening ends, his determination to rise to a higher status in the university's hierarchy has motivated his "successful" sexual pursuit of Martha.

The disclosure of these secrets supports Foucault's assertion that the confessional dynamic comprises "a ritual that unfolds within a power relationship, for one does not confess without the presence (or virtual presence) of a partner who is not simply the interlocutor but the authority who requires the confession, prescribes and appreciates it, and intervenes in order to judge, punish, forgive, console, and reconcile" (61). Until the film's final confessional scene, it is a third party that regularly discloses the secret, making the person who reveals the secret into a messenger for another who acts out of malice or revenge. Having learned of Honey's hysterical (or aborted) pregnancy through a private conversation with Nick, for example, George subsequently reveals the information before his wife and guests at a strategic moment when the disclosure will place him at an advantage to the now-humiliated Nick, with Honey's devastation written off as collateral damage. Similarly, throughout the film Martha treats her guests to a series of humiliating disclosures about George, including the fact that he never became the chair of the History Department or attained the rank of full professor and that she, her father, and the university community have consequently perceived him as a failure—or in Martha's words, "a big, fat flop."

Unlike Honey's hysterical pregnancy or George's professorial status, both of which involve confirmed actualities (Martha's invective-laden embellishments notwithstanding), the narrative includes one specific secret that remains integral to the film's structure as well as its manipulation of the hierarchy of knowledge. Just before the guests arrive, George alludes to a secret that he *forbids* Martha to disclose, yet he refrains from naming it despite the absence of anyone else within hearing distance. The nature of this secret remains a private matter known only to the couple until a second reference, at which time we learn, but never witness, that Martha appears to have just shared the forbidden secret with Honey while giving her guest a tour of the house, entirely offscreen. Honey's revelation has merely reiterated before the full group what Martha has just told her in private: George and Martha have a son. In the first case, it appears that the secret remains unrevealed only because we as viewers might otherwise learn it; in the second case, Honey's revelation once again reminds the audience of its disadvantaged status as powerless, unable to gather private information unless another, more privileged character becomes ready to publicize it. And in the second case, George appears to feel similarly disempowered, both because Martha has disregarded his warning about "the kid" and because he was not present when she broke the rule with Honey. In both references to the secret, then, the withholding and disclosure of information implicates the audience in relations of intimacy, privacy, and ultimately, power. The *Hollywood Reporter*'s suggestion that "The film seems so very seldom a drama, and almost a violation of privacy, captured with hidden cameras and microphones" (Powers) stems not only from its bravura performances, intricate close-ups, tight framings, and confining spatial configurations; the play between privacy and its publicization makes the audience uncomfortably complicit in the mind games that the characters play with one another. While the protagonists of *Who's Afraid of Virginia Woolf?* never break the fourth wall to address viewers directly, through such devices the film repeatedly emphasizes our uncomfortable presence in relation to the scene, as if, covertly and without permission, we were being made receptive to exchanges, disclosures, and confessions that we were not meant to overhear, and that situate us simultaneously as eavesdropping penitents and surrogate confessors.[4]

The games reach an apex in the film's final sequence, both because the secret or "truth" regarding George and Martha's child is ultimately exposed to all, and also because the exposure of this secret through the confessional act so entirely upends and destabilizes the matter of "truth" itself. Yet the act of verbalization central to the cathartic effect of both religious confession and psychotherapeutic disclosure also serves other purposes here. As Martha and Nick are having sex in the bedroom upstairs (George sees their silhouettes from the porch), inspired by Honey's report of bells ringing, George rehearses the painful news that he must tell Martha: a messenger has just come to their home to report that their son is dead. Rather than rendering this death "real," however, the act of verbalizing unmasks the fact that George has fabricated it, since the killing of the son so closely resembles a previously revealed plot point of the same "novel" that George has purportedly been writing. Commenting on sacramental confession months before the film's release in 1966, Rev. Stevenson suggested that "both psychotherapy and religion operate under the theory that ultimate security lies in facing reality" (14), and *Who's Afraid of Virginia Woolf* remains invested in this painful process of coming to terms with reality, even while it complicates the distinction between truth and illusion—a distinction that Martha accuses George of failing to understand, although she too has fallen victim to this failure. If to confess involves "doing something with words" according to Austin's model of the performative, what confession does in this film is to make real or "true" the fact that the son is himself not real, that his "reality" is based upon the couple's binding verbal contract not to discuss him with others. Accordingly, Martha has already initiated the process of murdering her son by discussing him openly with Honey, as George now prompts Martha to embellish her description of their imaginary son in the presence of witnesses whose own recently revealed bout with imaginary progeny renders them attentive and empathetic listeners as well as witnesses. Martha seals her unknowing complicity in the murder of "the kid" as George recites a mass for the dead in Latin. These synchronous verbalizations and disclosures ultimately bring the son to life one last time as they kill him and mark his passing.

The film's final moments suggest that the catharsis of "killing" the son has also initiated a therapeutic process of reconciliation: alone in the aftermath of this disclosure, George and Martha seem closer to one another than ever before, the finality and irreversibility of the confessional act having now released them from any possibility of ever reviving this "third term" of their relationship. By speaking openly about their long-held illusion, they have begun to come to terms with its illusory nature. Their verbalizations and responses now comprise brief, simple exchanges marked by softness and an intimacy of communication entirely lacking from their interactions in the previous two hours and seventeen minutes of running time. "Just us?" Martha asks. "Yes," George responds, as they complete each other's thoughts, acknowledging a mutual isolation that the camera transforms into togetherness through a close-up of hand upon hand in a gentle caress, illuminated by the first rays of dawn.

If these final moments seem promising and redemptive for George and Martha, this is because, for better or worse, and more by circumstance than by design, they are now living outside the realm defined by their own mutually held illusions. And it is only at this moment that their desperate need to cling to a fiction developed in order to give their lives meaning and purpose is revealed to have been a psychopathological symptom of dysfunction, an inability or unwillingness to accept the ramifications of a specific physiological condition so devastating that they could never speak of it before. The film's ending finally moves them outside of themselves, from a state of hermetic isolation to some place beyond it, by the act of speaking, and doing so in front of witnesses who can now attest to the veracity of the disclosure. The narrative never specifies what will come next for them after this irrevocable confession, even while emphasizing that they could never have confronted this necessary next step without the painful unburdening that they have just completed.

The ending of *Who's Afraid of Virginia Woolf?* acknowledges the desolation that the "unspeakable" condition of human infertility poses to some couples—a problem that verbalization cannot cure, and that, on a grand scale, poses great risks to the future by denying this future itself, or at least parental access to the future, to the extent that this involves the prospect of progeny and legacy. The topical nature of this problem is verified in a different context in Stanley Kramer's *Guess Who's Coming to Dinner* (1967), released eighteen months after *Who's Afraid of Virginia Woolf?* and several months before the implementation of the new rating system. The two films initially seem like polar opposites: the first instrumental in dissolving the Production Code in favor of a system that acknowledged the changing tastes and concerns of adult audiences; the latter film a "throwback" to Old Hollywood, to an age confined to envision only the morally unquestionable realm of an undifferentiated "general" audience.[5] At the same time, however, the two films are connected through the value they ascribe to notions of generational progression embodied by the figure of the child—in this case, the mixed-race child whom we never see because this child has not yet been conceived, but whose safety from harm in a world that is changing—but not changing fast enough—resonates everywhere in the anxieties of prospective grandparents. If *Who's Afraid of Virginia Woolf?* conveys a sense of the tragic through a fear that after one's death there will be nothing left of you, *Guess Who's Coming to Dinner* retains a delicate and qualified hopefulness that the children of future generations might find themselves in a more accepting and embracing world. *Who's Afraid of Virginia Woolf?* is concerned about endings and reconciliations that must happen but that seem to come too late, while *Guess Who's Coming to Dinner* focuses upon the promise of new beginnings that have come too early, before the world is ready to embrace them.

The film's take on contemporary social issues strives to forge connections between old and new Hollywood, and also to bridge the generation gap and bring into productive dialogue the proponents of opposing perspectives on the controversial issue of miscegenation, in the wake of the Supreme Court decision on the case of *Loving v. Virginia* in June of 1967, after production had concluded but six months before the film's release.[6] The older generation is represented by the casting of Spencer Tracy and Katharine Hepburn in the roles of Matt and Christina Drayton, a wealthy San Francisco couple whose daughter Joey (played by Katharine Houghton, Ms. Hepburn's niece) has just fallen in love with the accomplished physician John Prentice (Sidney Poitier), whom she intends to marry soon after the couple announces the engagement to their parents.[7] Joey never finds their racial difference to be problematic, and John's love for Joey overrides his concerns about any obstacles that the couple might face. Because Christina's parents are politically progressive, Joey anticipates no resistance from either of them, although the film frequently reminds its audience that these issues are being presented at a moment of indecision and profound change, with attitudes and perspectives in flux.

Given the controversial matter of the couple's racial difference at this historical moment, much of the first two acts are devoted to the suspenseful anticipation of reactions to the couple's intentions as they disclose their "secret" to family and various friends. The narrative aligns identification and perspective with the parents' reactions to the news. Christina is surprised, but although her demeanor and facial expression initially suggest that she might be withholding her emotions, she soon enough expresses her support and delight at seeing her daughter so happy. Accordingly, the narrative centralizes Matt's less enthusiastic response as the one bearing the most weight because John has vowed not to marry Joey unless he receives the blessing of *both* of her parents.[8] The film elevates Matt's perspective not only because he is the father, but also because the character is portrayed by an actor who carries the weight of more than three decades of popularity in the Hollywood film industry. The fact that Tracy died shortly after production of the film was complete, and a full six months before the film's release, adds resonance to the status and authority of this paternal character in his final performance with an actress with whom he had a long, close personal and professional relationship.[9]

Even after John's parents accept Joey's invitation for dinner in San Francisco, decision-making authority remains something that John has bequeathed to Matt, and that Matt alone retains the power to deny. Not long after John's parents arrive, Mrs. Prentice (Beah Richards) approves and bonds affectively with her son, but when John's father (Roy E. Glenn, Sr.) expresses reservations similar to Matt's about the marriage, John evokes political, generation-gap discourse to abruptly dismiss his father's sentiments as outworn and oppressive. "You think of yourself as a colored man," John proclaims. "I think of myself as a man," he adds, explaining that he owes his father nothing—as his parents have brought him into this world, he expects them to sacrifice everything for him, just as he will do for his own children. Besides the two fathers, the only other male character of influence in the film is the Catholic priest Monsignor Ryan (Cecil Kellaway), a family friend who volunteers to serve as an intermediary in the effort to solicit Matt's acceptance; indeed, Monsignor Ryan is a most enlightened representative of post-Vatican II Catholicism, suggesting to Matt that mixed marriages work better because they require partners to display more compassion, and playfully accusing Matt of being a phony liberal as the priest dances and blissfully sings the reconciliatory refrain of The Beatles's "We Can Work It Out."

Yet Matt resists this and all other attempts at intervention, and the stage is set for a climactic verbalization that will culminate in his decision on whether or not to sanction the marriage. The careful weighing and evaluating of ideas and options—at his own pace, rather than in accordance with the tight schedule and firm deadline that his daughter and prospective son-in-law have set—requires a private, reflective process that the narrative largely elides from dramatization. Mothers just decide and move on, but this father has found cause to deliberate more extensively and exhaustively. The power granted to the father, and the suspense that builds around his still unrevealed final decision, make the moments leading up to his declaration resemble the uneasy anticipation of a group of defendants (except perhaps for John's father) awaiting notice that a judge has reached a decision on their case after extended deliberation. Because the outcome remains unknown to all besides the father himself, Matt's final, elaborate and extended "speech" resonates as a confession, yet it remains unclear whether the speaker will be performing the role of confessor—ready to establish the terms of reconciliation for those who have committed or contemplated a transgression—or an apologist finally determined to unburden himself of his own transgressive acts in a plea for forgiveness. Matt insists that all interested parties—including Tillie (Isabel Sanford), the Draytons's African-American maid who has been openly suspicious about John since his arrival—gather before him as an attentive audience. "There's something I want to say," he proclaims, accentuating the difficulty of the forthcoming pronouncement, yet curiously, throughout his painstakingly detailed, sequential recounting of the day's encounters and developments that the narrative has already dramatized, and his acknowledgment of the roles that everyone in the room has played, he consistently refers to each family participant in the third person as they all listen in attentive silence.

The tremendous buildup to the revelation of the father's decision prefigures the moment of catharsis when Matt gives his blessing to the couple, even while acknowledging the difficulties they will inevitably face in what the father describes as the "stinking world" that may not be ready for them or their children. Explaining that upon reflection he has realized how little it matters what he or his wife think about the marriage, however, the question arises as to what actually motivates or warrants this elaborate and extended confession of his feelings. Especially given that John and Joey have reservations for a flight that will depart in a few hours, Matt might certainly have been more concise. What ultimately justifies the confession—both to Matt and to the audience—is that it provides the only means for him to work through the intricacies and ambiguities of his own process of reflection.[10] His feelings and values make sense to him only by speaking about them, yet this process of verbal self expression effects a reconciliation with not only his own conscience, but also with his fellow performers of this family drama. If the interaction of these participants has been limited to private groups of two and three up to this point, the closing scene evokes a sense of community that stresses the importance of their mutual connections, of the fact that everyone in the room is somehow implicated in this decision-making process and its outcome. Matt's investment in this process of "reaching out" is most poignant when he addresses Kristina, explaining how his recollection of their own love, courtship, and marital plans so many years ago has helped him to clarify his feelings about the present situation. Through this reference and acknowledgment of the past, however, his verbalization also forges other vital connections. If the older generation is reconciled with the new, with the feeling of love transcending the pettiness of what Matt ultimately describes as Joey and John's "pigmentation problem," the film also serves as a bridge between old and new Hollywood—one that was admittedly on shaky ground by 1967, and that acknowledges the elevated perspective of the authoritative white male even as he proclaims to everyone that his authority has no basis, at least in this case. As an example of therapeutic, confessional enlightenment, however, Matt's speech is also meant as an advancement toward the larger goal of forging cross-generational connections, and of articulating, engaging, and reconciling opposing perspectives on both the generation gap and interracial marriage, addressed to audiences within and beyond the scope of this diegesis.[11] As a confessional act, Matt's verbalized deliberation comprises an internal, reflective process that requires a subsequent "reaching out" to others affected by his decision. As a therapeutic enterprise, *Guess Who's Coming to Dinner* offers the treatment of an immediate problem, but by doing so it strives to address the larger context of social problems that it references.

Guess Who's Coming to Dinner concludes as the networks of communication have just opened up between both families, with the two fathers inaudibly conversing side by side as they follow their wives and children into the dining room for the anticipated group meal. While the matter of marital sanctioning has apparently been resolved (Mr. Prentice voices no further objections), however, the narrative offers no prediction or promise about what will come next for Joey and John after the now-sanctioned marriage takes place—only a sense of qualified optimism fueled by their mutual determination and the support network that the narrative has just evidenced. Three years later, the film industry would offer a counter-perspective on the efficacy of confession in relation to prevailing intergenerational problems with Bob Rafelson's *Five Easy Pieces* (1970), the director's subsequent release after *Head* (discussed in chapter 4). Dramatizing conflicts that cannot be resolved through open communication strategies, by negative example *Five Easy Pieces* reinforces the notion that, especially at a time when psychotherapy and religion have interconnected so closely, the confessional act requires very specific penitent/confessor circumstances and dynamics to bring about forgiveness and reconciliation.

A modest-budget film compared to the general-audience, behemoth productions of the Old Hollywood whose box-office failures had drawn some studios to the point of bankruptcy at the time of the film's release—*Five Easy Pieces* offers a close character analysis of Robert (Bobby) Dupea (Jack Nicholson), who has exiled himself from an affluent family of accomplished classical musicians living in Washington state. Having curtailed his training as a classical pianist against his family's wishes years earlier, Bobby is working on an oil rig as the film begins. While John Prentice's professional identity as an accomplished and renowned physician working globally for the World Health Organization aligns him with the social standing of the wealthy Draytons of San Francisco, to the degree where the matter of class is neither questioned nor examined, Bobby rebels against the trappings of professional high-culture that his siblings and father hold sacred. He lives in modest quarters and bowls on weekends with his workmate Elton (Billy Green Bush) and his girlfriend Rayette (Karen Black), even as he demeans her and lies to her to cover up his sexual affairs with other women. The traditional notions of success and professional accomplishment in *Guess* become precisely what Bobby Dupea is determined to rebel against, even if he is often prone to displays of class-based arrogance and superiority. Near the start of the film, for example, he calls Rayette "pathetic" and is embarrassed later on when she shows up at the Dupea family home instead of waiting patiently and indefinitely at the motel where he has dropped her off, but when a guest poetess at the house judgmentally belittles Rayette for her lower-class speech, Bobby instinctively lashes out at the woman for her haughtiness.[12]

In place of embraces, unions, and communicative connections that characterize the supportive family network of *Guess*, *Five Easy Pieces* substitutes intergenerational family alienation, frustrated and failed attempts at connection, and departures that lend validity to Roger Greenspun's suggestion that the film "is built around a series of good-bys (sic)" (26).[13] The tensions surface especially after Bobby's sister Tita (Lois Smith) urges him to return home to visit his father (William Challee), who has become incapacitated by a stroke. Addressed at home as "Robert" rather than "Bobby," he almost immediately regrets his decision to return after encountering his immobilized father, who maintains a bold, piercing stare while remaining silent and entirely unreceptive to his environment. Bobby's frustrated comment that "He doesn't even know who the hell I am" sets the stage for a final encounter that is structured as a confession, even if the catharsis fails to elicit the therapeutic reconciliation that Matt Drayton attained. In this post-Old Hollywood realm, the disparate circumstances of Bobby's attempt at reconnection complicate his attempt to gain forgiveness or to overcome his own sense of isolation.

Having moved his father by wheelchair to the seaside, Bobby arranges the confessional scene as a private encounter—one for which he remains mostly unprepared, having agreed to make this attempt only at Tita's insistence. While the closed circuit of the encounter might not in itself prevent the efficacy of the confession, Bobby also contends with the likely possibility that his father, who assumes the role of confessor, is not an active listener (though Tita still feels that he might be), and that his apology may literally be falling upon deaf ears. Despite the open-air setting, the uncertainty surrounding the condition of the listener, and the absence of witnesses attesting to the encounter, suggest the conditions of a confessional booth where a barely visible priest never outwardly reacts to the penitent's verbalization. Disorienting as these conditions become, however, they also produce an ideal, no-risk situation for Bobby, freeing him to speak about whatever comes to his mind without having to weigh the consequences of his words or actions. "My feeling is I don't know that if you could talk that we wouldn't be talking," he admits, even though these circumstances accentuate his discomfort as he realizes that he has so little to say: "The best that I can do is apologize. We both know that I was never that good at it anyway. I'm sorry it didn't work out," he admits, presumably referring to his decision to give up a career as a classical pianist, yet his admission applies equally to his relationship with a man whose present condition of physical unresponsiveness literalizes a broader sense of lifelong disconnection between father and son. Bobby's words might drop away and fail to convey meaning to his father, yet this confession comprises the only scene in the film where he openly reflects upon his own behavior and actions, where he registers as "truth" an emotional vulnerability powerful enough to move him to tears. The confession, however, ultimately produces no reconciliation with himself or his father through any mutual, participatory process; instead, it resonates as a final rite of passage, an acknowledgment of a source of influence that has now been relegated to the past, as if Bobby were speaking these final words to a corpse moments before the sealing of the coffin. This ambiguous outcome suggests that the therapeutic, reflective process that Bobby undergoes in the confessional scene ultimately fails to transcend the circumstances of the specific moment of encounter with his father, such that it might bear upon Bobby's future actions and decisions. Yet this alienated wanderer's emotional confession still serves as a prerequisite to his moving on, having now realized through experience that the conditions of communication with his father will not accommodate forgiveness or redemption, and that this final attempt cannot "undo the damage and set things right again" (O'Toole 147). And indeed, the film's closing scenes comprise two more departures: after exchanging goodbyes with Tita, in the final scene at a gas station Bobby hitches a ride from a truck driver, leaving Rayette behind without letting her know. If the interpersonal disconnections of *Five Easy Pieces* originate from a deeply rooted, longstanding conflict between father and son, the film ultimately configures its version of the generation gap less in terms of a problem readily resolvable through the strategies of open communication made universally accessible in *Guess Who's Coming to Dinner*, than as a lingering, existential condition of personal and interpersonal alienation ceaselessly plaguing this alienated 1970 protagonist.

Sex, Sexuality, and Confessional Discourse

Bobby's confession qualifies as a communicative "failure" because his intentions are ultimately out of sync with the results of his attempt to connect with his father and redeem himself in the process. The notion of failure becomes an aspect of the characterization of this alienated anti-hero, while also functioning thematically in the larger context of the narrative. Bobby *wants* to connect, but circumstances—some within his control, others not—intervene. Offering newly sanctioned "adult" entertainment that incorporated sex and erotic subject matter in ways that would not have been possible five years earlier, the confessional narrative dynamic would take new directions during this early period of American cinema under the new rating system, motivated by the promised revelation of sexual "secrets." In the context of overlapping psychotherapeutic and religious practices by the late 1960s, the confessions of these cinematic narratives "fail" in quite different ways. Often because choices of narrative structure and style interfere with the intentions and results of the confessional act, such confession becomes little more than a premise for sexual exploitation. It is worth considering two examples of these "failed" narratives in some detail, since their failure helps to illuminate the conditions required for the intricate, complex cinematic confessional narrative to follow through with its promise of forgiveness and reconciliation.

The promise of "full disclosure" dominates Ernest Lehman's 1972 cinematic adaptation of Philip Roth's controversial 1969 novel *Portnoy's Complaint*.[14] The novel comprises an extended first-person monologue narrated by the protagonist Alexander Portnoy and directed to the voiceless, uncharacterized psychiatrist Dr. Spielvogel, whom Portnoy consults on a regular basis because of his "problem": masturbation appears to be his primary means of sexual arousal. The entire novel is structured as a psychotherapeutically motivated act of disclosure—one involving Portnoy's guilt-ridden Jewish heritage and a series of unsuccessful relationships with women. An extreme example of the compulsion to transform sex into discourse, the novel's protagonist narrates (in first-person) the details of his sexual history in a way that forges an alliance between Portnoy, the reader, and Dr. Spielvogel—an alliance based, on one side, upon disclosure, and on the other, upon mutual silence and attentive listening that fuels the protagonist's compulsion to perpetuate his exhaustive narration. Strategically containing the scope of its audience to both the doctor/patient relationship of the psychotherapeutic setting, and to the narrator/reader relationship to which it extends, the narrative registers Portnoy's confession as a highly self-reflexive performance in which the act of verbalization recursively regenerates itself, eliciting neither therapeutic redemption nor a catharsis that might bring the verbalization to a halt, or even a pause. Accordingly, the novel's intended audience comprises not only Spielvogel and the reader, but also Portnoy, whose awareness of his own act of speaking spurs him on to continue.

Under these conditions, the adaptation of the psychotherapeutic confessional dynamic from novel to screen disorientingly violates these unspoken terms of the narrational and confessional agreement between Portnoy, Spielvogel, and an extra-diegetic "listener" whose part now appears to have been recast. Spielvogel occasionally appears in the film, usually to remind viewers that Portnoy is undergoing psychotherapy, but the cinematic narrative otherwise places Portnoy in a diegetic space located somewhere *outside* the therapeutic confessional setting. One scene, for example, features a medium-long shot of Portnoy and his recent sexual conquest, "The Monkey" (Karen Black), in bed together, apparently after having sex. Portnoy's abstract gaze is directed outward, with his partner's head resting upon his chest, her eyes barely visible as he proudly and eagerly relates in detail how he managed to conceal from his parents the visible evidence of his frequent acts of masturbation—a verbalization that includes his notorious erotic experiment with a piece of uncooked liver.[15] The presence of an embodied listener in the frame as Portnoy relates these transgressive acts reconfigures The Monkey as the intended listener of the confession, even though Portnoy never directly addresses her and they never exchange glances or make eye contact. The narration thereby divorces both the psychoanalyst and the viewer from the context of the confessional, therapeutic dynamic, substituting another, diegetically present listener whose investment in the confession remains undefined, verifying her identity as an attentive listener only through the occasional giggle that registers as an affirmative reaction to Portnoy's outrageous disclosure. The composite effect of such narrative devices and choices is to emphasize the importance within the confessional dynamic of configuring the identity of the listener—or group of listeners—as an agent whose investment in the verbalization authorizes the penitent to disclose, and who offers the speaker the verification or redemption sought through the prospect of such disclosure. Even though Portnoy often appears to be speaking primarily to and for himself, this cinematic translation of his confession reiterates that, as part of the implicit agreement of the confessional dynamic, listeners must possess specific qualifications in order to serve as effective and effecting witnesses. Without his qualification, the narrative reduces itself to an exploitation of the shock value of Portnoy's disclosures, substituting smug self-aggrandizement for reflective, verbalized contemplation.

Philip Roth's novel was certainly notorious, yet masturbation itself had shed much of its identity as a psychopathological phenomenon by the time of the novel's release, largely relegated to the background in relation to sexual disorders such as male impotence and what was now bearing the label of "female sexual dysfunction." In terms of suitability for onscreen representation, however, homosexuality remained a more controversial theme until the early 1960s, when it became one of the last of the topic restrictions that the Production Code Administration lifted. Even in the relatively permissive early years of the MPAA's rating system in the late 1960s, however, condemnatory treatments of the topic remained the norm in Hollywood cinema, with films such as *The Detective* (Gordon Douglas, 1968), *The Sergeant* (John Flynn, 1968), *The Gay Deceivers* (Bruce Kessler, 1969), and *Staircase* (Stanley Donen, 1969) continuing the industry's tradition of associating sexual difference with deviance and pathology. Until 1973, the American Psychiatric Association supported this pathologization of homosexuality by including it in the Diagnostic and Statistical Manual of Mental Disorders (DSM).

Increasingly visible in news media and popular culture, the notion of homosexuality as a *treatable* and potentially reversible pathology made it an especially appropriate candidate for confessional discourse in the realms of both religion (as a sin) and psychotherapy (as something repressed). Although *Doctors' Wives* (George Schaefer, 1971, based upon the Frank G. Slaughter novel) was unsuccessful at the box office, it exploited the topic of homosexuality—along with other disorders that replicate the sexual psychopathologies dramatized in *The Chapman Report*—while providing the opportunity for its sexually under-fulfilled, eponymous protagonists to transform sex into discourse, and, in this case, to also make good on a promise to transform discourse into sex. The film opens at a posh social club, where overworked male physicians discuss their recent cases over a game of poker while the women play cards out of earshot at a separate table, their conversation dominated by the sexually liberated Lorrie Dellman (Dyan Cannon), who diagnoses the wives' collective "problem" as "sexual malnutrition."[16] She graciously offers to test her diagnosis by having sex with each of their husbands, intimating that she has "already covered fifty percent of the territory." Yet Lorrie never gets the opportunity to complete her experiment or to repent for having proposed it: by the following morning, her husband Mortimer (John Colicos) has shot and killed Lorrie after finding her in bed with colleague Paul McGill (George Gaynes), who is critically wounded in the incident.

Lorrie's assessment of her friends' "condition" turns out to be astute, and the narrative proceeds with a comprehensive analysis of the causes, symptoms, and treatments of their sexual problems. The studio's advertising strategy for the film foregrounds this clinical method, with each woman manifesting her own specific means of "sublimation of problems" that includes "frigidity," "nymphomania," "alcohol," "tranquilizers and committees," and "golf" ("Box Office Analysis and Advertising Approach," Jack Atlas Papers). The last sublimation has become the preferred sexual substitute for Della Randolph (Rachel Roberts), but one that makes her no less bitter, enraged, or dismissive in the presence of her psychiatrist husband Dave (Gene Hackman), who persistently probes her to express her feelings. With the couple on the brink of separation after Lorrie's funeral, the scene is set for a confession that aligns with religious notions of sin, remorse, and reconciliation, along with psychological notions of insight, verbalization, and catharsis. Clinical and professionally detached, yet heavily invested in his wife's determination to reveal what plagues her, Dave becomes an ideal confessor, a most qualified therapeutic agent, and an attentive listener as Della—haunted by the sound of Lorrie's laugh (as an extreme close-up of her terrified expression verifies)—describes at length and in vivid detail a recent incident, when Lorrie succeeded in seducing her despite Della's protestations ("I told her to stop!") and ultimate revelation ("I wanted her to touch me—just once only. Only that night."). Despite Della's insistence that "I've hated her every minute since," Dave loses his composure and proceeds to beat his wife frantically with the morning newspaper. Checking his behavior immediately afterwards, however, he proceeds to hold Della in his arms as she sobs, attempting to comfort her after her well-earned moment of catharsis. She responds lovingly to the man who holds the sole power to forgive her, and their reconciliation intimates that the confessional process has not only entirely expiated Lorrie's guilt about the sexual encounter, but also *cured* Lorrie of both her lesbian desire and her marital problems—all in less than five minutes' time. In *Doctors' Wives*, then, confessional disclosure functions as a performative act that quickly remedies any predisposition or inclination for sexual experimentation outside the boundaries of heteronormativity. The prospect and manifestation of such a fast-acting "cure" remain out of sync with the practice of confession in either a psychological or religious context, even as it provides a convenient ideological tool for containing and expelling "perverse" sexualities. *Doctors' Wives* exploits both sex and sexual difference during a process of revealing painful, humiliating, and repressed "truths" through the vehicle of the confessional act.

In contrast, the confessional strategies deployed by the homosexual male characters of William Friedkin's *The Boys in the Band* (1970) align much more closely with the contemporaneous developments in psychotherapy and the Catholic Church after Vatican II. Indeed, the film's central protagonist Michael (Kenneth Nelson) is tied to both institutions, explaining early on that he is still "in therapy," and deciding as his final action in the narrative that he will now go to Mass. An adaptation of Mart Crowley's successful 1968 off-Broadway play,[17] the film is the product of a historical moment when the gay community's longstanding social and political oppression had only very recently begun to yield to gathering forces of resistance. It is, consequently, quite appropriate that the film uses the psychotherapeutic dynamic of confession so intently, since the narrative dramatizes the unveiling of secrets that had been both psychologically difficult and culturally dangerous to disclose, given a social climate where homosexuality was still considered aberrant and criminal.[18] At the same time, the ability to safely disclose these secrets in the context of theatrical or cinematic narrative gave voice to a silenced, oppressed community—a voice that other homosexuals might recognize, and that straight audiences might relate to as well.[19]

The first half of *The Boys in the Band* centers upon a group of friends' extended preparation for a party at Michael's Manhattan apartment to celebrate Harold's (Leonard Frey) birthday. The plans are interrupted when Michael's "straight" college friend Alan (Peter White) telephones, pleading with Michael to make time to see him that day. Michael prompts the others to tone down their gay banter when the uninvited guest arrives, and after Alan calls back to say that he cannot come after all, Michael and the entire group are relieved. The anticipation of a party and the prospect of close friends arriving and coming together make the tone of this first half of the film light, as accentuated by dynamic camera movement tracing the characters' intersecting paths as they move freely through the indoor and outdoor patio spaces of the apartment. The spirit of festivity reaches its peak when the men join together in an exuberant line dance filmed in medium-long shot to highlight the characters' closeness and connectedness.

And then, quite suddenly, the tone changes. Alan has decided to come after all, and now, several drinks into the evening, no one except the straight-acting Hank (Laurence Luckenbill) seems prepared or interested in accommodating his intrusive presence, least of all Emory (Cliff Gorman), who refuses to disguise his sexual identity for Alan's sake. Alan and Emory soon exchange insults and fight viciously just as Harold arrives for his celebration. Angry at Alan for mocking Avery's effeminacy, Michael decides to start drinking again, and he soon dominates the conversation, peppering it with sharp invective directed indiscriminately at his guests, who must now confine their activities to the closer quarters of the living room space because of a violent rainstorm. The camera becomes static, with close-ups and two-shots emphasizing the environment's claustrophobia,[20] exacerbated when Michael announces to the guests that they will now play a game, and that no one is permitted to leave.

The narrative traces a movement from open, social connection and communication to tightly compressed isolation and alienation—from exteriority to the realm of an interior that coincides with a shift to a mournful, contemplative tone aligned with the rules of Michael's game:

each man is challenged to telephone the person he has truly loved and confess this love to him. Disguised as an attempt to dispel hypocrisies by having each man express the painful "truth" of his feelings, the confessional game instead precipitates interpersonal conflict, resulting in shame, regret, and humiliation. As Michael goads his guests into deeper humiliation, the scenario begins to resemble a dysfunctional group support network, one in which the person exacting the confession of the other's "secret" is more interested in meting out punishment than facilitating absolution, catharsis, or forgiveness. Michael ultimately focuses his invective upon Alan, striving to unmask his friend's hypocrisy by coercing him to reveal the latent homosexuality that his friend ultimately denies.

Much like the roles that George and Martha alternately play to assert power and control in *Who's Afraid of Virginia Woolf?*, Michael's self-nomination for the role of confessor provides him with a momentary illusion of power that is ultimately decimated when Harold defies him.[21] Harold refuses to play the game, and he proceeds to reverse the power dynamics by transforming Michael into the penitent, publically revealing his friend's own "truths," including his sadness, self-hatred, his disgust at his own sexuality, and his inability to accept that it is not something he can ever change about himself. Exposed, shamed, and humiliated after his humiliated guests depart, Michael breaks down before Donald (Frederick Combs), the emotional anchor who has supported him unconditionally and without judgment. Michael cries, apologizes, and for only a brief moment willingly exposes his own vulnerability by confessing that he wants to commit suicide (see fig. 5.2). Once he has received his requisite share of solace, however, Michael quickly returns to his former self: "Show me a happy homosexual, and I'll show you a gay corpse."

While this drama results in emotional devastation, *The Boys in the Band* ultimately affirms the therapeutic value of confession in ways that resonate with the phenomenon's alliance with the fields of religion and psychology during the 1960s. Michael may want his friends to suffer as much as he is suffering, yet even in the context of the spiteful games he forces them to play, expressions of empathy and mutual comfort emerge. Sharing the weight of social oppression and human suffering, the group of gay friends finds opportunities to reach out to one another. Despite Michael's efforts to dispel this empathy, it surfaces as Emory consoles Bernard (Reuben Greene), who has become inconsolably regretful after the awkward phone call he has just finished. Other guests strengthen their mutual bond, especially the couple Hank and Larry (Keith Prentice), who have remained alienated from one another throughout the party because of tension over conflicting expectations regarding sexual monogamy, but who ultimately use the game format and dynamic as

Figure 5.2. Donald (Frederick Combs, right) consoles Michael (Kenneth Nelson, left) near the ending of *The Boys in the Band* (William Friedkin, Cinema Center Films/Leo Films, 1970). Digital frame enlargement.

an opportunity to proclaim their love for one another and to vow to respect their mutual differences. Indeed, with their vulnerabilities and limitations now exposed, even Emory and Alan find common ground and apologize for their former conflict. "If we could just not hate ourselves so much," Michael suggests. Were there ever a need for a cure, *The Boys in the Band* suggests, it would be a cure not for homosexuality but for the devastating psychological effects that social and cultural ostracization relentlessly inflicts upon his subjects. Here, confession becomes an antidote to silence, and while it cannot bring about such a cure, the connections and bonds that emerge and strengthen during this very dark night attest to the power of therapeutic healing through attempts at reaching out, even when the compulsion to retreat seems so comfortably familiar, and so tempting.

Ultimately, these connections harbor at least as much value as Michael's morning visit to the psychotherapist, or tonight's midnight Mass, since the efficacy of both of these therapeutic endeavors remained compromised by the historically specific conditions of American culture. Although *The Boys in the Band* never reveals much about the methods of Michael's psychiatrist, the fact remains that homosexuality was still listed as a disorder in the DSM-II in 1970. The Catholic Church that Vatican II had modernized a few years earlier had certainly not become so accepting to embrace Michael unless he tacitly agreed to continue to disguise or disavow his homosexuality, or unless his self-hatred remained such that he would invest in the power of the Church to make him heterosexual. The idiosyncrasies of his personality notwithstanding, however, the sense of connection and comfort that Michael finds after his cathartic confession to Donald could never be anything but momentary. Rather than an act that the Catholic Church devised as a panacea for mankind's inherent sinfulness, confession remains part of a lifelong process of coming-to-terms with oneself that Michael is unprepared to recognize. The more pressing problem is that he has misidentified his "sickness" as homosexuality itself, when his suffering more clearly derives from the guilt that he feels about his sexual predisposition. So, is Michael sick? Clearly not—were he living in another world, or at least in a future when homosexuality had not just begun to shed its association with psychopathology.

Conclusion

Despite the fame and notoriety that director William Friedkin would earn years later, *The Boys in the Band* is not a traditional Hollywood film. It features no actors with name recognition; instead, all of its players appeared in the off-Broadway production that premiered two years earlier. As a film of historical significance, however, it demonstrates a problem with which the American film industry was contending during its "darkest" financial period—a problem common to many of the cinematic productions discussed in this book. Therapy in the 1960s—as an institution-based professional practice or a sociocultural dynamic—is most successful an enterprise in American cinema when it is introduced in conjunction with a clearly defined problem. One reason is that the problem provides a functional tool for engaging and sustaining audience interest in the context of the "classical" narrative construction prominent in Hollywood cinema (along with many films produced outside of it), since problems anticipate resolutions. Also, on an ideological level, the therapeutic agent (psychiatrist, sex therapist, marriage therapist, or confessor) has the best chance of success when this agent confronts problems around which national consensus has already been established.

In the case of *The Boys in the Band*, the fact that the problem the narrative poses is only a problem to the extent that Michael misperceives it as such already limits the efficacy of the therapies that are introduced to confront it. Even if it qualifies as a "problem" at all, Michael's problem is not one that lends itself to definitive closure: while it manifests itself in aggression and scorn, the conflict remains internal, and his emotional breakdown anticipates no resolution. The more profound issue, however, is that no national consensus around the "acceptability" of homosexuality in American society had yet been attained by the time of the film's production or release. Indeed, among the film's remarkable achievements is that, despite its designation as an art-house release with limited distribution, the film brought a context of needless, senseless human suffering to the attention of the broader American public. As a case study on the efficacy of therapy, however, it falls short: any sense of interpersonal bonding, empathy and community is relegated primarily to the other characters, and not to Michael, the host who has instigated their humiliation. Meanwhile, Michael suffers.

The status and efficacy of therapy in *The Boys in the Band* is antithetical to that of *Guess Who's Coming to Dinner*, produced only three years earlier. Here, the framing of the problem is precise and on target: a father must decide whether to sanction or forbid his daughter's marriage. And although the national consensus around the issue of miscegenation had been only recently confirmed by the Supreme Court case of *Loving v. Virginia*, the official position—of the prevailing administration, at least—was that racial discrimination was incontrovertibly unjust. Accordingly, the white father succeeds in his mission as therapeutic agent, even though he wavers and deliberates for some time before verbalizing a decision that redeems him along with the narrative itself.

Across the five primary contexts of therapy examined here, instances of therapeutic success and failure follow patterns similar to those noted in *Guess Who's Coming to Dinner* and *The Boys in the Band*. Therapies for sexual dysfunction present an especially noteworthy case, since there is so little controversy inherent in the topic. Even if openly articulating or dramatizing such dysfunction in American cinema of the early 1960s was quite controversial, few would argue that a sustained inability to perform sexual acts was preferable to finding sexual pleasure or fulfillment. Accordingly, sexual dysfunction could be readily identified as a problem that could benefit from therapeutic treatment, and the psychoanalytic method used in *The Chapman Report* and *Marnie* proved especially effective not because it was necessarily the most suitable choice, but because audiences of this era were so accustomed to the psychoanalytic discourse that framed the "problem." As noted earlier, it initially seems curious that even after the film industry was granted license to confront sexual issues more frankly and explicitly, and even with the pharmaceutical, technological, and cultural advancements sanctioning the sexual revolution of the later 1960s, the industry still elected to produce films that constituted sex as a problem to be resolved. Given the status of the "problem" in narrative structure, however, the decision to focus upon resolving sexual dysfunction makes perfect sense: while an unrestrained celebration of sex on the screen might seem marketable in the context of the late 1960s or the early 1970s, the dramatization of sexual dysfunction is the option that anticipates a crisis and its resolution. Within such narratives of dysfunction, the emphasis upon male impotence also turns out to be most appropriate at a historical moment when second-wave feminist discourse was challenging male sexual dominance so overtly. The fact that *this* topic was controversial and potentially divisive, however, correlates with the necessity of Jonathan's therapeutic failure in *Carnal Knowledge*, a way of critiquing masculine excess and bravado while refraining from too overtly celebrating female power. (Indeed, women in the film are not offered much reason to celebrate.) Without the security of consensus, therapeutic strategies must fail, in order to ensure that audiences on neither side of the issue are excluded or unduly offended.

In chapter 3, I noted that even though many sociologists of the mid-1960s were less optimistic about the fate of marriage than psychologists and psychiatrists, the determination to preserve the marriage institution prevailed in popular discourse. This too required that marriage be constituted as a problem, even while steadily increasing divorce rates compromised the security of consensus. Making matters more complex, changes in the gender and political contexts of the problem would shift dramatically over the course of a decade. Comedic treatments of the institution in mid-1960s films such as *How to Murder Your Wife* and *A Guide for the Married Man* attempted to balance the scales of gender through ironic and satirical approaches to marriage, such that the institution was shown to jeopardize male sexual freedom even while cinematic narratives simultaneously criticized men for desiring such freedom. Shortly afterwards, the film industry even experimented with incorporating the matter of consensus itself into the plot of *Divorce American Style*, where a world in which husbands and wives no longer listen to each other signals a problem that must be corrected by making marriage stronger. As the influences of second-wave feminism gained momentum in the final years of the decade, films such as *Diary of a Mad Housewife* secured consensus by placing central female protagonists in circumstances of such extreme oppression that it became unthinkable for audiences of either gender to condone such treatment. Under the less extreme conditions of oppression that prevail in the early 1970s film *The Marriage of a Young Stockbroker*, in which the culprit of the marriage problem becomes more ambiguous, the matter of consensus is addressed through a curious process of cancelling out all imaginable ideological positions from the narrative, vilifying the feminist movement for its oppression of men *and* women while condemning the institution of marriage for the unreasonable demands and expectations it generates. Once the process of cancellation is complete and the ideologies removed, liberated ex-wife and ex-husband are left with nothing more than to embark upon an escapist celebration of untapped human potential.

The controversy surrounding psychedelic drug use presents issues that are equally difficult to negotiate cinematically. Since most of the American films focusing upon the use of LSD were released after the drug became illegal, after scientists were denied access to the hallucinogen for research purposes, and also after Timothy Leary was transformed into the national representative of hallucinogenic excess, overtly vilifying this chemical substance seemed a more reasonable fallback position for the film industry than exploring or celebrating its therapeutic uses. Adhering to this dominant discourse of vilification also perfectly aligned with the decision to constitute LSD use as a problem to be resolved. From the film industry's perspective, however, such logic was complicated by the fact that vilifying LSD also meant vilifying the thousands of members of the younger generation who were experimenting with it, and who also constituted the most likely audience for the genre. Far from foolproof, the strategy of playing to both sides of the generation gap—of securing the failure of LSD as a therapeutic agent while provoking curiosity about hallucinogenic experimentation—arose from a recognition of this dilemma, one that most often resulted in contradictory, paradoxical, and uneven narratives that puzzled critics and audiences alike.

And as the first chapter demonstrates, cinematic configurations of the therapist/patient dynamic are just as reliant upon the necessity of tangible problems and determinations of consensus. Cinema of the early 1960s framed psychopathological problems in both social and political terms, refraining from alienating audiences by anchoring narrative plots to such universally intolerable historical conditions as totalitarianism, Nazism, and white supremacy (*Pressure Point, Shock Corridor*). When the escalation of the Vietnam War disrupted political consensus by the middle of the decade, however, the therapist was demoted from professional healer and attentive listener to ineffectual (and most often pathetic) bystander in a series of romantic comedies that attempted to situate sex—or more specifically, how men might get more of it from women without giving much back in the way of "commitment"—as the problem around which consensus could be built. It was not until much later in the decade that the therapist would regain a place in a politicized interpersonal dynamic, in films that remained critical of the psychiatric profession while becoming more attentive to the advancements of the women's movement.

Through a period of slightly more than a decade, then, shifting historical conditions complicated the film industry's attempt to secure audience appeal in support of a therapeutic dynamic that would infiltrate the fields of psychology, psychiatry, pharmacology, politics, religion, sex and sexuality, and gender and race relations. The industry's dedication to formulating clearly defined problems to drive its narratives, and its equal attention to ensuring that these problems dovetailed with matters of national consensus, demonstrated its commitment to continue to apply "general" audience criteria to a composite viewership with vastly different priorities, ideologies, and expectations.

Further reflecting upon how historical, cultural, and institutional conditions enhance the prospect of therapeutic success, I close this study with a return to its starting point, in a reconsideration of the "sick society" that Robert Kennedy in 1968 so passionately urged Americans to counteract and rectify by practicing the principles of empathy, unity, and connectedness. Did America heed this call? A brief examination of subsequent developments in politics and cinema as the nation transitioned to a new decade offers a rather disheartening response to this question. The sociopolitical conditions of America that prompted Kennedy's 1968 plea definitely intensified in the years that followed: the nation's involvement in the Vietnam War would continue until 1973, and the circumstances surrounding the military's withdrawal from this prolonged Southeast Asian conflict, as well as its aftermath for the south Vietnamese people, provided neither a cause for celebration, nor any sense of redemption for the thousands of lives lost. Accordingly, as Bruce J. Shulman suggests, confidence in the effectuality of organized public resistance was also compromised, since despite the protests of the counterculture, "GIs invaded Cambodia and students died at Kent State" (15-16). Referencing an opinion poll of college students taken in the first years of the Nixon era, Terry H. Anderson relates that "half held no living American in high regard, and over 40 percent felt America was a 'sick society,' did not think that they shared the views of most citizens, and even considered moving to another country" (251).

If the therapeutic potential of empathy and human connectedness requires a sustained belief and investment in the value of trust—in others, and in a government that fairly represents its citizens—public revelations of government activities in the opening years of the new decade thwarted this potential. The release of the *Pentagon Papers* in 1971 brought to light a wealth of information on America's previously undisclosed aims and objectives by initiating and sustaining conflict in Southeast Asia. That this information deviated from, and often contradicted, the government's "official" line across several decades and presidencies resonated as both a drastic rewriting of international history and a grand-scale deception. If this was not enough to prompt Americans to be more cautious about unquestioningly believing the rhetoric and policies of top-level political figures, the gradual disclosure of the incumbent executive branch's instigation and cover-up of the Watergate scandal exacerbated an already growing sense of distrust and cynicism about the sincerity and integrity of its national leadership. American presidents had misrepresented their actions and intentions to the citizens whom they had been elected to serve, and the revelation of these lies resonated as a betrayal. As Shulman suggests, "The ideal of social solidarity, the conception of a national community with duties and obligations to one's fellow citizens, elicited greater skepticism during the 1970s" (xv).

This profound sense of national distrust contributed to the manifestation of what Robert Kolker aptly describes as a "cinema of loneliness," one that addresses "a continual impotence in the world" (10) and that "leaves its viewers bereft of hope for change or community" (xi). Kolker's intensive study of alienation, powerlessness, and loss of control spans across genres in the work of a number of directors, many of whom belong to what we now reference as the "Hollywood Renaissance." A brief examination of a handful of such early 1970s films evidences a remarkable perspectival shift from the therapeutic strategies that had prevailed in the very recent 1960s. As we have seen, concerns about loneliness, disconnectedness and an insidious, festering alienation brought about by technocracy remained prominent throughout much of this decade, yet the prospect of effective, successful therapeutic treatment—in professional analyst/patient relations, individual or group experiments with psychedelic drugs, or confessional settings—was consistently configured as a process of opening up or reaching out beyond the boundaries of the self, toward the realization of a sense of interpersonal connection and community. In the cinema of the early- to mid-1970s, however, the sense of disconnectedness is itself amplified, while the conviction to counteract or overcome it increasingly dissipates.

In some cases, this dissipation surfaces as therapeutic methods and objectives that once seemed so effective are either weakened or rhetorically reworked to serve counter-therapeutic purposes. For example, the recruitment strategies of the sinister, eponymous corporation of *The Parallax View* (Alan J. Pakula, 1974) reposition the therapeutic prospect of "living up to one's potential" in psychopathological terms, in an effort to breed efficient political assassins, with the corporation's recruiter Jack Younger (Walter McGinn) marveling at his success in the products he develops: "If I can earn their loyalty, I can give them a sense of their own worth." After a series of uncomfortably long pauses, the admirable efforts of Joanna (Katharine Ross) and Bobbie (Paula Prentiss) to foster nondomestic communication in a women's consciousness-raising group comprising the mostly mechanized neighbors of the "ideal" planned community in *The Stepford Wives* (Bryan Forbes, 1975) soon devolve into a series of bizarre confessions about failed ironing methods, culminating in the eager testimony of one of the robotically transformed guests that she would gladly appear for free in a television commercial for Easy-On Spray Starch. In *The Conversation* (Francis Ford Coppola, 1974), surveillance expert Harry Caul (Gene Hackman) belies the process of absolving himself in the church confessional booth, first admitting his concern for the young couple who may suffer because of the evidence he is collecting against them, and then clarifying that whatever happens to them is neither his doing nor his fault.

Harry's paradoxical, fault-free confession correlates with another prominent means by which a yearning for connectedness becomes compromised in these films, through the triumph of a nameless, faceless, yet overwhelming technocracy that thwarts the efforts of any therapeutic endeavor that might inspire citizens to resist what Carl Rogers, in the context of the 1960s, described as the "increasing dehumanization of our culture, where the person doesn't count" (10). *The Conversation* highlights technocracy's potential to reduce human investment in the integrity of cause-effect relationships, and also in the development of a sense of accountability for one's actions. Harry clearly struggles with this matter of accountability, but what he ultimately struggles *for* is the ability to disavow the extent to which his actions precipitate consequences that are often dire. The technocratic impulse of *The Conversation* becomes one that insidiously seeks to transform empathic human emotions—specifically, those that empower the subject with a sense of "reaching out" beyond the self, of forging connections with others—into a "value-neutral" arrangement of mechanized functions that invert this process of connection, forcing the subject to retreat into a state of alienation and isolation. No wonder, then, that instruments of technological "progress" vie for the status of central protagonist in these dramas. The entire credit sequence of *Klute* (Alan J. Pakula, 1971) appears over an extended, static take of a tape recorder playing back the private disclosures of Bree Daniels (Jane Fonda), while relegating to offscreen space the identity of the individual who has secured and initiated the playback of this recording. Throughout the film's climactic scene, as the villain Peter Cable (Charles Cioffi) shares with Bree his tape-recorded documentation of his murder of her friend, Cable himself remains offscreen, sociopathically disengaged from any responsibility for his crime, as the camera focuses upon a close-up of Bree's terrified and devastated reaction to the murder to which she is technologically bearing witness.

Cumulatively, these early 1970s films attest to a chronic societal illness, the culmination of a technocratic ideal that witnesses the triumph of a faceless, alienating force wholly proficient in transforming its subjects' investment in human trust—without which the therapeutic value of human communication cannot be realized—into doubt, anxiety, and suspicion. Indeed, in the dismal, alienating realms of this cinema, trust no longer forges or cements human bonds; instead, it has become a mechanism sought for the sole purpose of tricking someone else into investing in you, for their own duplicitous ends. Peter Cable is empowered to conduct his investigation into his colleague's "disappearance" as the pursuit of "truth" only because of the unquestionable authority that his high rank within the corporation lends him; disguised as a quaint rural utopia, the town of Stepford harbors "respectable" techno-criminals fine-tuning their plans for the construction of the ideal American wife, unbeknownst to the actual, human women who are being replaced one by one, Harry Caul tragically realizes that his alliances with the corporation that has hired him have been wholly misguided, and that both his clients and the technology that he has relied upon to do his job have duped him into accepting false truths. Indeed, Harry has even "learned" by experience to distrust anyone who might "threaten" him with human intimacy, including not only Amy (Teri Garr), the occasional lover of whom he quickly grows suspicious when she starts to ask him too many personal questions, but also Meredith (Elizabeth MacRae), the convention showgirl to whom he opens up briefly before realizing that one of his "friendly" industry competitors has tricked him by bugging his conversation with her. If the cinema of therapy in the 1960s managed to preserve the prospect of hope in the face of the sometimes seemingly insurmountable odds against realizing or benefitting from interpersonal and social connection, as the 1970s progress such a sense of connection appears inaccessible, as if it had already receded into some distant past.

Notes

Introduction

1. For a cogent example by the African-American press, see "A Sick Society," *Chicago Daily Defender*, 15 Aug. 1967, p. 13.

2. Thomas Schatz offers a detailed account of the financial successes and problems that the studios incurred during the 1960s in "The New Hollywood," *Film Theory Goes to the Movies*, edited by Jim Collins, Hilary Radner, and Ava Preacher Collins, Routledge, 1992, pp. 8–36.

Chapter 1

1. In a review written at the time of the film's release, *Motion Picture Daily* references a pro-social component that has not carried over into the DVD version of the film: "At the conclusion of the film, President Kennedy is seen and heard pleading for renewed support for efforts to further the care of the mentally ill among modern scientific lines." See Charles S. Aaronsen's review dated Aug. 15, 1963.

2. Although the *Newsweek* review of the film praised the absence of psychiatric jargon and pat explanations of psychopathology, the reviewer also noted a distancing mechanism inherent in films of this genre: "All thrillers, psychological or otherwise, succeed to the degree that audiences can identify with the beleaguered hero, and no one really identifies with a schizoid." See "Two for the Jigsaw," *Newsweek*, Dec. 31, 1962, p. 57.

3. *Life* praised the film for its realism: "It is a relief, too, to encounter a mental institution where most of the inmates are civilized, intelligent people, as many mentally disturbed people are in real life, and where the *Snakepit* type of ranting and raving is kept to a minimum." See Richard Oulahan, "A Touching, Tortured Lilith," *Life*, Oct. 2, 1964, p. 26.

4. The film inspired critical invective on a number of levels. Regarding cinematic form, the *Life* review noted that "No plot whatever develops out of this situation—just more situations, each less logical and connected than the last, until the whole thing collapses into a lengthy unmotivated chase of excruciating ineptitude." See "A Witless Junket to Too-Muchville," July 9, 1965, p. 12. *Newsweek*

comments that "the whole nasty business is tricked up to look like an exotic flowering of the avant-garde cinema—frenetic, disjointed (above all disjointed)—and it batters the senses with the mindless insistence of a discotheque loudspeaker." See "Out of Joint," July 1965, pp. 90-91. And Philip Hartung comments that "for a comedy that means to be so far out, this picture is amazingly clogged with clichés: Toulouse-Lautrec passing by in an outdoor café, O'Toole bumps into Richard Burton in a bar and says, 'Haven't we met before some place?' the obvious take-off on the whip scene in '8½,' and the many psychiatry jokes." See "The Screen: A Comic Knack," *Commonweal*, July 2, 1965, pp. 473-74.

5. Barbara Wilinsky's discussion of how European art cinema was promoted in the United States by exploiting sexual themes and content serves as a useful reference point here. See *Sure Seaters: The Emergence of Art House Cinema*, University of Minnesota Press, 2001.

6. Some reviewers found the inclusion of lobotomy problematic and out of sync with the tone of the remainder of the film. *The Hollywood Reporter* review (May 9, 1966) reports that "Since the atom bomb and funeral services already have been topics for black humor in the movies, brain operations may seem relatively tame stuff. It may be a matter of personal reaction, but to some, there is something about this situation that stills laughter. At any rate, these situations, dealing with the operation, are the weakest in the picture, and its genially rowdy mood never quite recovers from them." See "'Fine Madness' Fine Comedy with Sean Connery as Star."

7. It is entirely feasible that the Production Code Administration's suggested modifications (with which Universal Pictures complied) were at least partially responsible for the film's conflicted perspective on sex. The PCA found the first draft of the screenplay unacceptable. In a letter to Universal Pictures dated Mar. 2, 1964, Geoffrey Shurlock noted that "The story is totally preoccupied with the sex act—in this case, illicit sex. This preoccupation seems to us to be in itself a sound reason for rejecting the script. To explain—the dialogue and action deals exclusively with either attempting, plotting, lying about, or being interrupted in, seduction." PCA Files for *A Very Special Favor*, Special Collections, Margaret Herrick Library, Beverly Hills, CA.

8. One inspiration for the film, or what Ginsberg describes in this piece as a "haunting," was Valerie Solanas's shooting of Andy Warhol in June of 1968, days before the RFK assassination.

9. Karen Swenson suggests that this song served "not only . . . to reassure Daisy that it's OK to possess special gifts, but it was also a song about self-illumination and learning to accept one's *present life*" (23). See "One More Look at On a Clear Day You Can See Forever," *Barbra Quarterly*, no. 9, 1982, pp. 20-35.

Chapter 2

1. In "A Laboratory Study of Sexual Behavior," *Life*, Apr. 22, 1966, Albert Rosenfeld explains that "I don't see how the authors [of *Human Sexual Response*]

could have done it any other way if they were to avoid any hint of prurience" (8). And speaking of the first book again in a 1969 article, Masters clarifies that "In fact, we rewrote it to make the language as technical and non-inflammatory as we could. . . . I don't think we were dodging the issue, but the one thing we could not afford was any suggestion that this was pornographic. The suggestion was never made." See Tom Buckley, "All They Talk About Is Sex, Sex, Sex," *New York Times*, Apr. 20, 1969.

2. Expressing the perspective of a skeptic, Lois R. Chevalier notes that "their work ignored all the questions that it immediately raised in any ordinary person's mind—questions of morality, decency, human values. They wrote about men and women exactly as if they were writing about white mice" (26). See "Should This Sex Research Be Allowed To Go On?," *Ladies Home Journal*, May 1966.

3. Psychotherapeutic professional literature regularly attested to the high demand for sexual therapy. Describing their Rhode Island clinical practice modeled upon the Masters and Johnson method, therapists James O. Prochaska and Robert Marzilli explain that by 1973 they were experiencing a significant back-up in available human resources to treat their patients. Accordingly, the dearth of qualified therapists compelled them not to rely upon the two-person therapist team. They justified this modification as beneficial because "talking directly to [the patient's] spouse rather than through the therapist appears to keep transference problems to a minimum and also sets the stage for the post-therapy situation when the couple will have to work out other problems without a therapist" (294). See "Modifications of the Masters and Johnson Approach to Sexual Problems," *Psychotherapy: Theory, Research and Practice*, nos. 1–4 1973).

4. John Paul Brady, for example, details several cases in which Freudian therapists were incorporating behavioral techniques analogous to systematic desensitization. See "Psychotherapy by a Combined Behavioral and Dynamic Approach," *Comprehensive Psychiatry* vol. 9, no. 5, 1968, pp. 537–42.

5. The Production Code Administration was concerned about the exclusive focus on sex as well as the clinical, scientific, and frank discourse associated with the study of sexual dysfunction. In a letter from February 1, 1961, to Frank McCarthy after reviewing an early version of the screenplay, PCA president Geoffrey Shurlock explained that "The detailed scientific investigations out of which these involvements grow, are also expressed so clinically and in such blunt language, that we feel that a picture based on this script could not be approved under Code requirements." The Legion of Decency issued the film a "B" rating; in its report to the PCA, the Legion described the film as "a pseudo-scientific survey of female sexual behavior, whose only purpose seems to be sensationalism for its own sake, is of questionable value for a mass medium of entertainment." Production Code Administration Files on *The Chapman Report*, Special Collections, Margaret Herrick Library, Beverly Hills, CA.

6. "Just about the only thing most observers of frigidity agree upon," notes Michael Trask, "is that it manifests across the gamut of its patients as an unbridgeable distance between what they feel and what . . . they are supposed

to feel" (183). See *Camp Sites: Sex, Politics, and Academic Style in Postwar America*, Stanford UP, 2013.

7. Marnie's keen perception of male behavior and expectations offers a noteworthy counterpoint to Hitchcock's perverse observations on female sexual behavior. Among the "Inside Hitchcock—Quotes" section of the Universal City Studios Showman's Manual is the following: "The typical American woman is a tease—dresses for sex and doesn't give it. A man puts his hand on her and she runs screaming to mother" (2). Alfred Hitchcock Collection on *Marnie*, Special Collections, Margaret Herrick Library, Beverly Hills, CA.

8. Only five years after the film's release, by which point assessments of female sexual dysfunction were no longer limited to manifestations of neurotic behavior, Alan J. Cooper suggested that instances of sexual dysfunction could be construed as evidence of "toughmindedness" in women, and as "an obdurate and often aggressive refusal or inability to communicate with the male partner" (154). See "Some Personality Factors in Frigidity," *Journal of Psychosomatic Research*, no. 13, 1969, pp. 149–55.

9. As late as 1973 there continue to be references in psychiatric literature to the use of behavioral modification therapies to remedy the "disorder." See, for example, Edward J. Callahan and Harold Leitenberg, "Contingent Shock and Covert Desensitization," *Journal of Abnormal Psychology*, vol. 8, no. 1, 1973, pp. 60–72. Callahan and Leitenberg explain that both methods are found to be effective, used either in combination or alternation.

10. In *Three in the Attic*, fraternity brother Paxton Quigley (Christopher Jones) feigns homosexual trauma as a means of provoking Jan (Maggie Thrett) to "cure" his sexual dysfunction by seducing him out of sympathy.

11. Stanley Corkin's juxtaposition of the menacing urban decline of New York City with the welcoming embrace of a "less hostile" Florida offers an important historical contextualization of the film's narrative strategies. "As the bus traverses the interstate" in the closing sequence, Corkin, observes, the skies brighten and the world becomes greener" (630). See "Sex and the City in Decline: *Midnight Cowboy* (1969) and *Klute* (1971)," *Journal of Urban History*, vol. 36, no. 5, (2010), pp. 617–33.

12. The intense intimacy and competition between Sandy and Jonathan in the first segment of the film, and Jonathan's compulsion to have sex with Susan only after she has "gone all the way" with Sandy, seems to support Cynthia Fuchs's assertion that *Carnal Knowledge* is one of a number of early 1970s American films in which "the exclusion of women compelled overt condemnation of implicit and even explicit homoeroticism, as the texts worked precisely to keep such frightening feelings 'below the surface'" (196). See "The Buddy Politic," *Screening the Male: Exploring Masculinities in Hollywood Cinema*, edited by Steven Cohan and Ina Rae Hark, Routledge, 1993, pp. 194–210. At the same time, however, because the narrative manages to maintain such a critical (and ironic) perspective on Jonathan's too-aggressively protested (and ultimately compromised) masculinity, it could also be argued that *Carnal Knowledge* simultaneously engages in a critique of both misogyny *and* homophobia.

13. One reviewer suggests that "Bobbie is victim par excellence and the film's most powerful feminine argument. Totally molded by masculine fantasy, she is the incarnation of woman as siren. And her predicament lies in her servility to that very image." See Joy Gould Boyum, "A Case for Fem Lib, in Film," *Wall Street Journal*, Aug. 17, 1971.

14. One reviewer describes *Carnal Knowledge* as "a scrupulously honest portrayal of the sexual failure of the American male circa 1970—his adolescent attitude toward sex, his fear of emotional commitment, and ultimately his self-castrating fears of sexual inadequacy." See Winfred Blevins, "'Knowledge': Brilliantly Executed," *Los Angeles Herald-Examiner*, July 2, 1971, p. C-1.

15. The following discussion of *Everything You Always Wanted to Know About Sex (But Were Afraid to Ask)* and *Deep Throat* expands upon my analysis of these films in "1972: Movies and Confession," a chapter of the anthology *American Cinema of the 1970s: Themes and Variations* (Rutgers UP, 2007).

Chapter 3

1. Despite climbing divorce rates, in the 1966 article "May I Ask You a Few Questions about Love?" Sandford Brown reports that "three-quarters of all Americans, married and unmarried, feel that it is completely realistic to expect a husband and wife to love each other throughout their lives," and that Americans were not reporting "happier" marriages than their parents. *Saturday Evening Post*, Dec. 31, 1966, pp. 24–27.

2. *The Atlantic Monthly* published a number of negative responses to Cadawallader's article in its November 1967 issue, including the following: "Silence by our religious readers may tend to be interpreted as approval of Dr. Cadawallader's flagrant contempt for religious and moral principles, and civil laws which relate to the institution of marriage" (32).

3. The Italian film industry of the early 1960s was bolstered by government subsidies and a star system that was becoming internationally recognized. For a contemporary assessment of the industry's status, see Henry Gaggiottini, "Italian Film Boom Still Rolling: Exported Movies Help Reduce Rising Costs," *Chicago Daily Tribune*, Jan. 6, 1963, p. A2.

4. Bosley Crowther described the film as a "dandy satiric farce." See his review of *Divorce Italian Style* in the *New York Times*, 9 Sept. 9, 1962, p. 34.

5. Ironically, the Columbia Pictures pressbook for the film suggests a promotional strategy that accentuates a closer alignment with the discursive and interactional dynamics of *The Newlywed Game*: an invitation to viewers to win a judged competition in which they complete the following sentence: "It's Time For a 'Divorce American Style' "When . . . neighbors interrupt their own squabbles to listen to yours!," Pressbook, *Divorce American Style*, Columbia Pictures, 1967, p. 16. Margaret Herrick Library, Production Files.

6. Charles Champlin argued that the couple's "split is established as illogical anyway, thus setting us up for a sentimental happy ending." See "Marriage Rites or Wrongs in 'Divorce,'" *Los Angeles Times*, June 23, 1967. David Adams

finds the resolution exasperating: "make [marriage] the basis of semi-satirical and quite light-hearted humour—OK—and then impose a happy ending—ugh!" See the review in *Films and Filming*, November 1967.

7. That the film was responding to a sense of cultural alienation and disaffection becomes evident in the following comment in *Variety*'s review: "It's what's happening in the sex revolution. Morals are changing. People are more intelligent, more educated and more liberal than ever before. And yet, in our fast-paced, automated society, it's possible that people are losing their emotions, their capacity for joy, love and understanding." See Rela, Review of *Bob & Carol & Ted & Alice*, *Variety*, July 2, 1969, p. 3.

8. Esalen had received widespread publicity in the popular press by the time of the film's release, most notably in the extended piece by Leo E. Litwak, "A Trip to Esalen Institute—: Joy Is the Prize," *New York Times*, Dec. 31, 1967, pp. 119+.

9. Christie Milliken argues that the film "ultimately positions the couples as too decidedly (and comfortably) middle class and middle aged to embrace such an ethos [of free love]" (39). See "Rate It X? Hollywood Cinema and the End of the Production Code," *Sex Scene: Media and the Sexual Revolution*, edited by Eric Schaefer, Duke UP, 2014, pp. 25–52.

10. I discuss *Diary of a Mad Housewife*, *Lovers and Other Strangers*, and *The Marriage of a Young Stockbroker* with a focus upon expressions of homophobia during marriage conflicts in "Mispronouncing 'Man and Wife': The Fate of Marriage in Hollywood's Sexual Revolution," *Hetero: Queering Representations of Straightness*, edited by Sean Griffin, SUNY Press, 2008.

11. According to an NCOMP notice issued to Paramount on June 27, 1968, in addition to objections over its nudity and devil worship, "much more serious . . . is the perverted use which the film makes of fundamental Christian beliefs, especially the events surrounding the birth of Christ, and its mockery of religious persons and practices" (Production Code Administration Files, *Rosemary's Baby*, Margaret Herrick Library, Academy of Motion Picture Arts and Sciences). Critics including Charles Champlin strongly objected to the film on the basis of its morality and its configuration of evil ("'Rosemary's Baby' on Crest Screen," *Los Angeles Times*, Apr. 14, 1968). In her review published in *America* (20 Jul. 1968), Moira Walsh suggests that "It stands to reason that characters with a commitment to pure evil are going to act out baleful mirror images of Christian beliefs and practices. This is not the same thing as saying, as the NCOMP statement did, that the film makes perverted use of Christian beliefs. Perhaps a case can be made against the film but it would have to be made with some tentativeness and in the context of a familiarity with witchcraft and diabolism in literature over the centuries. . . . I don't think in practice it makes a great deal of difference how NCOMP rates *Rosemary's Baby* or any other film. It could make an enormous difference, however, if the organization found a way to reach 50 million people with sensible, informed and interesting critical statements about today's films, controversial and otherwise."

12. This ultimate reaffirmation of the central female protagonist's alliance with the audience is reiterated in Frank Perry's subsequent film *Play It As It Lays* (1972). In its closing moments, it is revealed that Maria (Tuesday Weld) has

been narrating her feature-length life story from the setting of a sanitarium to which she has been confined after witnessing the suicide of her best friend BZ (Anthony Perkins). "I know what nothing means, and keep on playing," Maria confesses in voiceover narration. In the final moments of this film, however, the protagonist simultaneously establishes alignments with the audience (once again, in close-up) and an unidentified, offscreen (or internal) male voice, who asks, "Why?" "Why not?" and a smiling Maria responds directly to the camera, thereby eliciting the possibility that the entire narrative has comprised a confessional "talking cure" in the presence of a never-visualized psychotherapist. Unlike *Diary of a Mad Housewife*, then, the closure of *Play It As It Lays* emphasizes a disaffected sense of resignation that more emphatically registers as pathology than personal enlightenment.

13. In his comprehensive review of literature pertaining to voyeuristic symptomatology and therapy, Spencer R. Smith distinguishes between "deviant" ("those that differ from the norm") and "perverted" sexual behaviors ("involving force or harm"). See "Voyeurism: A Review of Literature," *Archives of Sexual Behavior*, vol. 5, no. 6, 1976), pp. 585–608.

Chapter 4

1. Roszak was disconcerted by the hippie culture's preoccupation with hallucinogenic drug use, perceiving the phenomenon as an instrument that the dominant ideology might readily use to tame or quell the revolutionary spirit of the era. "If it is the case that the current mode of human being needs drugs to survive," he argues, "this spells the victory of the technocracy" (171).

2. Reflecting upon the prison experiment decades later, Ralph Metzner bemoaned the fact that the success of the research team, which had initially emphasized the importance of following-up on the conditions of participating prisoners after their release, was compromised by the inability to sustain such efforts. "Deep personality changes occurred," Metzner explains, "but in order to maintain changed behavior outside of the prison, some kind of halfway house or rehab program is essential." See Metzner, "Reflections on the Concord Prison Project and the Follow-Up Study," *Journal of Psychoactive Drugs*, vol. 30, no. 4, 1998, pp. 427–28. See also Rick Doblin, "Dr. Leary's Concord Prison Experiment: A 34 Year Follow Up Study," *Bulletin of the Multidisciplinary Association for Psychedelic Studies*, vol. 9, no. 4, Winter 1999/2000, pp. 10–18.

3. As Alpert (under the name Ram Dass) clarifies in the documentary *Dying to Know: Ram Dass & Timothy Leary* (Gay Dillingham, 2014), he and Leary had agreed to limit their experiments with hallucinogens to graduate students, and Alpert was dismissed after administering the drug to an undergraduate student to whom he was sexually attracted.

4. "After reading the guide," the authors promised, "the prepared person should be able, at the very beginning of the experience, to move directly to a state of non-game ecstasy and deep revelation" (6).

5. In a piece that synthesizes her experiences in the Haight-Ashbury district, Joan Didion asserts that the *Time* magazine article entirely overlooks the

political dimension of hippie culture. After drawing attention to the article's use of the phrase, "They call it bread," Didion notes that "this they're-trying-to-tell-us-something approach reached its apogee in July in *Time* . . . and remains the most remarkable, if unwitting, extant evidence that the signals between the generations are irrevocably jammed." See "The Hippie Generation," *Saturday Evening Post*, Sept. 23, 1967, pp. 25+.

6. Benshoff (39) places Oshinky's observation in the context of other contemporaneous reviews that noted the film's failed attempts to authentically recreate or represent the drug's hallucinatory properties.

7. Contemporary critics were attentive to these exploitative strategies. As Dale Munroe suggests in his 1967 review of *Riot on Sunset Strip*, "Someday a filmmaker may come along who will go onto the streets inhabited by the hippies, the addicts, the boozers—the mini-skirted girls and the scraggly-haired boys—and attempt to capture some of the reasons and meaning (or lack of meaning) behind these youngsters' chosen existence. To try to understand them—not to patronize them nor preach." See Dale Munroe, "Problem Exploited, But Never Explored," *Hollywood Citizen-News*, Apr. 7, 1967.

8. For a fuller and more detailed account of the conditions of the film's pre-production, see Benshoff (36–37).

9. The examples in this paragraph were gleaned from a file of advertising slogan ideas included in the collection of the James Raker Papers at the Margaret Herrick Library in Beverly Hills. While most of the entries included in this file appear in typed format, the last entry is handwritten: "The DeviL'S Drug."

10. As Benshoff discusses, in his memoirs Corman ultimately *did* admit to deliberately portraying this LSD trip as much more menacing than his own, positive experience with the drug (38).

11. As McGee asserts, the historical correlation between the narrative and the subsequent events in Chicago was reinforced when "Mayor Daley expressed concern over the possible repercussions of a sequence in the movie in which Washington's water supply is spiked with LSD. He ordered guards and barbed wire around Chicago's reservoirs" (260).

12. The 26th Amendment, by which the national voting age was changed from 21 to 18, was not ratified until March of 1971.

13. Reviews of *Wild in the Streets* highlighted contradictions and paradoxes that most critics found to be unresolved by the narrative. As Kevin Thomas comments, "here is a picture that's aimed directly at youthful audiences yet tells them if they ultimately took over the world they'd turn into fascists." See "'Wild in the Streets' Opens," *Los Angeles Times*, July 18, 1968. In a similar vein, Joseph Morgenstern asserts that the film "is the latest in a lengthening line of shoddy goods that serves youth what it wants, or what adults think it wants, or what adults are willing to pretend it wants if there's enough money in the pretense," adding that it is at once "anti-Vietnam, antiwar, anti-foreign policy (any foreign policy), antirationalist (the President's 'brain trust' consists of little lotus eaters, pot smokers and mind blowers) and, certainly, anti-youth." See "Kiddie Coup," *Newsweek*, June 3, 1968. In a revealing piece about director Barry Shear's own

account of the target marketing strategies, Shear confesses that he was unsure that older audiences would be drawn to the film, and that "some adults see it as a put-down of the younger generation." Shear described his film with the enthusiasm of a man who had engineered a put-down of both ends of the audience scale. He hastened to add, then, that 'for the rough overall portrait, it's a put-down of The Establishment.'" See Lawrence DeVine, "Story of a 20-Day Teenage Instant Classic," *Los Angeles Herald-Examiner*, July 21, 1968, p. G-1.

14. See Benshoff (43, note 27). I am indebted to Benshoff and his research on the film's reception for bringing Hoberman's review of the film to my attention.

15. In a letter to the Motion Picture Academy Library dated May 31, 1991, Cannon explains that before Preminger experimented with the drug, "I had gone to a lecture with two suited ex-academicians, Richard Albert [sic] and Tim Leary . . . and was excited by the potential. Also, sociologically, and culturally with how it was changing the mindset of people." Doran William Cannon Papers, Margaret Herrick Library, Beverly Hills, CA.

16. Benshoff explains that after *Skidoo*, the LSD film "devolved back into its generic origin" in exploitation and horror cinema (40).

Chapter 5

1. Black explicitly documents a case in which New York Archbishop Francis Spellman issued such a directive to parishioners regarding the film *Baby Doll* (Elia Kazan, 1956), which was written by Tennessee Williams.

2. Critical reviews upon the film's release identified the notion of technocracy to be at the heart of its satirical strategy. *High Times* suggests that the film "mocks everything frightful about modern electronic fascism" (Oct./Nov. 1975), while *The Film Daily* finds that the film "envisages a depersonalized society in which fear and suspicion, generated through advanced electronics, become the master of men" (Dec. 21, 1967).

3. Bishop Gerald Kennedy, head of the Methodist Church of Southern California and Arizona, explains that "I have felt for some time that it is ridiculous to assume that we can expect only movies which every parent will be willing to have his children attend. We do not do this in any other realm that I know about and certainly not with books nor stage plays. There are serious themes which movie producers ought to deal with and not feel constrained to treat on the level of childhood." See Mark Gibbons, "Warm Praise By Methodist Leader For Adults Policy On 'Woolf.'" *Exhibitor*, June 8, 1966.

4. Eileen M. Condon suggests that in cinematic depictions of the Catholic confessional act such as *I Confess*, viewers cannot help but be implicated in voyeuristic observation and judgmental participation in the scene: "contemporary films which portray the Sacrament of Penance question the active and passive facets of relationships and roles between clergy and laity, men and women. Movies like these ask how penitents, as well as confessors, must consider the values of privacy alongside the dangers of deception" (55). See "Confession in

the Movies: The Transmission of Sacramental Tradition through Film," *Catholic Education*, vol. 4, no. 1, 2000.

5. A February 1967 memorandum from Production Code Administration chief Geoffrey Shurlock to Frankovich regarding *Guess Who's Coming to Dinner* called for changes to "coarse and vulgar expressions which we feel we would not be able to approve in a picture of this caliber and importance, which should naturally appeal to the largest possible audience."

6. Aligned with his effort to forge connections, director Stanley Kramer showed the film on nine college campuses and promoted a dialogue with students on the efficacy of the film's representation of social issues. "As for a general comment," Kramer explains, "this new unsmiling generation may occupy itself with the dire foreboding of its music, the serious faces and apartness of its dance—but I wish for its vast multitude of film makers a little more humor—about themselves and about us. Even if they blame us for the whole Goddam mess, let it not be because we've been evil—but rather because we were somewhat ridiculous" (13). See "Nine Times Across the Generation Gap: 'On the Campuses Anything Less Than the Ultimate Is A Cop-out,'" *Action*, Apr./May 1968.

7. The Columbia Pictures production notes describe the film as a "reunion picture" for Hepburn and Tracy.

8. As Murray Pomerance's observes, Joey "has a romantic but ultimately powerless mother and a father whose public positions and private sentiments are in conflict" (185), and the traditional stratification of power by gender remains integral to the film's plot and its narrative strategies. See "1967: Movies and the Specter of Rebellion," *American Cinema of the 1960s: Themes and Variations*, Rutgers UP, 2009, pp. 172–92.

9. Susan Courtney suggests that the audience's foreknowledge of Tracy's death intensifies the moment in the film when "he finally declares openly his passion for the woman long known as the primary but unofficially recognized woman in his life" (266). See *Hollywood Fantasies of Miscegenation: Spectacular Narratives of Gender and Race, 1903–1967*, Princeton UP, 2005.

10. One reviewer aptly describes the film as "a wrestling-through by a troubled and decent human, of emotional tangles that are inherent in us all." See James Powers, "GWCTD' Big BO: Kramer's Release for Col Poignant," *The Hollywood Reporter*, Dec. 6, 1967, p. 3.

11. Arthur Knight suggests that the film "ventilates through [screenwriter] conscientious dialogues, the conflicting emotions of both whites and Negroes toward a mingling of the races." See "The Now Look," *Saturday Review*, Dec. 16, 1967. The *Variety* review explains that "story ends on an upbeat note, leaving audiences not only entertained but with many a new thought on how they would face similar situations." See Murf's review in *Variety*, Dec. 6, 1967.

12. Mimi White asserts that whatever the film's perception of the upper class on the basis of its characterization of Bobby's family members, "The working-class characters are not only down to earth, they're also stupid; their simple pleasure are also exposed as simple mindedness" (39). See "1970: Movies and the Movement," *American Cinema of the 1970s: Themes and Variations*, Rutgers UP, 2007, pp. 24–47.

13. In one of a series of cogent letters to the editor blasting both Greenspun's and Peter Schjeldahl's largely negative reviews of the film, Suzanne Lego comments that the film centers upon "man's alternately reaching out for and running away from emotional contact." See "'Pieces Is So Easy to Love," *New York Times*, Oct. 11, 1970, p. 119.

14. I examine the film as an example of confessional narrative in a historical context in "1972: Movies and Confession," in *American Cinema of the 1970s: Themes and Variations*, edited by Lester Friedman, Rutgers UP, 2007, pp. 88–90.

15. Several contemporary critics draw attention to problems that ensue in this adaptation of novel to screen. One reviewer notes that in many of these confessional monologues, "the movie goes about its business of quoting verbatim all the dog-eared pages of the novel. Nothing outrageous actually appears on the screen in this prep school Portnoy, which projects the sensibility of a locker-room loudmouth blathering about his sexual prowess, or lack of it, stroke by stroke." See the review of the film in *Playboy*, Oct. 1972. Fred M. Hechinger asserts that "the device of pretending that the story is nothing but a tale told from Dr. Spielvogel's psychiatric couch, moderately successful in the novel, in Mr. Lehman's hands fails to turn cinematic reality into believable stream of consciousness" ("An Anti-Jewish Joke," *New York Times*, July 16, 1972). And Charles Champlin argues that "what the screening process has done, in fact, is to screen out all of the author's shaping consciousness, all the uses of irony, exaggeration, all the deliberate posturings and feignings which constituted the comic masking over of Roth's (or Portnoy's) underlying rage, tenderness and fear" ("Portnoy Travels From Page to Screen," *Los Angeles Times*, July 16,1972).

16. One critic comments that "sex in the movie is treated as some sort of hysterical affliction that only attacks women." See "Misanthropic Movies," *New Yorker*, Mar. 13, 1971.

17. Kylo-Patrick Hart is among the latest critical voices to express that the film became outdated by the time of its release after the Stonewall incidence of June 1969. See *Queer Males in Contemporary Cinema*, Scarecrow Press, 2013.

18. Vito Russo rightly suggests that *The Boys in the Band* "was a gay movie for gay people, and it immediately became both a period piece and a reconfirmation of the stereotypes" (177). See *The Celluloid Closet*, Harper & Row, 1981.

19. Toward this end, in promotional materials and press interviews Friedkin insistently proclaimed that the film was less about gay culture than universal emotions. The Publicity section of the Cinema Center Films Pressbook explains that "Although the sexual implications of 'The Boys in the Band' break new ground in the film industry, Friedkin says that is incidental to the strong points the movie makes. 'Crowley was writing about something else,' Friedkin emphasizes, 'of self-destruction and how you can stand in your own way of achieving anything.'" Margaret Herrick Library, Beverly Hills, CA.

20. In his overwhelmingly positive review of the film, Roger Ebert notes that the already claustrophobic staging of the play is intensified in the film version— "the room isn't big enough for these people" and we are presented with "tight, sweating, desperate closeups, which tend to violate OUR territorial imperatives and to make us restless." See his review in *Chicago Sun Times*, Mar. 23, 1970.

21. Several critics correlated the two films. Mary Knoblauch suggests that "there is a theory that 'Virginia Woolf' was written to be played by two homosexual couples. 'The Boys in the Band' is quite definitely about homosexuals, but a case could be made that the boys are really heterosexual couples in disguise." See her review of the film in *Chicago Today American*, Mar. 19, 1970.

Works Cited

Aaronson, Charles S. "The Caretakers." *Motion Picture Daily*, 15 Aug.1963.
Abrahamson, Leslie H. "1968: Movies and the Failure of Nostalgia." *American Cinema of the 1960s: Themes and Variations*, edited by Barry Keith Grant. Rutgers UP, 2009, pp. 193-216.
Adams, David. Review of *Divorce American Style*. *Films and Filming*, Nov. 1967.
"All About the New Sex Therapy." *Newsweek*, 27 Nov. 1972, pp. 65-67.
Alpert, Hollis. "SR Goes to the Movies: A Wandering Samurai." *Saturday Review*, 15 Sep. 1962, p. 26.
———. Review of *Bob & Carol & Ted & Alice*. *Saturday Review*, 11 Oct. 1969.
Anderson, Terry H. *The Movement and the Sixties: Protest in America from Greensboro to Wounded Knee*. Oxford UP, 1995.
"An Epidemic of Acid Heads." *Time*, 11 Mar. 1966, p. 56.
Austin, J. L. *How to Do Things With Words*, 2nd ed. Harvard UP, 1975.
Bach, Dr. George R., and Peter Wyden. *The Intimate Enemy: How to Fight Fair in Love and Marriage*. William Morrow & Company, 1969.
Baumeister, Roy F., and Kathleen S. Placidi. "A Social History and Analysis of the LSD Controversy." *Journal of Humanistic Psychology*, vol. 23, no. 4, 1983, pp. 25-58.
Benshoff, Harry M. "The Short-Lived Life of the Hollywood LSD Film." *The Velvet Light Trap*, no. 47, 2001, pp. 29-44.
Black, Gregory D. *The Catholic Crusade Against the Movies, 1940-1975*. Cambridge UP, 1998.
Blevins, Winfred. "'Knowledge': Brilliantly Executed." *Los Angeles Herald-Examiner*, 2 Jul. 1971, p. C-1.
The Boys in the Band. Pressbook. Cinema Center Films, 1970. Special Collections, Margaret Herrick Library, Beverly Hills, CA.
Boyum, Joy Gould. "A Case for Fem Lib, in Film." *Wall Street Journal*, 17 Aug. 1971.
Brady, John Paul. "Psychotherapy by a Combined Behavioral and Dynamic Approach." *Comprehensive Psychiatry*, vol. 9, no. 5, 1968, pp. 537-42.
Brown, Sandford. "May I Ask You A Few Questions About Love?" *Saturday Evening Post*, 31 Dec, 1966. pp. 24-27.

Buckley, Tom. "All They Talk About Is Sex, Sex, Sex." *New York Times*, 20 Apr. 1969, p. SM28.

Burlingame, Gary M., and Scott Baldwin. "Group Therapy." *History of Psychotherapy*, edited by John C. Nordcross et al., 2nd ed., pp. 505-15.

Burnham, John C. "The Influence of Psychoanalysis Upon American Culture." *American Psychoanalysis: Origins and Development*, edited by Jacques M. Quen and Eric T. Carlson. Brunner/Mazel, 1978, pp. 52-72.

Cadawallader, Mervyn. "Marriage as a Wretched Institution." *The Atlantic Monthly*, Nov. 1966, pp. 62-66.

Callahan, Edward J., and Harold Leitenberg. "Contingent Shock and Covert Desensitization." *Journal of Abnormal Psychology*, vol. 81, no. 1, 1973, pp. 60-72.

Canby, Vincent. "'Bob & Carol & Ted & Alice' Twits 'New Morality.'" *New York Times*, 17 Sep. 1969, p. 50.

Cannon, Doran William. Letter to the Motion Picture Academy Library, 31 May 1991. Doran William Cannon Papers. Margaret Herrick Library, Beverly Hills, CA.

Cantor, Donald J. "The Right of Divorce." *The Atlantic Monthly*, Nov. 1966, pp. 67-71.

Cautin, Robin L. "A Century of Psychotherapy, 1860–1960." *History of Psychotherapy: Continuity and Change*, edited by John C. Nordcross et al., 2nd ed. American Psychological Association, 2011, pp. 3-38.

Celli, Carlo, and Marga Cottino-Jones. *A New Guide to Italian Cinema*. Palgrave Macmillan, 2007.

Champlin, Charles."Marriage Rites or Wrongs in 'Divorce.'" *Los Angeles Times*, 23 Jun. 1967.

———. "'Rosemary's Baby' on Crest Screen.'" *Los Angeles Times*, 14 Apr. 1968.

———. "Carrie Snodgrass Star Rises in 'Mad Housewife.'" *Los Angeles Times*, 11 Oct. 1970.

———. "Portnoy Travels from Page to Screen." *Los Angeles Times*, 16 Jul. 1972.

The Chapman Report. Letter to Mr. Frank McCarthy from Geoffrey Shurlock, 1 Feb. 1961. Production Code Administration Files, Special Collections, Margaret Herrick Library, Beverly Hills, CA.

———. "Analysis of Film Content: Legion of Decency Report," 2 Apr. 1962. Production Code Administration Files, Special Collections, Margaret Herrick Library, Beverly Hills, CA.

Chevalier, Lois R. "Should This Sex Research Be Allowed To Go On?" *Ladies Home Journal*, May 1966, pp. 26, 36.

"Children of Darkness." *Time*, 28, Dec, 1962, p. 64.

Cloud, Dana L. *Control and Consolation in American Culture and Politics: Rhetorics of Therapy*. Sage Publications, 1998.

Condon, Eileen M. "Confession in the Movies: The Transmission of Sacramental Tradition through Film." *Catholic Education*, vol. 4, no. 1, 2000, pp. 42-56.

"The Confession Controversy." *Time*, 3 Dec. 1965, pp. 78-80.

Cooper, Alan J. "Some Personality Factors in Frigidity." *Journal of Psychosomatic Research*, no. 13, 1969, pp. 149-55.

Corkin, Stanley. "Sex in the City in Decline: *Midnight Cowboy* (1969) and *Klute* (1971)." *Journal of Urban History*, vol. 36, no. 5, 2010, pp. 617–31.

Couglan, Robert. "The Chemical Mind-Changers." *Life*, 15 Mar. 1963, pp. 81+.

Courtney, Susan. *Hollywood Fantasies of Miscegenation: Spectacular Narratives of Gender and Race, 1903–1967*. Princeton UP, 2005.

Crowther, Bosley. "The Screen: Story of the Thief Who Was Spared." *New York Times*, 11 Oct. 1962, p. 47.

———. "Screen: Plotting a Spouse's Demise." *New York Times*, 27 Jan. 1965, p. 26.

DeAngelis, Michael. "1972: Movies and Confession." *American Cinema of the 1970s: Themes and Variations*, edited by Lester Friedman. Rutgers UP, 2007, pp. 71–94.

———. "Mispronouncing 'Man and Wife': The Fate of Marriage in Hollywood's Sexual Revolution." *Hetero: Queering Representations of Straightness*, edited by Sean Griffin. SUNY Press, 2008, pp. 129–52.

DeLeon, Patrick H. et al. "Psychotherapy: 1960 to the Present." *History of Psychotherapy: Continuity and Change*, edited by John C. Nordcross et al., 2nd ed. American Psychological Association, 2011, pp. 39–62.

DeVine, Lawrence. "Story of a 20-Day Teenage Instant Classic." *Los Angeles Herald-Examiner*, 21 Jul. 1968, p. G-1.

Didion, Joan. "The Hippie Generation." *Saturday Evening Post*, 23 Sep. 1967, pp. 25+.

Divorce American Style. Columbia Pictures Pressbook, 1967, p. 16. Production Files, Margaret Herrick Library, Beverly Hills, CA.

Doblin, Rick. "Pahnke's 'Good Friday Experiment': A Long-Term Follow-Up and Methodological Critique." *The Journal of Transpersonal Psychology*, vol. 22, no. 1, 1991, pp. 1–28.

———. "Dr. Leary's Concord Prison Experiment: A 34 Year Follow Up Study." *Bulletin of the Multidisciplinary Association for Psychedelic Studies*, vol. 9, no. 4, Winter 1999/2000, pp. 10–18.

Doctors' Wives. "Box Office Analysis and Advertising Approach." Jack Atlas Papers, 3 Jun 1970. Margaret Herrick Library, Beverly Hills, CA.

"Doing the Garrote." *Newsweek*, 28 Oct. 1968, p. 114.

Ebert, Roger. "The Boys in the Band." Review. *Chicago Sun Times*, 3 Mar. 1970.

Everett, Anna. "1961: Movies and Civil Rights." In *American Cinema of the 1960s: Themes and Variations*, edited by Barry Keith Grant. Rutgers UP, 2009, pp. 44–66.

Farrell, Barry. "Scientists, Theologians, Mystics, Swept Up in a Psychic Revolution." *Life*, 25 Mar. 1966, pp. 30–32.

"Fight Together, Stay Together." *Time*, 1 Feb. 1969, pp. 64–66.

"'Fine Madness' Fine Comedy with Sean Connery as Star." *The Hollywood Reporter*, 9 May 1966.

Fleming, Alice. "Frigidity—The Myth That Plagues Too Many Women." *Redbook*, Mar. 1969, pp. 69+.

Foucault, Michel. *The History of Sexuality, Volume I: An Introduction*, translated by Robert Hurley. Vintage Books, 1990.

Friedan, Betty. *The Feminine Mystique*. W. W. Norton, 1963.
Fuchs, Cynthia. "The Buddy Politic." Screening the Male": *Exploring Masculinities in Hollywood Cinema*. Routledge, 1993, pp. 194–210.
Fulbright, J. W. "The Great Society Is a Sick Society, Says Senator Fulbright." *New York Times*, 20 Aug. 1967, pp. SM 30+.
Gabbard, Glen O., and Krin Gabbard. *Psychiatry and the Cinema*, 2nd ed. American Psychiatric Press, Inc., 1999.
Gabbard, Glen. "Psychotherapy in Hollywood Cinema." *Australasian Psychiatry*, vol. 9, no. 4, 2001, pp. 365–69.
Gaggiottini, Henry. "Italian Film Boom Still Rolling: Exported Movies Help Reduce Rising Costs." *Chicago Daily Tribune*, 5 Jan. 1963, p. A2.
Gibbons, Mark. "Warm Praise by Methodist Leader for Adults Policy on 'Woolf.'" *Exhibitor*, 8 Jun. 1966.
Gillespie, C. Kevin, S.J. *Psychology and American Catholicism: From Confession to Therapy?* The Crossroad Publishing Company, 2001.
Ginsberg, Milton Moses. "Essay by Director Milton Moses Ginsberg." *Coming Apart*. DVD, Special Features, Kino Video 1990.
———. "How to Fall Into Oblivion and Take Your Movie With You: Coming Apart." *Film Comment*, vol. 35, no. 1, 1999, pp. 4–6.
Grant, Barry Keith, ed. *American Cinema of the 1960s: Themes and Variations*. Rutgers UP, 2009.
Greenfeld, Sidney M. "Love and Marriage in Modern America: A Functional Analysis." *The Sociological Quarterly*, vol. 6, no. 4, 1963, pp. 361–77.
Greenspun, Roger. "Rafelson's 'Five Easy Pieces' Bows." *New York Times*, 12 Sep. 1970, p. 26.
Grob, Gerald N. *From Asylum to Community: Mental Health Policy in Modern America*. Princeton UP, 1991.
Guess Who's Coming to Dinner. Production Notes. Columbia Pictures, 1967. Beverly Hills, CA: Margaret Herrick Library.
"Guess Who's Coming to Dinner." Review. *Variety*, 6 Dec. 1967.
Gurman, Alan S., and Douglas K. Snyder. "Couple Therapy." *History of Psychotherapy*, edited by John C. Nordcross et al., 2nd ed., pp. 485–97.
Hacker, Andrew. "If the 18-year-Olds Get the Vote. . . ." *New York Times Magazine*, 7 Jul. 1968, pp. 6–7+.
Hall, Agnes Regina. "Revitalizing the Sacrament of Confession." *Worship*, vol. 40, no. 2, 1966, pp. 97–102.
Halleck, Seymour L., M.D. *The Politics of Therapy*. Science House, 1971.
"Hallucinations." *Newsweek*, 10 Dec. 1962, p. 56.
Hanisch, Carol. "The Personal Is Political." February 1969. http://www.carol-hanisch.org/CHwritings/PIP.html. Accessed 12 Apr. 2016.
Harris, Thomas. *I'm OK, You're OK: A Practical Guide to Transactional Analysis*. Harper & Row, 1969.
Hart, Kylo-Patrick. *Queer Males in Contemporary Cinema*. Scarecrow Press, 2013.
Hartung, Philip T. "The Screen: Sang-Freud." *Commonweal*, 4 Jan. 1963, pp. 389–90.

———. "The Screen." *Commonweal*, 4 Oct. 1963, pp. 45–48.

———. "The Screen: A Comic Knack." *Commonweal*, 2 Jul. 1965, pp. 473–74.

Hechinger, Fred M. "An Anti-Jewish Joke." *New York Times*, 16 Jul. 1972.

Herbstman, Mandel. "The Caretakers." *Film Daily*, 16 Aug. 1963.

"The Hippies." *Time*, 7 Jul. 1967: pp. 22+.

Hoberman, J. "Head Trips: *Skidoo*." *Village Voice*, 17 Mar. 1998.

———. *The Dream Life*. The New Press, 2003.

How to Murder Your Wife. Pressbook. United Artists, Mat 501, 1965. Production Files, Margaret Herrick Library, Beverly Hills, CA.

Hunt, Morton M. "Freudians are wrong, the behaviorists say—: A Neurosis is 'Just' a. . . ." *New York Times*, 4 Jan. 1967, pp. SM20+.

Hymer, Janet. "The Therapeutic Nature of Confessions." *Journal of Contemporary Psychotherapy*, vol. 13, no. 2, 1982, pp. 129–43.

"I Love You, Alice B. Toklas." Review. *Variety*, 28 Aug. 1968.

"Impotence: the result of female aggressiveness—or what?" *Mademoiselle*, Feb. 1972, pp. 122–25.

Johnson, Nora. "A Marriage on the Rocks." *The Atlantic Monthly*, 1 Jul. 1962, pp. 48–51.

Jones, Beverly, and Judith Brown. "Toward a Female Liberation Movement." *Redstockings*. Gainesville, FL, 1968.

Kaplan, Helen Singer. "Friction and Fantasy: No-Nonsense Therapy for Six Sexual Malfunctions." *Psychology Today*, Oct. 1974, pp. 77–86.

Kauffmann, Stanley. "Diary of a Mad Housewife." *New Republic*, 12 Sep. 1970.

Kawin, Bruce F. *Mindscreen: Bergman, Godard, and First-Person Film*. Princeton UP, 1978.

Kennedy, Robert F. "Remarks on the Assassination of Martin Luther King, Jr." Delivered in Indianapolis, IN, 4 Apr 1968. *American Rhetoric: Top 100 Speeches*. http://www.americanrhetoric.com/speeches/rfkonmlkdeath.html. Accessed 14 Oct. 2016.

Knight, Arthur. "SR Goes to the Movies: View from the Couch." *Saturday Review*, 5 Jan. 1963, p. 30.

———. "SR Goes to the Movies: Who's Morbid?" *Saturday Review*, 10 Aug. 1963, p. 34.

———. "The Now Look." *Saturday Review*, 16 Dec. 1967.

Knoblauch, Mary. "The Boys in the Band." Review. *Chicago Today American*, 19 Mar. 1970.

Kobler, John. "The Dangerous Magic of LSD." *Saturday Evening Post*, 2 Nov. 1963, pp. 31–40.

Koempel, Leslie. "Why Get Married?" *Saturday Evening Post*, 13 Feb. 1965, pp. 10, 15.

Kolker, Robert. *A Cinema of Loneliness*. 4th ed. Oxford UP, 2011.

Kramer, Stanley. "Nine Times Across the Generation Gap: 'On the Campuses Anything Less Than the Ultimate Is A Cop-out.'" *Action*, Apr./May 1968, pp. 11–13.

Kreuz, Roger J., and Richard M. Roberts. "On Satire and Parody: The Importance of Being Ironic." *Metaphor and Symbolic Activity*, vol. 8, no. 2, 1993, pp. 97–109.

Leary, Timothy, et al. "A New Behavior Change Program Using Psilocybin." *Psychotherapy: Theory, Research and Practice*, vol. 2, no. 2, 1965, pp. 61–72.

———. *The Psychedelic Experience: A Manual Based on the Tibetan Book of the Dead*. Citadel Press, 1992.

Lederer, William J., and Don D. Jackson. *The Mirages of Marriage*. W. W. Norton 1968.

Lee, Martin A., and Bruce Shlain. *Acid Dreams: The Complete History of LSD: The CIA, The Sixties, and Beyond*. Grove Press, 1985.

Lego, Suzanne. "'Pieces' Is So Easy to Love." *New York Times*, 11 Oct. 1970, p. 119.

Leslie, Gerald R. "Conjoint Therapy in Marriage Counseling." *Journal of Marriage and the Family*, vol. 26, no. 1, 1964, pp. 65–71.

Levit, Herbert I. "Marital Crisis Intervention: Hypnosis in Impotence/Frigidity Cases." *American Journal of Clinical Hypnosis*, vol. 14, no. 1 (1971), pp. 56–60.

Lewis, Jon. *Hollywood v. Hard Core: How the Struggle over Censorship Saved the Modern Film Industry*. New York UP, 2000.

Litwak, Leo E. "A Trip to Esalen Institute—: Joy Is the Prize." *New York Times*, 31 Dec. 1967, pp. 119+.

Lumen Gentium (Light of the Nations). *The Documents of Vatican II*, edited by Walter M. Abbott, S.J. Herder and Herder Association Press, 1966, pp. 14–101.

Mahoney, John. "'Alice B. Toklas' One of Best Comedies in Years." *The Hollywood Reporter*, 28 Aug. 1968.

Mainardi, Pat. "The Politics of Housework." *Redstockings*, 1970.

Marnie. Universal City Studios Studios Showman's Manual. "Inside Hitchcock—Quotes." Alfred Hitchcock Collection, Special Collections, Margaret Herrick Library, Beverly Hills, CA.

Martin, Peter A. "Treatment of Marital Disharmony in Collaborative Therapy." In *The Psychotherapies of Marital Disharmony*, edited by Bernard L. Greene. The Free Press, 1965, pp. 83–101.

Masters, William, and Virginia Johnson. *Human Sexual Response*. Boston: Little, Brown and Company, 1966.

———. *Human Sexual Inadequacy*. Boston: Little, Brown and Company, 1970.

McConnell, Theodore A. "Confession in Cross-Disciplinary Perspective." *Journal of Religion and Health*, vol. 8, no. 1, 1969, pp. 76–86.

McGee, Mark Thomas. *Faster and Furiouser: The Revised and Fattened Fable of American International Pictures*. McFarland & Company, Inc., 1996.

Metzner, Ralph, PhD. "Reflections on the Concord Prison Project and the Follow-Up Study." *Journal of Psychoactive Drugs*, vol. 30, no. 4, 1998, pp. 427–28.

Miller, Timothy. *The Hippies and American Values*, 2nd ed. University of Tennessee Press, 2011.

Milliken, Christie. "Rate It X? Hollywood Cinema and the End of the Production Code." *Sex Scene: Media and the Sexual Revolution*, edited by Eric Schaefer. Duke UP, 2014, pp. 25–52.
"Misanthropic Movies." *New Yorker*, 13 Mar. 1971.
Moore, Burness E. "Frigidity: A Review of Psychoanalytic Literature." *The Psychoanalytic Quarterly*, vol. 33, 1964, pp. 323–49.
Morgenstern, Joseph. "Kiddie Coup." *Newsweek*, 3 Jun. 1968.
"Most in Poll Say U. S. Is Not 'Sick': Negroes and Whites Differ on Question by Gallup." *New York Times*, 3 Jul. 1968, pp. 24.
Munroe, Dale. "Problem Exploited, But Never Explored." *Hollywood Citizen-News*, 7 Apr. 1967.
Nobile, Philip. "What is the New Impotence, and Who's Got It?" *Esquire*, Oct. 1972, pp. 95–98+.
"No Illusions." *Newsweek*, 10 Jun.1963, pp. 92–93.
Nordcross, John C. et al., editors. *History of Psychotherapy: Continuity and Change*, 2nd ed. American Psychological Association, 2011.
Ofiesh, Lt. Colonel Gabriel D. "Modern Woman and Modern Marriage: Men Are Actually the Weaker Sex." *Vital Speeches of the Day*, 15 May 1961: 471–77. Delivered at Colorado Woman's College, Denver, 2 Mar 1961.
O'Neill, Nena, and George O'Neill. *Open Marriage: A New Life Style for Couples*. M. Evans and Company, Inc., 1972.
Oshinsky, Sy. Review of *The Love-Ins*. *Motion Picture Herald*, 16 Aug. 1967.
O'Toole, James M. "In the Court of Conscience: American Catholics and Confession, 1900–1975." *Habits of Devotion: Catholic Religious Practice in Twentieth-Century America*, edited by James O'Toole. Cornell University Press, 2004, pp. 131–85.
Otto, Herbert A. "Has Monogamy Failed?" *Saturday Review*, 25 Apr. 1970, pp. 23–25, 62.
Oulahan, Richard. "A Touching, Tortured Lilith." *Life*, 2 Oct. 1964 p. 26.
"Out of Joint." *Newsweek*, 12 Jul. 1965, pp. 90–91.
"'Pieces Is So Easy to Love." *New York Times*, 11 Oct. 1970, p. 119.
Pomerance, Murray. "1967: Movies and the Specter of Rebellion." *American Cinema of the 1960s: Themes and Variation*s, edited by Barry Keith Grant, Rutgers UP, 2009, pp. 172–92.
"Portnoy's Complaint." Review. *Playboy*, Oct. 1972.
Powers, James. "'GWCTD' Big BO: Kramer's Release for Col Poignant." *The Hollywood Reporter*, 6 Dec. 1967, p. 3.
Powers, James. Review of *Who's Afraid of Virginia Woolf? Hollywood Reporter*, 22 Jun. 1966.
"The President's Analyst." Review. *The Film Daily*, 21 Dec. 1967.
"The President's Analyst." Review. *High Times*, Oct./Nov. 1975.
Prochaska, James O., and Robert Marzilli. "Modifications of the Masters and Johnson Approach to Sexual Problems." *Psychotherapy: Theory, Research and Practice*, nos. 1–4, 1973.
"Raymond Durgnat finds fun without corpses. . . ." *Films and Filming*, Oct. 1965.

Reed, Rex. "Woody Allen's Sex Satire Is Inspired Lunacy." *Daily News*, 11 Aug. 1972, p. 54.
Rela. Review of *Bob & Carol & Ted & Alice*. *Variety*, 2 Jul. 1969, p. 3.
Reuben, David. "Male Sexual Inadequacy." *McCall's*, Oct. 1970, pp. 26, 29.
Riot on Sunset Strip Ad Mats. American International Pictures, 1967. Margaret Herrick Library, Beverly Hills, CA.
Robinson, Leonard Wallace. "Hearing Color, Smelling Music, Touching a Scent." *New York Times*, 22 Aug. 1965, pp. 14+.
Rogers, Carl. *Carl Rogers on Encounter Groups*. Harper & Row, 1970.
Rosemary's Baby. Production Code Administration Files, Margaret Herrick Library, Beverly Hills, CA.
Rosenfeld, Albert. "A Laboratory Study of Sexual Behavior." *Life*, 22 Apr. 1966, pp. 8, 12.
Roszak, Theodore. *The Making of a Counter Culture: Reflections on the Technocratic Society and Its Youthful Opposition*. University of California Press, 1995.
Rubin, Theodore J. "My Impotent Husband." *Ladies' Home Journal*, May 1973, p. 40.
Russo, Vito. *The Celluloid Closet*. Harper & Row, 1981.
Sarachild, Kathie. "Consciousness-Raising: A Radical Weapon": *A Radical Feminist Revolution: Redstockings of the Women's Liberation Movement*. New York: Random House, 1975, pp. 144–50. Originally delivered 27 Nov. 1968.
Satir, Virginia. *Conjoint Family Therapy*, 3rd ed. Science and Behavior Books, Inc.,1983.
Schatz, Thomas. "The New Hollywood." *Film Theory Goes to the Movies*, edited by Jim Collins, Hilary Radner, and Ava Preacher Collins. Routledge, 1992, pp. 8–36.
Schickel, Richard. "Running a Good Thing Right into the Ground." *Life*, 8 May 1964, p. 14.
———. "Overpraised Quickie on a Vital Theme: Wild in the Streets." *Life*, 26 Jul.1968.
"Schizoid Sensations." *Time*, 2 Oct. 1964, p. 144.
Shulman, Bruce J. *The Seventies: The Great Shift in American Culture, Society, and Politics*. Da Capo Press, 2002.
Shurlock, Geoffrey. Letter to Frank McCarthy, on *The Chapman Report*, 1 Feb. 1961. Special Collections, Production Code Administration Files, *The Chapman Report*, Margaret Herrick Library, Beverly Hills, CA.
———. Letter to Mrs. Kathryn McTaggart, Universal Pictures, Inc. on *A Very Special Favor*, 2 Mar. 1964. Special Collections, Production Code Administration Files, *A Very Special Favor*, Margaret Herrick Library, Beverly Hills, CA.
———. Memorandum to M. J. Frankovich on *Guess Who's Coming to Dinner*, 20 Feb. 1967, Special Collections, Production Code Administration Files, *Guess Who's Coming to Dinner*, Margaret Herrick Library, Beverly Hills, CA.
"A Sick Society." *Chicago Daily Defender*, 15 Aug. 1967, p. 13.

"The Silver Snuffbox." *Time*, 19 Mar. 1966, p. 97.
Siskel, Gene. "Everything on sex, Woody Allen style." *Chicago Tribune*, 5 Aug. 1972, p. B6.
Smith, Spencer R. "Voyeurism: A Review of Literature." *Archives of Sexual Behavior*, vol. 5, no. 6, 1976, pp. 585–608.
Stevenson, Rev. Beaumont. "Confession and Psychotherapy." *The Journal of Pastoral Care*, vol. 20, no. 1, 1966, pp. 10–15.
Swanson, Ana. "144 Years of Marriage and Divorce in the United States, in One Chart." *The Washington Post*, 23 Jun. 2015. https://www.washingtonpost.com/news/wonk/wp/2015/06/23/144-years-of-marriage-and-divorce-in-the-united-states-in-one-chart/. Accessed 1 June 2016.
Swenson, Karen. "One More Look at On A Clear Day You Can See Forever." *Barbra Quarterly*, no. 9, 1982, pp. 20–35.
Taylor, Chloe. *The Culture of Confession from Augustine to Foucault: A Genealogy of the 'Confessing Animal.'* Routledge, 2009.
Thomas, Kevin. "'Wild in the Streets' Opens." *Los Angeles Times*, 8 Jul. 1968.
Todd, Elizabeth. "The Value of Confession and Forgiveness According to Jung." *Journal of Religion and Health*, vol. 24, no. 1, 1985, pp. 39–48.
Trask, Michael. *Camp Sites: Sex, Politics, and Academic Style in Postwar America*, Stanford UP, 2013.
"*The Trip*: Advertising Slogan Ideas." American International Pictures. James Raker Papers, Margaret Herrick Library, Beverly Hills, CA.
The Trip. Liner Notes. American International Pictures. Core Collection, Margaret Herrick Library, Beverly Hills, CA.
"The Trip." Review. *Films and Filming*, Sep. 1967, pp. 41–42.
Trombley, William. "Small-Budget Triumph: David and Lisa." *Saturday Evening Post*, 16 Mar. 1963, pp. 56–60.
"Two for the Jigsaw." *Newsweek*, 31 Dec. 1962, p. 57.
"U's 'Housewife' a BO Winner." *Hollywood Reporter*, 31 Jul. 1970.
Walker, Janet. *Couching Resistance: Women, Film and Psychoanalytic Psychiatry*. University of Minnesota Press, 1993.
Walsh, Moira. "Marriage Italian and American Style." *America*, 6 Feb. 1965.
———. Review of *Rosemary's Baby*. *America*, 20 Jul. 1968.
Weiler, A. H. "Screen: Romantic Middle-Aged Men and Women: 'Shock Corridor.'" *New York Times*, 12 Sep. 1963, p. 32.
White, Mimi. "1970: Movies and the Movement." *American Cinema of the 1970s: Themes and Variations*, edited by Lester D. Friedman. Rutgers UP, 2007, pp. 24–47.
Wild in the Streets: Advertising Slogans. American International Pictures, 1967. James Raker Papers. Margaret Herrick Library, Beverly Hills, CA.
Wild in the Streets: Pressbook. American International Pictures, 1967. Margaret Herrick Library, Beverly Hills, CA.
Wilinsky, Barbara. *Sure Seaters: The Emergence of Art House Cinema*. University of Minnesota Press, 2001.
"Willfully Delicate." *Newsweek*, 12 Oct. 1964, p. 116A.

Williams, Linda. *Hard Core: Power, Pleasure, and the 'Frenzy of the Visible.'* University of California Press, 1989.

———. "Film Bodies: Gender, Genre, and Excess." *Film Quarterly*, vol. 44, no. 4, 1991, pp. 2–13.

"A Witless Junket to Too-Muchville." *Life*, 9 Jul. 1965, p. 12.

Wolfe, Linda. "When Men Lose Interest in Sex." *McCall's*, Apr 1973, pp. 30–36.

Yalom, Irvin D. *The Theory and Practice of Group Psychotherapy*, 4th ed., Basic Books, 1995.

Yoder, Robert M. "Help for the Living Dead." *Saturday Evening Post*, 22 Oct. 1955, pp. 42–43, 66–67, 71.

Young, Robert. "LBJ Disputes Notion U. S. Is a Sick Nation: Notes Needs for Unity, Progress, However." *Chicago Tribune*, 12 Jun 1968, p. A9.

Youngblood, Gene. " 'The Trip' Makes It Sexually, Cinematically." *Los Angeles Free Press*, 15 Sep. 1967, p. 13.

Yulli, Chris. "Forgetting and Remembering Alienation Theory." *History of Human Sciences*, vol. 24, no. 2, 2011, pp. 103–19.

Zimmerman, Paul. "Forbidden Fruitcake." *Newsweek*, 28 Oct. 1968.

Index

Advise and Consent (Otto Preminger, 1962), 148
alienation, 122
Alpert, Richard, 126, 129–31, 201n3 (chap. 4)
American International Pictures (AIP), 138, 140–42
Anatomy of a Murder (Otto Preminger, 1959), 148
Antonioni, Michelangelo, 76–77
Austin, J. L., 156

Baby Doll (Elia Kazan, 1956), 203n1 (chap. 5)
Bach, George, and Peter Wyden, 113–15, 117
Batman (ABC, 1966–1967), 148
behavior therapy, 4, 7–9, 18, 51, 55, 57, 62, 127; and behavior modification, 67, 69, 72, 116; in *Deep Throat*, 80–81; and focus upon the present, 16, 67, 86, 101; in *A Very Special Favor*, 42
Benshoff, Harry, 135, 202n6 (chap. 4), 202n8 (chap. 4), 202n10 (chap. 4), 203 n14 (chap. 4), 203n16 (chap. 4)
Bob & Carol & Ted & Alice (Paul Mazursky, 1969), 102–108, 110, 166; critical reception of, 106–107, 200nn7–9 (chap. 3)

Boston Strangler, The (Richard Fleischer, 1968), 45–46; critical reception of, 45
Boys in the Band, The (William Friedkin, 1970). 11, 182–86, 187–88, 205–206nn17–21
Breen, Joseph, 163
Brown, Helen Gurley, 40, 60, 62
BZ, 125

Candid Camera (1960–1967), 47
Cannon, Doran William, 203n15 (chap. 4)
Caretakers, The (Hal Bartlett, 1963) 22–26, 30, 51, 195n1 (chap. 1)
Carnal Knowledge (Mike Nichols, 1971), 7, 72–75, 81–82, 189, 198–99n12–14 (chap. 2), 204n12 (chap. 5)
castration anxiety, 69
catharsis: in *The Boys in the Band*, 184–85; in *Doctors' Wives*, 182; in *Guess Who's Coming to Dinner*, 175; in *Portnoy's Complaint*, 179; in *Who's Afraid of Virginia Woolf?*, 171
Catholic Church. *See* confession; Legion of Decency
Chapman Report, The (George Cukor, 1962), 7, 61–63, 65, 79–80, 181; concerns of the Production Code Administration, 197n5; and the

Chapman Report, The (continued)
perception of scientific depictions of sex, 61–62
Chayefsky, Paddy, 71
CIA (Central Intelligence Agency), 9, 124–25, 143–44
Civil Rights Movement, 24, 30, 32–33
Cloud, Dana, 12, 15, 33, 52
Cold War, 9, 122, 124–25, 130, 143; anxiety in *Shock Corridor*, 26
Coming Apart (Milton Moses Ginsberg, 1969) 6, 46–53, 196n8 (chap. 1)
communication: as confession, 11; and marriage, 8, 85, 97–100; sexual intercourse as, 58; and spiritual satisfaction, 157; compromised by stereotyping, 25; and therapy, 5, 7, 16–18, 87–88
Community Health Centers Act (1963), 24
Concord State Prison experiment, 126, 149
confession, 5, 10–11, 13, 22, 78; in *The Boston Strangler*, 46; and catharsis, 165; and the Catholic mass, 159; as communication, 161–62; as dialogue, 159; in *Diary of a Mad Housewife*, 113; Michel Foucault on, 166; legal dimension of, 155–56; as narrative climax, 165; and narrative closure, 165; and contrition, 157, 159; and psychoanalysis, 154–57; as reconciliation, 160, 166; and sin, 157–59; the "talking cure" as, 156; and truth, 155–56
consciousness-raising, 108–109, 121; and *Diary of a Mad Housewife*, 110–12; and *The Marriage of a Young Stockbroker*, 117–18; and *Rosemary's Baby*, 110–11; in *The Stepford Wives*, 192; v. therapy, 109
Conversation, The (Francis Ford Coppola, 1974), 193
Corman, Roger, 139–41, 202n10 (chap. 4)

Cuban Missile Crisis, 33, 122

David and Lisa (Frank Perry, 1962), 20–23, 25, 30; critical reception of, 31, 195n2 (chap. 1)
de Beauvoir, Simone, 108
Deep Throat (Gerard Damiano, 1972), 79–82
DeSalvo, Albert: 1. See also *The Boston Strangler*
Detective, The (Gordon Douglas, 1968), 181
Devil in Miss Jones, The (Gerard Damiano, 1973), 81
Diary of a Mad Housewife (Frank and Eleanor Perry, 1970), 8, 110–13, 116, 189
Didion, Joan, 201–202n5 (chap. 4)
Divorce American Style (Bud Yorkin, 1967), 96–100, 115, 189, 199–200nn4–6 (chap. 3)
divorce: and the Catholic church, 90, 93–94; and capitalism, 90–91, 96–99; legal aspects of, 98–99; in the postwar period, 84, 88, 96, 102, 199n1 (chap. 3)
Divorce Italian Style (Pietro Germi, 1961), 8, 90–92, 107, 110
Doctors' Wives (George Schaefer, 1971), 181–82, 205n16 (chap. 5); promotional strategies of, 181
double standard, 67, 105–106; Masters and Johnson on, 67–68
Dr. Strangelove, or How I Learned to Love the Bomb and Stop Worrying (Stanley Kubrick, 1964), 26
Dying to Know: Ram Dass & Timothy Leary (Gay Dillingham, 2014), 201n3 (chap. 4)

Easy Rider (Dennis Hopper, 1969), 150
encounter group therapy, 8, 86, 100, 121; and marathon sessions, 103, 166
Esalen Institute, 103, 108, 200n8 (chap. 3)

Escobeda v. Illinois (1964), 156
Everett, Anna, 30–31
Everything You Always Wanted to Know About Sex* (*But Were Afraid to Ask) (Woody Allen, 1972), 75–79, 81
Everything You Always Wanted to Know About Sex* (*But Were Afraid to Ask) (book by David Reuben, 1969), 75–76

Fail Safe (Sidney Lumet, 1964), 26
family therapy, 17, 118
female sexual dysfunction, 7, 55–57, 59–64, 69, 79–80, 181, 197–98n6 (chap. 2), 198n8; in *The Chapman Report*, 60–63; in *Deep Throat*, 79; in *Marnie*, 63–64
A Fine Madness (Irvin Kershner, 1966), 38–41, 196n6 (chap. 1)
Five Easy Pieces (Bob Rafelson, 1970), 176–79
Foucault, Michel, 166, 169
Freud (John Huston, 1962), 19–20, 31
Friedan, Betty, 40, 60, 62, 83, 85; on the logic of the "feminine mystique," 84, 108
frigidity. *See* female sexual dysfunction
Five Easy Pieces (Bob Rafelson, 1970), 11, 176–78, 205m13 (chap. 5)
Fuchs, Cynthia, 198n12 (chap. 2)
Fulbright, J. W. (Senator), 1

Gabbard, Glen: on the "cathartic cure," 17–18; on family dysfunction, 21; on the "Golden Age" of psychiatry, 19, 32–33, 37; on race relations in cinema, 29
Gaudium et Spes (Joy and Hope), 1965), 158
Gay Deceivers, The (Bruce Kessler, 1969), 181
generation gap, 9, 123, 136, 146, 148–49, 175
gestalt therapy, 101
Ginsberg v. New York, 55
"Good Friday" Experiment, 127–28

Greenfeld, Sidney M., 88
Greer Germaine, 85
group sex, 106–107
group therapy, 17; in *Bob & Carol & Ted & Alice*, 103; in *The Caretakers*, 23–24, 103; and the Concord State Prison Experiment, 126; and confession, 161; in *A Very Special Favor*, 42. *See also* encounter group therapy
Guess Who's Coming to Dinner (Stanley Kramer, 1967), 172–78, 188, 204nn5–11
Guide for the Married Man, A (Gene Kelly, 1967), 95–96, 107, 110, 189

Halleck, Seymour, 15–17
Hallucination Generation (Edward Mann, 1966), 135–38
hallucinogenic drug therapy: and the treatment of alcoholism, 126; and mystical experience, 127, 131; and political activism, 128; and recidivism, 127–28; the roles of "set" and "setting" in, 127. *See also* LSD; psilocybin
Hart, Kylo-Patrick, 205n17 (chap. 5)
Head (Bob Rafelson, 1968), 134
healing, 12, 15
hippies, 9, 123–24, 128, 133–37, 145–47, 149, 151
Hoberman, J., 34
Hoffmann, Albert, 124
Hollywood Renaissance, 192
homophobia, 76–77
homosexuality: in *Doctors' Wives*, 182; in *Midnight Cowboy*, 69–71; in *Reflections in a Golden Eye*, 64–66; in *Three in the Attic*, 70
Hospital, The (Arthur Hiller, 1971), 7, 71–72
How to Murder Your Wife (Richard Quine, 1965), 92–97, 99, 107, 110, 189; critical perspectives on, 94
human potential movement, 86, 101–102; and *Bob & Carol & Ted & Alice*, 103; and *The Marriage of a*

human potential movement *(continued)*
    Young Stockbroker, 118–19; and *On a Clear Day You Can See Forever*, 151
Human Sexual Inadequacy (1970), 55, 57–58, 67, 72. *See also* William Masters and Virginia Johnson
Human Sexual Response (1966), 57, 75. *See also* William Masters and Virginia Johnson
hypnosis, 52, 116

I Confess (Alfred Hitchcock, 1953), 166–67, 203–204n4 (chap. 5)
I Love You, Alice B. Toklas (Hy Averback, 1968), 145–47; critical reception of, 146–47
I'm OK, You're OK (Thomas Harris), 51–52
impotence. *See* male sexual dysfunction
Inside Deep Throat (Fenton Bailey & Randy Barbato, 2005), 79

Jackson, John D., 87
John XIII (pope), 154, 157
Johnson, Lyndon B., 1; and the Great Society platform, 34
Jung, Karl, 156, 161–62

Kazan, Elia, 4, 163
Kennedy, Robert, 1–2, 191
Kinsey, Alfred, 60, 80; on sexual dysfunction, 56, 62
Klute (Alan J. Pakula, 1971), 193–94
Kolker, Robert, 192

La Dolce Vita (Federico Fellini, 1960), 89–90
Laing, R. D., 122
Leary, Timothy, 9; 126–31, 139, 141, 149, 190
Lederer, William J., 87
Lee, Martin A. & Bruce Schlain, 124–25, 127, 129, 131, 133

Legion of Decency, 4, 11, 19, 59, 162–65; film classification system of, 164; reaction to *Who's Afraid of Virginia Woolf?*, 168. *See also* National Catholic Office of Motion Pictures
Lewis, Jon, 162, 169
Lilith (Robert Rossen, 1964), 35–36; critical reception of, 36, 195n3 (chap.1)
Love and Death (Woody Allen, 1975)
Love-Ins, The (Arthur Dreifuss, 1967), 135–38, 142
Lovers and Other Strangers (Cy Howard, 1970), 8, 113–16
Loving v. Virginia (1967), 173
LSD (lysergic acid diethylamide), 9–10, 13, 121, 134–45, 147–51, 190; and chromosomal damage, 130; and mind control, 124–26, 129, 150
Lumen Gentium (*Light of the Nations*, 1964), 158, 160
Luther, Martin, 158

Mainardi, Pat, 112
Making of a Counter Culture, The (1968), 122
male sexual dysfunction, 188–89; and alienation, 71–72; and homosexuality, 7, 64–66, 69–70; and machismo, 73–74; and masturbation, 180–81; sources of, 67; in relation to the Women's Liberation Movement, 68–69, 114
Manchurian Candidate, The (John Frankenheimer, 1962), 26
Manson, Charles, 138, 151
Man with the Golden Arm, The (Otto Preminger, 1955), 148
marijuana, 145
Marnie (Alfred Hitchcock, 1964), 7; 63–64, 79–80, 198n7
marriage: and male sexual freedom, 89–95; as problem, 189 sociological perspectives on, 88–89

Marriage Italian Style (Vittorio De Sica, 1964), 8, 90–92. See also open marriage
Marriage of a Young Stockbroker, The (Lawrence Turman, 1971), 8, 75, 116–19, 189
marriage therapies: collaborative model, 86; concurrent model, 86; conjoint model, 87, 100
Masters, William and Virginia Johnson: 7, 62, 66, 68, 75, 77, 80–81, 196–97nn1–3 (chap. 2); public impact of, 59; and interpersonal communication, 58; and male v. female orgasm, 57; in relation to David Reuben, 75; therapeutic methodologies of, 57–58. See also open marriage
Mental Health and Mental Retardation Act (1966), 32
Metzner, Ralph, 131, 201n2 (chap. 4)
Midnight Cowboy (John Schlesinger, 1970), 7, 69–71, 81, 198n11
Minnelli, Vincent, 20
Miranda Prorsus (*On Entertainment Media*, 1957), 164
Miranda v. Arizona (1966), 156
Momism, 22
Monkees, The, 134
Moon Is Blue, The (Otto Preminger, 1953), 4, 163
movie rating system, 34, 55, 60, 64, 123–24, 155, 166, 169, 179. See also Production Code Administration
Myra Breckenridge (Michael Sarne, 1970), 77

National Catholic Office of Motion Pictures (NCOMP), 10, 110, 200n11 (chap. 3)
"New Frontier," 33
New Left, 123, 128
Newlywed Game, The (ABC, 1966–1971), 97

nuclear war, 33–34, 122; anxiety in *Shock Corridor*, 26

Office Catholique International du Cinéma (OCIC), 163
On a Clear Day You Can See Forever (Vincente Minnelli, 1970), 6, 82, 196n9 (chap.1); hypnotherapy in, 51–53; and reincarnation, 52–53
O'Neill, Nena and George, 102, 105
open marriage, 102, 105, 115

Pahnke, Walter. See "Good Friday" Experiment
Parallax View, The (Alan J. Pakula, 1974), 192
Pentagon Papers, 191
Pillow Talk (Michael Gordon, 1959), 93
Pius XII (pope), 11, 163
Play It As It Lays (Frank Perry, 1972), 200–201n12 (chap. 3)
Portnoy's Complaint (Ernest Lehman, 1972), 75, 179; critical perspectives on, 205n15 (chap. 5); and the role of the implied listener, 180
Preminger, Otto, 4, 147–48, 163
President's Analyst, The (Theodore J. Flicker, 1967), 11, 167–68, 203n2 (chap. 5)
Pressure Point (Hubert Cornfield, 1962), 27–31, 190; critical reception of, 31
Production Code Administration (PCA), 4, 6, 11, 18, 34, 38, 55, 59, 90, 100, 104, 148, 162–64, 166, 168, 181
Project MKUltra, 125
Psilocybin, 126; in the "Good Friday" Experiment, 127
Psychedelic Experience, The (1964), 131–32
Psycho (Alfred Hitchcock, 1960), 45, 63
psychoanalysis: and Catholicism, 156–57; and collaborative therapeutic

psychoanalysis *(continued)*
  models, 86; and confession, 154, 160; and countertransference, 86–87; and *Deep Throat*, 80–82; and depiction of male sexual dysfunction, 64–67; and the focus upon the past, 2, 16, 57, 59, 62; and gradual psychotherapeutic transition from, 17; and treatment of female sexual dysfunction, 55–57
Psychology Today, 66
psycholytic therapy, 125
psychomimesis, 125, 144
psychotherapy: co-administration with behavior therapy, 59; and confession, 153–61; in *Divorce American Style*, 97–98; and exoticism in analyst/patient relationships, 39; political dimensions of, 20–31; power relations in, 47–53; and "reaching out," 2–5; and the characterization of sexual dysfunction, 59–66; and sexualization of analyst/patient relationships, 34–44

race relations, 18; 24; in *Guess Who's Coming to Dinner*, 173–76; in *Pressure Point*, 28–30, 34; in *Shock Corridor*, 27
Ray, Nicholas, 20
realism in cinema, 31–32, 36
recidivism, 126
reconciliation, 33, 155, 160, 164, 166, 179; in *Doctors' Wives*, 182; in *Five Easy Pieces*, 177–78; in *Guess Who's Coming to Dinner*, 174–75; in *Who's Afraid of Virginia Woolf?*, 171–72
Reflections in a Golden Eye (John Huston, 1967), 64–66, 69–70
Reuben, David, 75–77
Riot on Sunset Strip (Arthur Dreifuss, 1967), 135–38; critical reception of, 202n7 (chap. 4); promotional strategies for, 137

Rogers, Carl, 103, 193; and confession, 156; and focus upon the "here and now," 2; on group encounter therapy, 100–103, 105
Rosemary's Baby (Roman Polanksi, 1968), 110–12; and the Catholic Church, 165, 200n11 (chap. 3)
Roszak, Theodore, 122–23, 19, 131, 133, 144–45, 149; perspective on psychedelic drug use, 201n1 (chap. 4)
Russo, Vito, 205n18 (chap. 5)

Sandoz Laboratories, 124–25, 129
Sarachild, Kathie, 109
satire, 90–92, 94–96, 99–100
Satir, Virginia, 87, 103
schizophrenia, 9; in *David and Lisa*, 22; LSD as a treatment for, 125
self-actualization, 8, 102, 154
Sergeant, The (John Flynn, 1968), 181
Shock Corridor (Samuel Fuller, 1963), 26–28, 190; critical reception of, 31–32
Shurlock, Geoffrey, 163–64
"sick society," 1–2, 45, 151, 191
Singer, Helen Kaplan, 66
Sirk, Douglas, 20
Skidoo (Otto Preminger, 1968), 10, 147–51
Speck, Richard, 1
Staircase (Stanley Donen, 1969), 181
Stepford Wives, The (Bryan Forbes, 1975), 193–94
St. John's Summer Institute (1954), 157
"swinging" phenomenon, 104–107
systematic desensitization, 57, 66, 116
Szasz, Thomas, 126

technocracy, 2, 9, 101, 122–23, 131, 133, 146, 148–49, 192–93, 201n2 (chap. 4); in *The Conversation*, 193; *The President's Analyst*, 168; in *Skidoo*, 149

Thalidomide, 130
Three in the Attic (Richard Wilson, 1968), 70, 198n10
Tingler, The (William Castle, 1959), 135
totalitarianism, 30
Tracy, Spencer, 173
Trip, The (Roger Corman, 1967), 138–41, 147, 202nn8–9 (chap. 4); promotional strategies for, 140–41; reviews, 141

Vatican II (Second Ecumenical Council), 10, 13, 154, 156–61, 174, 182, 185; on contraception, 160. *See also* confession
Very Special Favor, A (Michael Gordon, 1965), 93, 196n7 (chap. 1): gender and power relations in, 40–44: nationalism in, 40
Vietnam War, 6, 40, 45, 122, 134, 190–91
voyeurism, 116, 201n13 (chap. 3)

Walker, Janet, 12, 15–16, 19, 35–36, 51, 59
Wallace, George, 1, 27, 33
Watergate scandal, 192
What a Way to Go! (J. Lee Thompson, 1964), 36–37

What's New Pussycat? (Clive Donner and Richard Talmadge, 1965), 37–38, 40–41, 78, 194–95n4 (chap. 1)
White, Mimi, 204n12 (chap. 5)
Who's Afraid of Virginia Woolf? (Mike Nichols, 1966), 168–72, 184, 206n21 (chap. 5); and the Production Code, 4, 168
wife swapping. *See* "swinging"
Wild in the Streets (Barry Shear, 1968), 9, 141–45, 148, 202–203nn11–13 (chap. 4); promotional strategies for, 144; reviews, 144
Williams, Linda, 80–82
Wolpe, Joseph, 57
Women's Liberation Movement, 6; 8. 121, 190; and *Carnal Knowledge*, 74; and *Diary of a Mad Housewife*, 110–12; and gender identity, 113–14; and *Lovers and Other Strangers*, 113–14; and *The Marriage of a Young Stockbroker*, 117–18; Masters and Johnson on, 67–68; in relation to male sexual anxiety, 56, 68–69, 189; and *On a Clear Day You Can See Forever*, 51; and radical feminism, 108–10; and *Rosemary's Baby*, 110; stereotyping of, 117; and *A Very Special Favor*, 40

Yalom, Irvin D., 101

www.ingramcontent.com/pod-product-compliance
Lightning Source LLC
Chambersburg PA
CBHW030648230426
43665CB00011B/1006